The New York Times

KEEP CALM AND CROSSWORD ON

The New York Times

KEEP CALM AND CROSSWORD ON
200 Easy Puzzles

Edited by Will Shortz

ST. MARTIN'S GRIFFIN ❧ NEW YORK

ACROSS

1 Doctrine
6 "___ of the D'Urbervilles"
10 Bit of hair standing up
14 Targeted, with "in on"
15 Fe, on the periodic table
16 Burn soother
17 Nimble
18 Entangle
19 Fort ___ (gold repository)
20 "Go!"
23 Doctor's charge
24 Glimpsed
25 Big name in copiers
26 "Look how perfectly I performed!"
27 Vigorous
31 Aviated
34 Web address, for short
36 Wood for black piano keys, once
37 V.I.P.'s transport
38 Separate . . . or a hint to this puzzle's theme
41 Razor brand
42 Billy the Kid, for Henry McCarty
44 Bygone Russian space station
45 "Fargo" director
46 Messed up, as a message
49 Eat like a bird
51 Anglo-Saxon writing symbol
52 No. starting with an area code
53 Firms: Abbr.
56 Sherlock Holmes phrase, when on a case
60 Horse's halter?

61 Temperate
62 ___ ball soup
63 Big rabbit features
64 Salinger heroine
65 Animal that plays along streams
66 Shade of color
67 More's opposite
68 All set

DOWN

1 Grain husks
2 Scalawag
3 Author Zola
4 Farmer's place, in a children's ditty
5 Black Sea port
6 Dance in "The Rocky Horror Picture Show"
7 Cleveland's lake
8 Vile
9 Underhanded

10 Surprised and flustered
11 Bone that parallels the radius
12 Groceries
13 Moniker for a Lone Star cowboy
21 Italian city where "The Taming of the Shrew" is set
22 Sharpen, as a knife
26 Going in side-by-side pairs
28 Mr. ___, John P. Marquand detective
29 About, on a memo
30 Greenish blue
31 Old Glory, for one
32 Reader's Digest co-founder Wallace

33 Arab ruler
35 Take it on the ___ (flee)
39 Dangerous ocean currents
40 Oak and teak
43 Hit hard, as a baseball
47 Tooth cover
48 Death
50 Hullabaloo
53 Terra ___ (tile material)
54 Seeped
55 Tale
56 Southeast Asian cuisine
57 Tooter
58 Classic street liners
59 Destiny
60 Drenched

by Jill Denny and Jeff Chen

ACROSS

1 Voice above tenor
5 Cross: Christianity :: ___ : Judaism
9 Interior design
14 Cries from Homer Simpson
15 Very very
16 Going brand?
17 Number between eins and drei
18 Neeson of "Clash of the Titans"
19 Track-and-field events
20 *"Ocean's Eleven" actor
23 Follower of spy or web
24 Any Beatles song, now
25 *Tweaks
28 Enters Facebook, maybe
30 Annoys incessantly
31 Female flock member
32 N.B.A. nickname
36 Film units
37 *Small sci-fi vehicle
40 Rapper's crew
43 Director Apatow
44 Obstruction for salmon
47 Culmination of a Casey Kasem countdown
49 Book size
52 *"Get Smart" device
56 Toothpaste with "green sparkles"
57 Falsity
58 *Blastoff spot
60 Uses sleight of hand on
62 Head of Québec
63 French girlfriend
65 Aerodynamic
66 Tied, as a score
67 "Boy Meets World" boy

68 Late
69 Organize alphabetically, say
70 Chips in the pot

DOWN

1 Carpenter's curved cutter
2 Uncalled-for insult, say
3 U2 guitarist
4 Brother and husband of Isis
5 Arias, usually
6 Robin Hood or Jesse James
7 "Same here"
8 Director Polanski
9 Obama, e.g.: Abbr.
10 Performed, as one's duties
11 Purify
12 Quaker breakfast offering
13 Prescriptions, for short
21 Keanu Reeves's role in "The Matrix"
22 Middling grade
24 Chilean cheer
26 Poi source
27 Aves.
29 Foreign policy grp.
33 Pilgrimage to Mecca
34 Kwik-E-Mart clerk
35 Proof ending
37 Well-regarded
38 Fall through the cracks?
39 A.S.A.P.
40 A TD is worth six: Abbr.
41 "So beauuutiful!"
42 Unwanted plot giveaway

44 "Yeah, like that'll ever happen"
45 Groveled
46 Blondie, to Alexander and Cookie
48 Rangers' org.
50 "That's awful"
51 Fleecy fiber
53 Hall's musical partner
54 ___ Laredo, Mexico
55 Go in
59 50 ___ ("Candy Shop" rapper)
60 Winter clock setting in Nev.
61 Heavens
64 Storm center . . . or, phonetically, letter that can precede the ends of the answers to the five starred clues to spell popular devices

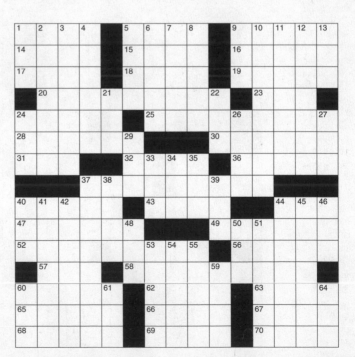

by José Chardiet

ACROSS

1 Veracruz's capital
7 Its motto is "Semper paratus": Abbr.
11 Bonobo, for one
14 You can count on it
15 Kelly of "Live with Regis and Kelly"
16 Word with band or sand
17 Command to a French composer at an intersection?
19 Conciliatory gift
20 Pen
21 Tickle response
22 Uccello who painted "The Battle of San Romano"
24 Don Corleone
25 Loading locale
27 City south of Luxor
30 Command to a Hungarian composer at the piano?
34 Activities
36 Jacques Cousteau's middle name
37 "Tippecanoe and Tyler ___"
38 Move like mud
39 Sophia of "Marriage Italian-Style"
41 Fringe benefit
42 Sch. supporter
43 Author who famously ended a short story with the line "Romance at short notice was her specialty"
44 Cell on a slide
46 Command to a German composer on a baseball diamond?
49 Lessen, as fears
50 Jay Gatsby's love
51 Mayberry boy
53 Leaf holders
55 Czar of Russia between Feodors
57 Initials at sea
60 Snap, Crackle or Pop
61 Command to an Austrian composer on a scavenger hunt?
64 Freudian concept
65 Adm. Zumwalt, chief of naval operations during the Vietnam War
66 Word before a sentence
67 Guerra's opposite
68 Does, e.g.
69 "Woo-hoo!"

DOWN

1 Injures with a pencil, say
2 Somewhat
3 Unlike a go-getter
4 Point of no return?
5 Green skill
6 Plus
7 What an addict fights
8 Symbol of simple harmonic motion
9 Tax pro, for short
10 Bachelorette party attendees
11 Hard core?
12 Game involving banks
13 Fair
18 Denny's competitor
23 Talent agent ___ Emanuel
24 Roof topper
26 Relative of an aardwolf
27 Make one's own
28 Truth, archaically
29 1939 title role for Frank Morgan
31 Like much poetry
32 1964 title role for Anthony Quinn
33 Hungarian wine
35 Hearty helpings of meat loaf, say
40 "Go ahead"
41 It may be+or−
43 Moved, as a horse's tail
45 "But of course!," in Marseille
47 Symbol of strength
48 Device making a 53-Down
52 "Little" digit
53 Sound made by a 48-Down
54 Kurylenko of "Quantum of Solace"
56 Febreeze target
57 Succor
58 Parcel (out)
59 ___ terrier
62 Hearty quaff
63 Take in slowly

by Will Nediger

ACROSS

1 Point that marks the beginning of a change
5 Rainbows, basically
9 Blunder
14 Palo ___, Calif.
15 Jacket
16 Affliction said to be caused by worry
17 One of 12 for the Alcoholics Anonymous program
18 Robust
19 More courteous
20 Special offer at an airline Web site
23 Japanese electronics brand
24 Scottish castle for British royals
29 Special offer at a supermarket
32 "___ your age!"
35 Scuba tankful
36 Midwest tribe
37 Depressed
38 Place for phys. ed.
39 "The Murders in the Rue Morgue" writer
41 Depressed
42 Way too weighty
44 Arrow shooter
45 Attempt
46 Special offer at a diner
50 Element with the symbol Ta
51 Rotini or rigatoni
56 Special offer at a car dealership
59 One of three people walking into a bar, in many a joke
63 Fox's "American ___"
64 Sir Geraint's wife, in Arthurian legend
65 François's farewell

66 Mission control org.
67 Prince Charles's sister
68 ___ pole (Indian emblem)
69 Campbell who sang "Rhinestone Cowboy"
70 Corrosive alkalis

DOWN

1 Groups on "Saturday Night Live"
2 The "U" of UHF
3 Writer Gertrude
4 Opium flower
5 Yearn (for)
6 What buffalo do in "Home on the Range"
7 .45, e.g., for a firearm
8 Upright, inscribed stone tablets
9 TV western that ran for 20 seasons
10 Muhammad ___, opponent of 53-Down
11 TV monitor?
12 Lawyer's charge
13 Blunder
21 Bit of real estate
22 Santa's helper
25 ". . . ___ quit!"
26 Henhouse perch
27 Egypt's Sadat
28 Like many old water pipes
30 What a farmer bales
31 Edge
32 Skyward
33 Snake that a snake charmer charms
34 Sixth-grader, usually
38 Flower also known as a cranesbill
39 Campaign pro

40 "Wise" bird
43 Put in rollers
44 Having two methods
47 "Shine a Little Love" rock grp.
48 Really angry
49 Passer of secret documents
52 "What ___!" (possible response to 20-, 29-, 46- and 56-Across)
53 ___ Liston, opponent of 10-Down
54 Bale binder
55 Much of Chile
57 Sniffer
58 Verve
59 Double-crosser
60 Hubbub
61 Chomped (on)
62 Busy one?

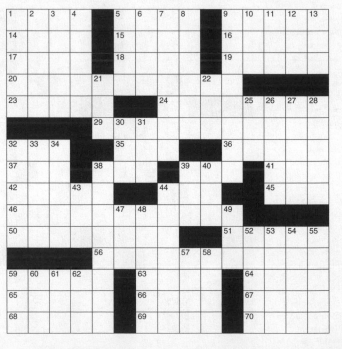

by Freddie Cheng

ACROSS

1 Tiny scissor cut
5 Sphere
10 Annoyance at a barbecue
14 Lug
15 "I'm outta here!"
16 Aachen article
17 Nice through and through . . . or not
20 Mother, in Milan
21 Pin's place
22 Charlemagne's dominion: Abbr.
23 Like some stares
25 Levy on cigarettes and booze
27 Really digs . . . or not
33 Woman who raised Cain
34 58 minutes past the hour
35 Hogwash
38 Portland, Ore., college from which Steve Jobs dropped out
40 Uses a dagger
42 33-Across's partner
43 Invite to the penthouse, say
45 Some Iroquois
47 2008 Super Bowl M.V.P. Manning
48 Most wretched . . . or not
51 One of academia's Seven Sisters
53 Many a 16-year-old Southern belle
54 Bridge expert Culbertson
55 Maryland athletes, for short
59 Shepherded, in a way
63 Speaks with brutal honesty . . . or not

66 Rock's Mötley ___
67 Club that doesn't beat much
68 "L'___ c'est moi": Louis XIV
69 Terse order to a chauffeur
70 Evaluate
71 Title girl in a 1922 hit

DOWN

1 Flower stalk
2 Exploding star
3 Couple on a gossip page
4 Learner's ___
5 Priestly attire
6 Train transportation
7 Singer James
8 Kind of tide
9 "Gunsmoke" star James

10 ___-Xer
11 Certain vigilante
12 End of ___
13 Bygone communication
18 America's Cup entry
19 "Can I give you ___?"
24 Some evergreens
26 Writer Ephron
27 Juno's counterpart
28 Connecticut and Virginia, in Monopoly: Abbr.
29 Defect
30 Monopoly purchase
31 Japanese seaport
32 Book of the Apocrypha
36 Buddies
37 Give off

39 Nicknames
41 Bit of watermelon waste
44 11th-grade exams, for short
46 Ingemar Johansson or Ingrid Bergman
49 Tater Tots maker
50 Funnyman Conan
51 Climbing legume
52 Old Oldsmobile
56 Itinerary parts: Abbr.
57 Bonus
58 "The Bicycle Thief" director Vittorio De ___
60 Bus driver on "The Simpsons"
61 Lab container
62 "Cómo ___?"
64 Stan who co-created Spider-Man
65 Lock opener

by Peter A. Collins

ACROSS

1 "Roger that" sayer
5 Cakes with a kick
10 "A ___ on you!"
13 ___-kiri
14 Laughing gas, for one
15 Mixologist's instruction
16 Fine-tune, as a script
17 Finland-based communications giant
18 Wee bit
19 "Yada yada yada"
20 Ironic weather forecast?
22 KFC servings
24 Alluringly slender
25 What to do at a drive-thru window
26 Do some cardio
29 Thin as ___
30 It's under a foot
31 Bullet-point item
33 Ironic marriage plan?
38 Grows darker
39 Ride for Hawkeye or Radar
41 Chipped in
45 "Making something out of nothing and selling it," per Frank Zappa
46 Like dogs in packs
47 Carrier crew
49 Classic Sinatra topper
50 Ironic exam schedule?
54 Nellie who circled the world
55 "How could ___ this happen?"
56 Agent Swifty
57 Dust jacket bits
58 Ruing the workout, maybe
59 Where élèves study

60 Prom night worry
61 Helpful connections
62 Overhauled
63 Army NCO

DOWN

1 Orange munchies
2 Ball field error
3 Monty Python member
4 Unpopular mobster
5 Boss's good news
6 Neural transmitter
7 Steven ___, subject of "Cry Freedom"
8 Point before "game," maybe
9 Clothes lines
10 Sometimes-dyed dog
11 Bested at Nathan's on July 4, e.g.
12 Got an inside look at?

15 Yearning sort
20 Stock unit: Abbr.
21 Cameo shapes
23 Turned right, like Dobbin
26 Midrange Volkswagen
27 None of the above
28 All skin and bones
31 Paternity test factor
32 Quarterly payment recipient, for short
34 Of yore
35 Spun 45s, say
36 Gym class set to music
37 Like many magazine subscriptions
40 Jungle gym, swings, etc.
41 Home of St. Francis
42 "S.N.L." alum Kevin

43 Home runs, in slang
44 Be melodramatic
46 Palin parodist
48 Buc or Niner
49 Got along
51 Where "They're off!" may be heard
52 Preppy shirt brand
53 "The Persistence of Memory" artist
57 Many undergrad degs.

by Michael Black

ACROSS

1 Aids for treasure hunters
5 Babble on
10 "Ali ___ and the 40 Thieves"
14 "The Time Machine" people
15 Environmentalist in a Dr. Seuss story
16 Muscat's country
17 "Yes, go on"
19 William ___, Hopalong Cassidy player
20 Spotted cat
21 Supers oversee them: Abbr.
23 Dove's sound
24 1969 Stevie Wonder hit
27 Harvard color
29 T on a test
30 Wedding dress material
31 Sony rival
33 Famed '50s flop
37 Eggs in labs
38 Former host of TV's "Last Comic Standing"
41 The way, in philosophy
42 "You'll love the way we fly" airline
44 Con's opposite
45 Suffix with Oktober
46 On ___ with (equal to)
49 Salad greens
51 Big name in paint
55 Meadow
56 Dark shade of blue
57 Go over again with a blue pencil
60 Eye part
62 Location in a Donizetti opera
64 Scrabble piece
65 Actress Graff

66 Florence's river
67 Lemon peel
68 These: Sp.
69 Without ice, as a drink

DOWN

1 "Take ___ your leader"
2 Baldwin of "30 Rock"
3 Tending to cause an argument
4 Words before "And here I thought . . ."
5 Great deal
6 CD-___
7 Clamoring
8 La Brea attraction
9 University attended by J. K. Rowling
10 ___ for apples
11 BP partner

12 Louisiana waterway
13 Compound conjunction
18 Comfy footwear, for short
22 Like some Kraut
25 Suffix with depend
26 Club ___
27 Dummkopf
28 Four-star review
32 Electric guitar need
34 Longshoreman
35 Simplicity
36 Auction groups
38 Where Mount Fuji is
39 Utah city
40 Toast recipients
43 ___ Mahal
45 What many a young boy wants to grow up to be

47 Charlotte ___, capital of the U.S. Virgin Islands
48 Coke and Pepsi, e.g.
50 No idle person
51 Fast-moving attack
52 Hair-raising
53 Tough as ___
54 Citi Field player, for short
58 New Rochelle campus
59 Horse's gait
61 Card game based on matching groups of three
63 Letters after L

by David Blake

ACROSS

1 Like the air in a cigar bar
6 In heaps
11 Medallioned vehicle
14 Soup server's implement
15 Dins from dens
16 Ill temper
17 Davy Jones's locker
19 Hoops org.
20 Irksome type
21 Look forward to
22 Foot problem, perhaps
23 Motel extra
25 Playful puppies, at times
27 S'more ingredient
32 Frisk, with "down"
33 "Gone with the Wind" plantation
34 Loonlike bird
37 VW or BMW
39 "Hold the rocks," at a bar
42 ___ mater
43 "All ___ is metaphor, and all metaphor is poetry": G. K. Chesterton
45 Shaker contents
47 Pop music's ___ Lobos
48 Site of London's Great Exhibition of 1851
52 Yucky, in baby talk
54 Cap-and-crown org.?
55 Shore washer
56 Rich soil deposit
59 Repairs some tears
63 Big fuss
64 Veneration of a cult image
66 Turkey piece
67 ___ Street, Perry Mason's secretary
68 Name associated with the starts of 17-, 27-, 48- and 64-Across
69 Sterile hosp. areas
70 "As You Like It" forest
71 Food for birds

DOWN

1 Barely edible fare
2 Knight's club
3 Keatsian works
4 Coffee ___ (social gathering)
5 Cash in Kyoto
6 Ship's front
7 Least bit
8 Monterrey miss, e.g.
9 Rated X
10 Mil. award
11 Rags-to-riches heroine
12 Shady area
13 Grizzlies, e.g.
18 Dynamic Duo member
22 Setting for a Marx Brothers farce
24 Cheerios grain
26 UPS delivery: Abbr.
27 Transcript nos.
28 Brother of Fidel
29 Responders to "Sic 'em!"
30 ___-Magnon
31 Mrs. Gorbachev
35 Coll. football star, e.g.
36 Life of Riley
38 One way to eat ham
40 Low-___ (for dieters)
41 City across the Rio Grande from Ciudad Juárez
44 Cheat, in 43-Across
46 Little bit
49 Electrician's alloy
50 Ineligible for kiddie prices, say
51 Old TV canine
52 Author Calvino
53 Fall drink
57 Magazine title that's a pronoun
58 Trumpeting bird
60 "Pride and Prejudice" actress Jennifer
61 Like jokers, sometimes
62 1974 Gould/Sutherland spoof
64 Mrs. McKinley
65 N.F.L. ball carriers

by Ed Sessa

ACROSS

1 "Impression, Sunrise" painter
6 Gives the thumbs-up
9 Dreamworks's first animated film
13 Site of some rock shows
14 End of a boast
16 Pitcher Derek
17 A heap
18 Flair
19 Subject of many Georgia O'Keeffe paintings
20 Disaster
23 Skill
24 Woman's name meaning "weary" in Hebrew
25 Of this world
27 Swelter
30 Word before and after "for"
32 Airport info: Abbr.
33 Maryland athlete, for short
34 They're often eaten with applesauce
38 Bard's "below"
40 Place to put a bud
42 Like J in the alphabet
43 Flirtatious one
45 See 53-Down
47 Suffix with Brooklyn
48 Made tidy, in a way
50 Bibliographic abbr.
51 Experience a mondegreen, e.g.
54 Agenda unit
56 ___ carte
57 Lover's woe . . . or something found, literally, in the 4th, 5th, 8th and 11th rows of this puzzle
62 Brass component

64 When doubled, popular 1980s–'90s British sitcom
65 Alexander the Great conquered it ca. 335 B.C.
66 Appendices with some studies
67 SAT taker, e.g.
68 Don
69 Genesis man
70 Date
71 Editors' marks

DOWN

1 Like bueno but not buena: Abbr.
2 Filmdom's Willy, for one
3 "Cool beans!"
4 It's ultimate
5 French cup
6 "Psst!"
7 Metric prefix
8 Pretty vistas, for short
9 The Greatest
10 Singer Jones
11 Pirouette
12 Full of spice
15 Rope for pulling a sail
21 Lacking spice
22 Mess-ups
26 French bean?
27 French bench
28 Uh-Oh! ___ (Nabisco product)
29 Where many a veteran has served
31 Distinct
33 Information superhighway
35 Make a sweater, say
36 "At Last" singer James
37 Poet/illustrator Silverstein

39 Rear
41 Slow alternative to I-95
44 Rip into
46 Breadth
49 Lower class in "1984"
50 Manage
51 Protegé, for one
52 Poem with approximately 16,000 lines
53 With 45-Across, largest city in California's wine country
55 Sends by UPS, say
58 Painter Paul
59 Chip or two, maybe
60 Real knee-slapper
61 Bronzes
63 Video shooter, for short

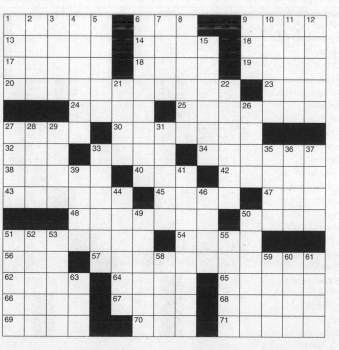

by Oliver Hill

10

ACROSS

1 Musical pace
6 Tractor maker John
11 Do (up), as a fly
14 Bird-related
15 Opposite of exit
16 ___ Today (newspaper)
17 County ENE of San Francisco
19 Was ahead
20 ___ & Tina Turner Revue
21 Greek H's
22 Debate topics
24 Hall-of-Famer Williams
25 End of many U.R.L.'s
26 ___ Easton Ellis, author of "American Psycho"
27 What a programmer writes
32 They get an eyeful
35 Take to court
36 Nutritionists' nos.
37 Hit with a hammer
38 "No ___!" ("Uncle!," in Spanish)
39 Evenings in Paris
40 Coup d'___
41 Lowest-priced gas grade: Abbr.
42 Japanese religion
43 Monica player on "Friends"
46 Language in Lahore
47 Broadcast
48 China's Three Gorges project
51 Alternative to a Quarter Pounder
54 Photographed
55 "Yes, madame"
56 Palindromic girl's name
57 Winter afflictions

60 Observer of Yom Kippur
61 Eating pork, to an observant 60-Across
62 Dark, as a room
63 Pose a question
64 Does' companions
65 Irascible

DOWN

1 Implied
2 Draw forth
3 Extracted ore
4 Butter serving
5 Publicly known
6 Leave suddenly
7 Grandson of Adam
8 Org. that produces college entrance exams
9 Pensioner
10 Blackboard accessory

11 Native of eastern South Africa
12 "Oh, right"
13 Goalie protectors
18 Elementary units
23 Largest of the Virgin Islands
26 A/C measures
27 Vitamin brand promoted as "Complete from A to Zinc"
28 Custom
29 Chief Norse god
30 Missile that might be tipped with curare
31 Old U.S. gas brand
32 Source of some of the oil for 31-Down
33 Attend
34 Hawaiian feast
38 It might start with "Starters"

39 Clever travel suggestion
41 British soldier in the American Revolution
42 Offspring
44 Political pamphlets
45 Brutes in "Gulliver's Travels"
48 Ken and Barbie
49 Cheating bookkeeper's fear
50 "Play ___ for Me"
51 Lower California, for short
52 Burl who won an Oscar for "The Big Country"
53 Get an eyeful
54 Pollution that may sting the eyes
58 Deg. from Wharton
59 Last number in a countdown

by Janet R. Bender

ACROSS

1 Pet welfare org.
5 Nobel Peace Prize city
9 This puzzle has 78
14 Georgetown athlete
15 Stack-serving chain, for short
16 Slowly, on a score
17 The whole ___
19 Pindar, notably
20 Had a bug
21 Mementos of a caning
23 Autodom's Beetle is one, slangily
25 The whole ___
30 Double curve
31 Nail-biting margin of victory
34 William Jennings Bryan, for one
35 Regain consciousness suddenly
37 React to a crowing rooster, say
38 The whole ___
42 Twosome
43 Raptor's grippers
44 Lover in a Shakespeare title
47 Cabinet position: Abbr.
48 B'way success sign
51 The whole ___
53 Ran through, as a credit card
55 Expels forcefully
58 Battery terminal
59 Subtly suggest
63 The whole ___
65 Shampoo brand
66 Rock music's Rush, for one
67 Revivalists, informally
68 Potter's potions professor

69 What the sun does at dusk
70 This, in Toledo

DOWN

1 Bundle, as wheat
2 Track bettors play them
3 Presoak, wash and rinse
4 Sounded content
5 Salad bar bowlful
6 Clarinetist Artie
7 Prospector's strike
8 Gems from Australia
9 Ninth-inning hurler, often
10 Took charge
11 Prefix with -form
12 U.F.O. crew
13 Sighter of pink elephants
18 "Beats me!"

22 Even if, briefly
24 Vehicle on a trailer, perhaps
26 St. ___ (Caribbean hot spot)
27 Suffix with problem
28 Munch on chips, say
29 College sr.'s test
32 Rotisserie rod
33 Lab burners of old
35 Biblical sin city
36 Gawk at
38 Align
39 "Hell ___ no fury . . ."
40 Around-the-house footwear, for short
41 Nonetheless
42 "___ Boot"
45 Get cozy
46 Talk, talk, talk
48 Future ferns

49 Mark of a rifle's laser sight
50 "The Battleship Potemkin" port
52 Most Monopoly income
54 Totally absurd
56 Electrician's hookup
57 Foul mood
59 Modern navigation tool, for short
60 Directional suffix
61 ___ Party movement
62 Tour de France peak
64 Aurora's counterpart

by Mike Torch

12

ACROSS

1 Declines, with "out of"
5 Professor says "Stocking stocker," pupil suggests . . .
10 Badlands formation
14 Mata __
15 Model glider material
16 Still unfilled
17 With 27-, 49- and 63-Across, the story behind 5-, 36-, 39- and 70-Across
20 Public commotion
21 Like much Vegas stagewear
22 Postgraduate field
23 Ramirez of "Spamalot"
25 1040 entry
27 See 17-Across
32 Ready to rock
33 Neighbor of Arg.
34 Bonny young girl
36 Professor says "Qualifying races," pupil suggests . . .
38 MGM motto ender
39 Professor says "Ax wielder," pupil suggests . . .
43 Buzzard's fare
45 Suffix with Brooklyn
46 Biblical witch's home
49 See 17-Across
52 Simple bit of plankton
54 Some reddish deer
55 "__ liebe dich"
56 Has in view, archaically
60 "Twice as much for a nickel" sloganeer, once
63 See 17-Across
66 Hodgepodge

67 Like limousines
68 Un-P.C. suffix, to many
69 "Hud" Oscar winner
70 Professor says "Equine restraint," pupil suggests . . .
71 Those, in Toledo

DOWN

1 Resistance units
2 Parisian picnic spot
3 Goes for a spot on the team
4 Prepare to turn
5 Kobe sash
6 Turned state's evidence
7 "Play it, Sam" speaker
8 Genesis twin
9 "Amazing" magician
10 Soccer or hockey follower
11 Feature of TV's "The Fugitive"
12 Halvah ingredient
13 Respond to a knock
18 Ex-Spice Girl Halliwell
19 Force units
24 Fighting it out
26 Docket item
27 Directly
28 ". . . __ mouse?"
29 Earth, in sci-fi
30 "__ ride" ("Don't change a thing")
31 Poet whose work inspired "Cats"
35 Ed of "The Bronx Zoo"
37 Kilt wearer
40 Signs of leaks
41 Jocular suffix with "best"

42 Flying Cloud automaker
44 Came about
46 "Speaking machine" developer
47 Paris's "The Simple Life" co-star
48 Mexico's national flower
50 Beatlesque dos
51 Tiny
53 Anne of "Archie Bunker's Place"
57 Life sci. course
58 Gait slower than a canter
59 Pentagonal plate
61 Madrid Mlle.
62 Fateful day in the Roman senate
64 Solid geometry abbr.
65 Onetime U.A.R. member

by Howard Baker

ACROSS

1. Angers, with "up"
6. Forest
11. Protrude
14. Disney's "little mermaid"
15. Facing the pitcher
16. French "a"
17. Recipe guideline for a hot dish
19. Railroad stop: Abbr.
20. Cozy lodging
21. Lure for Simple Simon
22. Smidgens
24. Persian Gulf leader
26. Family divided by divorce
30. Barber's tools
32. Deep hole
33. Fat used for tallow
34. Captain of Jules Verne's Nautilus
35. Name in a family restaurant chain
37. Football scores, for short
38. High-stakes draw in Las Vegas
41. Place for a baby to sit
44. Fish often destined for cans
45. Medical success
48. Gear for gondolas
50. Gradually slowing, in music: Abbr.
51. Pacific island garment wrapped around the waist
53. Pastrami, for one
56. Greek liqueur
57. Fainthearted
58. Spain's Costa del ___
60. Ob-___ (med. specialty)
61. Rope-a-dope boxer

62. "Sure, go ahead" . . . and a literal hint to what's found in 17-, 26-, 38- and 53-Across
67. IV adjusters
68. Oil directly from a well
69. 12" stick
70. Golf peg
71. Entered via a keyboard
72. Chasm

DOWN

1. More risqué
2. Certain triathlete
3. Treat as a celebrity
4. "Yikes!"
5. Sales receipt
6. Transaction at a racetrack
7. Slugger Mel
8. Kimono closer
9. Hoover ___
10. Gertrude who wrote "Rose is a rose is a rose is a rose"
11. Hot off the press
12. Wild
13. Dishes for doll parties
18. Penpoints
23. Cries of excitement
25. Frolic
27. Do surgery
28. Old Testament books labeled I and II
29. Sicilian erupter
31. Tooth or plant part
35. Jeans fabric
36. Family rec facility
39. Many a northern Iraqi
40. Continental currency

41. Skill that no one has anymore
42. "Now We Are Six" poet
43. Declaration sometimes made with crossed fingers behind the back
46. More or less
47. They help digest food
49. Vacation at Vail, maybe
51. Store (away)
52. Dead ducks
54. Formal decree
55. Queried
59. Turkey's currency
63. Give it a shot
64. Dine
65. "___ on a Grecian Urn"
66. Rubber ducky's spot

by Lynn Lempel

14

ACROSS

1 Muscat's land
5 Asset
9 Coffee choices
14 Clinton's 1996 opponent
15 Woodcarver's tool
16 Tortoise or hare
17 Actress Swenson of "Benson"
18 ___ de vivre
19 Milo of "Romeo and Juliet"
20 Astronomer's aid
22 Means
24 With 41- and 54-Across, group with a 1967 ballad version of 39-, 41-, and 42-Across
26 Word after "does" and "doesn't" in an old ad slogan
27 Glass on a radio
28 Audio input location
33 Wraps (up)
36 One who can't keep off the grass?
38 One of the Mannings
39 With 41- and 42-Across, 1964 Beatles hit
41 See 39-Across
42 See 39-Across
44 "The Star-Spangled Banner" preposition
45 Join the staff
48 Pinnacle
49 Keeps from happening
51 Western defense grp.
53 Broadcast
54 See 24-Across
59 Women, quaintly, with "the"
63 12:30 a.m. or p.m., on a ship
64 Bubbling

65 Cord material
67 Et ___
68 Zellweger of "My One and Only"
69 Button between * and #
70 Fronted, in a way
71 Piglike
72 Look inside?
73 Some jeans

DOWN

1 Keats, for one
2 The 6 in 6/8/10, e.g.
3 Pond buildup
4 Close call
5 Some are flannel
6 Parkinsonism drug
7 Israeli arm
8 Appear
9 See 40-Down

10 Having less forethought
11 Repeated message?
12 Thistle or goldenrod
13 Ladies of Spain: Abbr.
21 Damage
23 Villa d'___
25 Earliest time
29 Edit menu option
30 Job rights agcy.
31 Grad
32 Marriage, for one
33 Word before "You're killing me!"
34 Fancy pitcher
35 Bra insert
37 Lemony
40 With 9-Down, group with a 1962 hit version of 39-, 41-, and 42-Across

43 Really enjoys oneself
46 About, on a memo
47 "Private - keep out"
50 Isn't all the same
52 O'Neill's "The Hairy ___"
55 Old Testament prophet who married a harlot
56 Martinique volcano
57 Dior-designed dress
58 Strips in front of a window?
59 Old MacDonald had one
60 Busy as ___
61 Table salt is composed of them
62 PlayStation 2 competitor
66 Auto loan inits.

by Peter A. Collins

ACROSS

1 Flexible blades
6 Machines that run Panther or Leopard
10 Bean curd
14 Prefix with brewery
15 Home of King Harald V
16 Eye part
17 Part of a drug lord's income, maybe
19 Burping in public, e.g.
20 Eye part
21 Field of expertise
22 Small particles
23 Shogun's capital
24 Fruity soda
26 "Slumdog Millionaire" setting
28 Still
29 Watch furtively
30 Res ___ loquitur
33 You might get your feet wet with this
34 Boldly patterned warblers . . . and a hint to 17-, 24-, 50- and 59-Across
38 Minute Maid drink brand
41 Big film shower
42 Eye shade
46 Powerless
49 Singer portrayed in film by Jennifer Lopez
50 Rolling Stones hit of 1967
54 Liq. measures
55 Prepare to recite the Pledge of Allegiance
56 Hidden valley
57 "Comin' ___ the Rye"
58 Trillion: Prefix
59 Certain mason
61 City in Utah
62 Prefix with physics
63 Many-___ (large, as an estate)
64 Half, quarter or eighth follower
65 ___-bitsy
66 ___ nova

DOWN

1 Insignia
2 Amassed
3 Rental car choice
4 Cupid's Greek counterpart
5 Stuff sold in rolls
6 Actress Mary Tyler
7 Co-star of 6-Down in 1970s TV
8 Cloudless
9 ___ milk
10 Cassiterite, e.g.
11 Like a good speaking voice
12 Deft touch
13 Base entertainment
18 When doubled, a fish
22 When Emperor Henry IV was dethroned
24 Fred Astaire prop
25 Oenophile's concern
27 Staten Isl., for one
30 Doctrine
31 Educ. group
32 "Yakety ___," 1963 hit
35 Target of Pierre's prayers
36 Place with a gym
37 "The best pal that I ever had," in song
38 Author Zora Neale ___ of the Harlem Renaissance
39 Not yet born
40 1966 musical based on "I Am a Camera"
43 Gentle breezes
44 Sides accompaniers
45 World Series-winning manager of 1981 and 1988
47 How famous people are known
48 Brit. company name ending
49 Went under
51 Everglades wader
52 Skirt features
53 Break down
57 ___ Bell
59 ASCAP alternative
60 Science course requirement, maybe

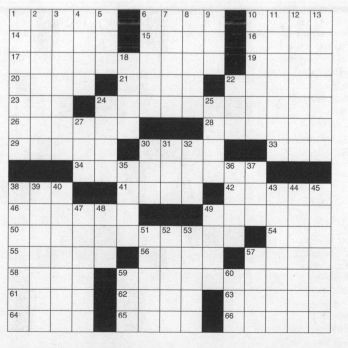

by Gary Whitehead

16

ACROSS

1 The Crimson Tide, informally
5 Swiss peaks
9 Rand McNally product
14 Author Haley of "Roots" fame
15 "___ Caesar!"
16 Result of an armistice
17 1980s TV series starring Michael Landon
20 Confused
21 Fill to excess
22 Sail holder
23 A sharpshooter needs a good one
25 Golf pro Ernie
27 2002 Tom Hanks/Paul Newman film
36 Easter roast
37 Actress Sorvino
38 Organization for geniuses
39 Japanese port
42 Catch red-handed
43 Cranium contents
44 Parking space adjunct
45 Elevator inventor Elisha
47 Big Japanese computer maker: Abbr.
48 Onetime Alaska boondoggle
52 One in a blue state majority: Abbr.
53 A pair
54 Yard entrance
57 Time of danger for Caesar
61 Occupied, as a lavatory
65 Traveler's option . . . or what you won't get on a 17-, 27- or 48-Across?
68 Near the center
69 Burden

70 Rough-___ (not smoothly finished)
71 Impoverished
72 Reserved parking space for an exec, maybe
73 Bones, anatomically

DOWN

1 ___ Men ("Who Let the Dogs Out" group)
2 Touched down
3 Computer capacity, in brief
4 Cutting part of a lumberjack's tool
5 Idea person's exclamation
6 Puts down
7 ___ bread
8 One-armed bandit
9 Animal that beats its chest
10 Professional truck driver
11 Volcano's output
12 King beaters
13 Already in the mail
18 World repeated before "Don't Tell Me!"
19 Obey
24 Pop's partner
26 What a do-it-yourself swing may hang from
27 Obllique-angled, four-sided figure
28 Western, in slang
29 Classic violin maker
30 ___ grigio (wine)
31 Muse of love poetry
32 Isarel's Yitzhak
33 Nonsensical
34 Willow whose twigs are used in basketry
35 F.D.R. veep John ___ Garner
40 Blushed
41 Encourage
46 Drunkard
49 Send out, as rays
50 Hitler started it: Abbr.
51 Top dog
54 Sheepish look, maybe
55 Popular steak sauce
56 Something to sing along to
58 Go south, as a stock market
59 "___ kleine Nachtmusik"
60 Thing on a cowboy's boot
62 Hawaiian instruments, informally
63 Stitches
64 Sicily's Mt. ___
66 Drought-stricken
67 "Shame on you!"

by Mark Feldman

ACROSS

1 Pet rocks, once
4 Prebirth event
10 Message runner
14 Top-of-the-charts number
15 It may come before the end of a sentence
16 Not get merely by accident
17 Intermittent, as a relationship
20 Host of a nightly TV show taped in Burbank
21 Sunburned
22 Lift the spirits of
23 Spearheaded
25 Plumlike fruit
27 Leaves the main topic temporarily
35 Playground retort
36 Pub deliveries
37 Apply brakes to
38 Org. with audits
39 Gearbox option
42 Day of anticipation
43 ___-do-well
45 One you dig the most
46 More exquisite
48 Start to exit an Interstate
51 Old El ___ (food brand)
52 Simile connection
53 Fall bloom
56 Resinous tree
58 Stick it in your ear
62 Trade places . . . or a hint to parts of 17-, 27- and 48-Across
66 Smuggler's unit
67 Francis of old game shows
68 Show hosts, for short
69 Dish simmered in a pot
70 Negotiator's refusal
71 Dig in

DOWN

1 Jester
2 Rice who wrote "The Vampire Chronicles"
3 College V.I.P.
4 Place to relax
5 Arrangement of locks
6 River of Normandy
7 Alternative to an iron
8 Little help?
9 Whistle blower, in brief
10 Limbs for movie pirates
11 Tiny battery
12 Sand
13 Feminine suffix
18 Uses an iron or a 7-Down, say
19 Time in Earth's history
24 Get an ___ effort
25 Quadraphonic halved
26 Scottish miss
27 Last step at a bakery
28 Delhi wrap: Var.
29 Beginning
30 Arizona tribe
31 Pain reliever brand
32 ___ Kagan, Obama nominee to the Supreme Court
33 Caesar's nine
34 Impudent nobody
40 Terrestrial salamanders
41 Bad grades
44 Aid for skiing uphill
47 Modern dweller in ancient Ur
49 Crack officer?
50 Hot breakfast cereal
53 Questions
54 Loretta of "M*A*S*H"
55 Scrabble piece
56 Bow out of a poker hand
57 "Now it's clear"
59 Big book
60 Member of a Pre-Columbian empire
61 It's attention-getting
63 ___ Solo, Harrison Ford role
64 Voting yes
65 ___ Aviv

by Jill Winslow

ACROSS

1 ___ Cohn, 1991 Grammy winner for Best New Artist
5 Rent-___
9 "War is not the answer" people
14 Elizabeth Taylor role, in brief
15 Khrushchev's impromptu gavel
16 Slightly ahead
17 Followed the Hippocratic oath, in a way
19 Either of two peaks in Greek myth
20 Sporty, powerful auto
22 Collapsible place to collapse
23 Not idling
24 "It's ___!" ("I give up!")
26 Racy, low-budget film
31 "Cool" amount
34 Checked out
35 Beatlemania reaction
36 Plebe's place: Abbr.
38 Check for freshness, in a way
41 Ladies' man
42 Ladies' man
44 "___ bien!"
46 Slot-car track section
47 Undergarments that show a little of the chest
51 101
52 Software instruction file heading
56 Easter lead-in
58 Messages on an Apple device
61 Youngest-ever French Open winner Michael ___

63 Some Election Day surveys
64 It may bring a tear to your eye
65 Word on a biblical wall
66 Sheryl Crow's "___ Wanna Do"
67 Fake-book contents
68 "With a wink and ___"
69 Closing bell org.

DOWN

1 Early 15th-century year
2 Many a day laborer
3 Make even deeper
4 ___ eel
5 Common car door fixtures, once
6 Activity in a virtual room
7 Simplest of choices
8 Send a tickler
9 Hollow-point bullets
10 ___-out clause
11 Yea-or-nay event
12 Prefix with skeleton
13 Pants part
18 Midwest air hub
21 Knock over, so to speak
25 Some eaters at troughs
27 Half a score
28 One of TV's Bunkers
29 Notes in pots
30 Reaches 0:00:00 on a countdown clock, say
31 Sportcaster Albert
32 Scissors, for "cut," on a PC
33 Knucklehead

37 Prefix meaning 27-Down
39 Common party night: Abbr.
40 Discovered after a search, with "out"
43 "Go ahead" hand gestures
45 High, as a price
48 Bit of advice
49 Conceptual framework
50 Margaret Mead interviewee
53 Waste time
54 Rumor sources?
55 Bovine in ads
56 Some PX patrons
57 "Yikes!"
59 Beasts in a span
60 Spanish boy
62 Seasonal quaff

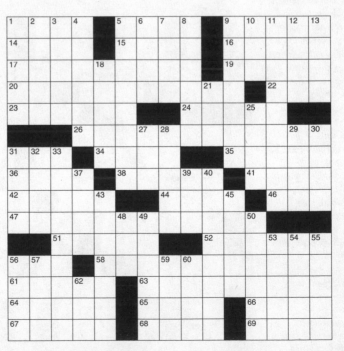

by Joe Krozel

ACROSS

1 Leftover bit of cloth
6 "The Zoo Story" playwright Edward
11 Manx or Siamese
14 "Remember the ___!" (cry of 1836)
15 Sounds SSTs made
16 Color shade
17 "It ain't hard!"
19 Ill temper
20 Go like a bunny
21 Wedding dress material
22 Kind of sleeve named after a British baron
24 With 46-Across, "It ain't hard!"
25 Chop-chop
26 Nadir's opposite
29 School time when kids aren't studying
30 Without an escort
31 Irritated
32 Potpie vegetable
35 Playful bites
36 Tennis great Monica
37 Source of linen
38 Big beagle feature
39 Farm tracts
40 Work like a dog
41 Be against
43 Hung around
44 Singer Flack or Peters
46 See 24-Across
47 Mama Cass ___
48 Autobiographer's subject
49 Follow the coxswain's calls
52 Sidewalk stand quaff
53 "It ain't hard!"
56 Not Rep. or Ind.
57 "The Odd Couple" slob

58 Bird on a U.S. quarter
59 B'way sellout sign
60 Attempts at baskets
61 Live in fear of

DOWN

1 Pageant entrant's wear
2 Advertising award
3 Multistory parking garage feature
4 Guitarist's accessory, for short
5 Foul the water, e.g.
6 Taken ___ (surprised)
7 Get whipped
8 Drag queen's wrap
9 Hugs tightly
10 Made a getaway
11 "It ain't hard!"
12 Hearing-related

13 Pint-size
18 To ___ his own
23 U.S.O. show audience members
24 Rackets
25 T. ___ (fearsome dinos)
26 Grey who wrote westerns
27 Charles Lamb alias
28 "It ain't hard!"
29 C.S.A. general
31 Vice ___
33 Roof overhang
34 Abruptly dismissed
36 Like many tartan wearers
37 Pajamas' rear opening
39 Pertinent
40 Like a taxidermist's work

42 Rock and Roll Hall of Fame architect I. M. ___
43 Without an escort
44 Uses a Kindle, e.g.
45 Like a big brother
46 Tarot card readers, e.g.
48 Ad-libbing vocal style
49 Violent 19-Across
50 State with a panhandle: Abbr.
51 Whacked plant
54 ___-friendly (green)
55 Indy 500 entry

by Fred Piscop

ACROSS

1 Fresh talk
4 Female TV dog played by males
10 Alphabet enders, to Brits
14 Letters on a wanted poster
15 Sitcom pal of 46-Down
16 Plains Indians
17 Kitten call
18 Governing body of a municipality
20 South-of-the-border outlaws
22 Conductor Zubin
23 12:50 or 1:50
24 Bay Area law enforcement org.
26 1965 Vivien Leigh movie
29 Gateways or Dells, briefly
32 Georgia home of the Allman Brothers
33 Baseball Triple Crown stat
34 Excellent, slangily
35 Safe havens
36 Word game . . . or a word that can precede the starts of 18-, 26-, 43- and 54-Across
38 Suffix for the wealthy
39 ___-Ball (arcade game)
40 Rawls of R&B
41 Strait of Hormuz vessel
42 "The buck stops here" prez
43 Old comics boy with the dog Tige
46 Rope fiber
47 Board game turns
48 Briquette residue
51 Delivery entrance, maybe

54 Center of attention around a campfire, say
57 Palm Treo, e.g.
58 Deborah of "The King and I"
59 Deck treatments
60 Often-replaced joint
61 Swing in the breeze
62 Hallucinogen-yielding cactus
63 To this point

DOWN

1 Souvlaki meat
2 Swedish home furnishings chain
3 Hockshop receipt
4 Make privy to, as a secret
5 Many
6 Remove, as a branch
7 Confessional list

8 Abbr. in co. names
9 Fair-hiring letters
10 Like most urban land
11 Impress deeply
12 Two-thirds of D.I.Y.
13 Ward of "The Fugitive," 1993
19 Stereotypically "blind" officials
21 Topple from power
24 Cries out loud
25 Move like a moth
26 Box-office hit
27 Pays attention
28 "Are you in ___?"
29 Field of Plato and Aristotle
30 Rod with seven batting championships
31 Howard of satellite radio

34 Like sorted socks
36 Market surplus
37 Nozzle site
41 "Heads" side of a coin
43 At it
44 The Brat Pack's Estevez
45 Porcupine or gopher
46 Former boyfriend of 15-Across
48 Queries
49 Ratatouille or ragout
50 Bar mitzvah dance
51 Leave in stitches
52 Occasionally punted comics canine
53 Totally absorbed
55 Dose amt.
56 Summer on the Seine

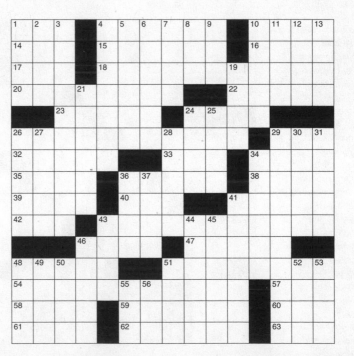

by Barry C. Silk

21

ACROSS

1 "Still mooing"
5 Old flames?
10 Forage storage
14 Old flames
15 Job made almost obsolete by voice recorders
16 Privy to
17 Tots
19 Upper hand
20 Plaza de toros cry
21 First murderer
22 "Entourage" agent Gold
23 Moor's deity
25 Make fine adjustments to
30 Home of the Stars
32 Fictional airline on "Lost"
33 Wine label datum
36 "It's ___-brainer"
37 "On the Waterfront" Oscar winner
41 Actress Larter of "Heroes"
42 Stars that exhibit the "lighthouse effect"
43 Tortilla chip brand
46 Need leveling, perhaps
50 With 60-Across, ink a contract . . . or a feature of 17-, 25- and 37-Across
53 Shop group
54 Trellis climber
55 "Drat!"
57 "Usual gang of idiots" magazine
58 One of Spot's masters
60 See 50-Across
63 Graph line
64 Film director Kershner
65 Fit for duty
66 Substance
67 Kind of question
68 Line to Penn Sta.

DOWN

1 Time-consuming task for a musketeer
2 Armpit, anatomically
3 Pass along, as gossip
4 Ballpark fig.
5 Away from harbor
6 Stiff-upper-lip sort
7 Temporary tattoo dye
8 St. Louis-to-Cleveland dir.
9 "Sending out an ___" (much-repeated line in a Police hit)
10 Jagged mountain range
11 Hoosier
12 Captain's journal
13 Diet-drink calorie count
18 Toast at a bar mitzvah
22 Mt. Rushmore neighbor of Teddy
24 Menlo Park middle name
26 Pricey seating areas
27 Winter fisherman's tool
28 Salon job
29 Prefix with -cide
31 Attach with a click
34 Target for Teddy Roosevelt
35 Feel awful
37 Morlocks' victims, in an H. G. Wells story
38 Birthplace of eight U.S. presidents
39 Roughly
40 Publisher's 13-digit ID
41 Billboard displays
44 Buy gold, e.g.
45 Water pistol or popgun
47 Bahamas getaway
48 Temporary wheels
49 Win over
51 Sharp products, for short
52 Opposite of "take out"
56 Setting for the movie "Sister Act"
58 Problem for a copier
59 Send packing
60 Handyman's letters
61 Miner's find
62 "U R funny!"

by Alex Boisvert

22

ACROSS

1 Some British sports cars, briefly
5 Contest specifications
10 Third piece of a three-piece suit
14 Baghdad's home
15 Separately
16 x or y, on a graph
17 In ___ of (replacing)
18 Copy, for short
19 Wang of fashion
20 Dreamy state
22 "Star Trek" weapon
24 The Beatles' "Abbey ___"
25 Schreiber who won a Tony for "Glengarry Glen Ross"
26 Broadcast with little room for mistakes
29 Unshackle
33 Card that may be "in the hole"
34 Early morning hour
36 Exxon merged with it
37 Appear
39 Provide with a blind date, say
41 Anti-attacker spray
42 Politico Palin
44 Aired again
46 Stag party attendees
47 Clearly confused, e.g.
49 ___ party (sleepover)
51 Pinnacle
52 Green gem
53 Isn't an odd one out
56 Gilda Radner character on "S.N.L."
60 Side x side, for a 4-Down
61 Hacienda material
63 Fizzless, as a Coke
64 Long skirt
65 Lethal cousin of the cobra
66 $50 for Boardwalk, in Monopoly
67 Founded: Abbr.
68 Put in prison
69 Pair with a plow

DOWN

1 Jack's partner in rhyme
2 Mozart's "Il mio tesoro," e.g.
3 Celt or Highlander
4 Equilateral quadrilateral
5 One in a million
6 Overturn
7 "Columbo" org.
8 Make a boo-boo
9 "Cut that out!"
10 "Hubba hubba!"
11 They've gone their separate ways
12 Retired racehorse, maybe
13 Peter the Great, e.g.
21 Oodles
23 Captain's place on a ship
25 Ring-tailed primate
26 Rodeo ring?
27 Mountaineer's tool
28 Small American thrush
29 Go past midnight, say
30 First president not born in the continental U.S.
31 Words to an attack dog
32 2008 Olympics tennis champion Dementieva
35 Copy, of a sort
38 1961 hit for the Shirelles
40 Owner of the largest bed Goldilocks tried
43 Pueblo Indian
45 Zilch
48 Put a new title on
50 Curly ethnic hairstyle, colloquially
52 "Star Wars" villain ___ the Hutt
53 Renown
54 401(k) cousins
55 Communicate like many teens
56 Fail miserably
57 Trebek of "Jeopardy!"
58 What moons do after full moons
59 Abbr. before a name on a memo
62 Beaver's construction

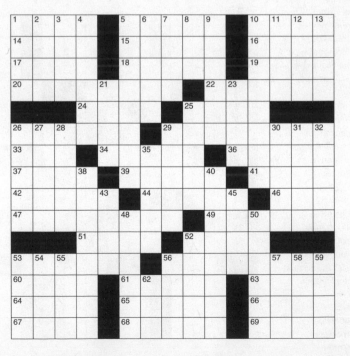

by Joel Fagliano

ACROSS

1 AARP or the National Rifle Association
6 Without: Fr.
10 French city in 1944 fighting
14 "Bird on ___" (1990 film)
15 Lafayette's state?
16 Singer India.___
17 Kind of code
18 Super star
19 Poetic foot
20 Asian cat
23 Blue Jays, on a scoreboard
24 Net
25 Heroine of Verdi's "Il Trovatore"
27 Euro forerunner
29 Slo-o-ow leak
31 Santa ___ winds
32 Makeshift seat at a rodeo
34 Penn, for one: Abbr.
35 Alarm bell
39 With 41- and 43-Across, cop cruiser . . . or a description of the five animals named in this puzzle
41 See 39-Across
43 See 39-Across
44 Form of many a diploma
46 Smidge
48 Sign to be interpreted
49 "The dog ate my homework," maybe
50 "You love," to Livy
52 Thurman of "Pulp Fiction"
53 Some track-and-field training
57 Move stealthily
59 Decorative pond fish
60 Shamu, for one
64 "Back in the ___"
66 Porky Pig, e.g.
67 Building usually without a 13th floor
68 Penury
69 "La Belle et la ___" (French fairy tale)
70 At ___ for words
71 Actress Sedgwick of "The Closer"
72 Cornerstone abbr.
73 Like the review "Hated it," e.g.

DOWN

1 Track units
2 Wilson of "Wedding Crashers"
3 Like some vision
4 Melee
5 Bellowed
6 Potential enamorada
7 On
8 Like some exercises
9 Ogle
10 ___ tai (drink)
11 Poetic Muse
12 Island near Java
13 Equus quagga
21 Prominent features of Alfred E. Neuman
22 "What should I ___?"
26 ___ cheese
27 Wanes
28 Class after trig
30 One of the 2008 Olympic mascots
33 Cause of a beach closure, maybe
36 Flight training equipment
37 Thing
38 "99 Red Balloons" singer, 1984
40 "Hogan's Heroes" colonel
42 Made less intense
45 1970 #1 hit whose title follows the lyric "Speaking words of wisdom . . ."
47 Bob ___, 2008 Libertarian candidate for president
51 "Who cares?"
53 Polecat
54 Actress Parker
55 Choir support
56 Tart fruits
58 Intact
61 Former Mississippi senator Trent
62 Minus
63 Ultimatum ender
65 Nutritional abbr.

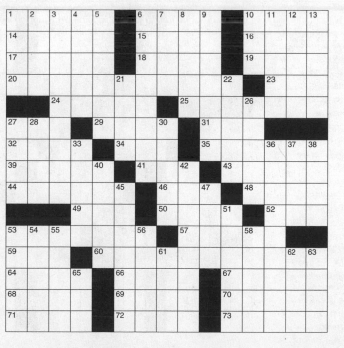

by Peter A. Collins

24

ACROSS

1 Harry James's "___ the Craziest Dream"
5 Knotted up
9 Bedding item
13 Marisa of "The Wrestler"
15 Georgetown athlete
16 Rabbit punch target
17 Conk the "You Were Meant for Me" singer?
19 Major in astronomy?
20 Attempts, with "at"
21 Did improv
23 Rogers and Bean
25 The "A" of A.D.
26 Truckers' breaks
30 Has contempt for
33 Dernier ___
34 Goes well with
36 Org.
37 Cause of head-scratching, perhaps
39 1943 penny material
41 Architect Saarinen
42 House arrestee's bracelet site
44 Instrument that's usually played cross-legged
46 Tbsp., e.g.
47 Some farm machinery
49 "Billy Budd" and "Of Mice and Men"
51 Radiate
52 Nike competitor
53 Pigeonholed, in moviedom
57 Site of a 1976 South African uprising
61 Speller's words of clarification

62 Scratch the "2 Legit 2 Quit" rapper?
64 Car door ding
65 Cousin of an eagle
66 Sends to blazes
67 Torah holders
68 Floored it
69 Defense grp. since 1949

DOWN

1 Trigger finger problem?
2 Dance done to "Hava Nagila"
3 Andy's partner in old radio
4 White Label Scotch maker
5 Everyday article
6 Early caucus state
7 Checked out
8 Miss Ellie's soap
9 Revolver feature, perhaps
10 Protect the "Kiss From a Rose" singer from the cops?
11 Cathedral recess
12 Drink in "Beowulf"
14 Bars at Fort Knox
18 Festive
22 Quechua speaker
24 Rotisserie parts
26 Programming class locale, perhaps
27 "Three Sisters" sister
28 Amuse the "Get the Party Started" singer?
29 Oktoberfest memento
31 Singer of the "Casta diva" aria
32 Tartan hose wearers

35 Play by a different ___ rules
38 Mendeleev's tabulation
40 Like an inaugural ball
43 Children's author Carle
45 Do a musketeer's job
48 IHOP servings
50 Wyatt Earp, e.g.
53 "Look what I did!"
54 River through Flanders
55 Break one's resolution, say
56 ___ Modern (London gallery)
58 Austen classic
59 Camper's carry-along
60 Roughly
63 Got hitched

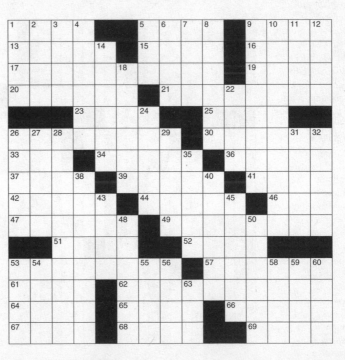

by Kristian House

ACROSS

1 Part of a flower or wineglass
5 "Exodus" author Leon
9 "Aladdin" villain
14 Volcano output
15 Quarter of a bushel
16 Had dinner at home
17 Jai ___
18 Sycamore or cypress
19 Diploma receivers, for short
20 The best place to sleep
23 Drought relief
24 This-and-that dish
25 Most strange
28 They may be tapped for fraternities
32 Singer in Abba
33 Give up a poker hand
34 "Vive le ___!"
35 The best place to sit
39 Vietnamese New Year
40 Abhor
41 Make up (for)
42 Long journeys
45 Name holders
46 "Little piggies"
47 About, on a memo
48 The best place to see
54 Narrow openings
55 Ending with peek or bug
56 Place to order a ham on rye
57 Secret stash
58 Take care of, as a store
59 Prez, e.g.
60 Like a stamp pad
61 Guitarist Townshend
62 Carve in stone

DOWN

1 Response to a rude remark
2 A fisherman might bring back a big one
3 Sen. Bayh of Indiana
4 They show you to your table
5 Ready for a challenge
6 Second airing
7 Summer coolers in tiny cups
8 ___-Ball (arcade game)
9 Alternative to a Mercedes or BMW
10 In jeopardy
11 Burlesque show accessory
12 Capitol Hill worker
13 E.R. workers
21 Attacks
22 Loses hair, as a dog
25 "We're ___ See the Wizard"
26 Hung on the clothesline
27 Prank that's not nice
28 Yachts, e.g.
29 Otherwise
30 On one's way
31 Trig functions
33 Whip
36 Where VapoRub may be rubbed
37 Training group
38 Conference-goer
43 Relieve
44 Felt
45 Like secret messages
47 "Not gonna do it"
48 Custard dessert
49 Highway exit
50 Theater award
51 Student's book
52 Monthly util. bill
53 Having megamillions
54 Chem. or biol.

by Mike Nothnagel

26

ACROSS
1 Not a hologram, say
5 First mate?
9 Somewhat, slangily
14 Kind of clef
15 Whittle (down)
16 Fiery feeling
17 "There's a call for you, Mr. Gates"
19 Talk big
20 Swatch rival
21 Rummy
22 In tune
23 Milk, on an Rx
25 Garbage boat
27 "Calm down, Mr. Wahlberg"
32 Faithful servant in "Otello"
36 Inits. on a telly
37 Mick Jagger and fellas, with "the"
39 Singer k. d. __
40 Sufficient, informally
42 Blackens, in a way
43 Suffix with electro-
44 Hart family sitcom
45 Build up, as a river's edge
47 Coffee holder
48 In poor taste
50 "Get out of the chair, Mr. Boone"
52 Swarm
54 Trial lawyer's advice
55 TV doctor
58 Part of F.W.I.W.
61 Popular exercise system
65 One way to read
66 "Clean up, Mr. Stewart"
68 Bing Crosby's record label
69 Toledo's lake

70 Event not run in the Olympics
71 Sausage flavor
72 Hold sway
73 What a ring doesn't have

DOWN
1 Fully absorbed
2 K–12
3 Positron's place
4 Unfriended
5 P.D. alert
6 Honoree's place
7 A Guthrie
8 Turns to mush
9 Comic book blast
10 "Press on, Mr. Smith"
11 Bismarck's locale: Abbr.
12 One tablespoon, e.g.
13 A bit pretentious

18 Boards, e.g.
24 Colorful marble
26 Some corporate planes
27 Critic Roger
28 Capp lad
29 Look at coral reefs, maybe
30 Part of an accusation in the game Clue
31 Old TV features
33 Simple two-pointer
34 The "I" in IUD
35 Cut taker
38 Louisiane ou Floride
41 "At once, Mr. Owens"
46 Coach Rockne
49 Prime time
51 "Alas!"
53 Silas Marner, e.g.

55 Rolls of dough
56 Boron or bohrium: Abbr.
57 Bats
59 Drive-__
60 Potter's buy
62 Land of poetry
63 Typeface option
64 Sapphic works
67 Minuscule

by Timothy Powell

ACROSS

1 Bunsen burner fuel
4 Womb contents
9 Identical socks
14 Dadaist Jean
15 ___ Sea, home of the Isle of Man
16 Unfriendly way to respond
17 Muumuu accessory
18 Queen's place
20 "Tsk tsk" elicitor
22 Pushed around, as food
23 Listen here
24 Sunburned
25 Queens place
31 Fall behind
34 Race assignment
35 Voting second in a voice vote
36 Comstock ___
37 U.S. rocket with a name from classical myth
38 Dr. Bartolo in Mozart's 4-Down
40 "Put a lid ___!"
41 Cushiony forest seat
42 #2
43 "The African Queen" scriptwriter
44 "Say 'ah'" doc
45 Queens place
48 Call ___ day
49 ___ Plaines, Ill.
50 Snack bar content
54 Hoedown staples
58 Queen's place
60 King Kong, e.g.
61 Bubbling on the stove
62 Attribute
63 Straight out of the box
64 Is wide open, as a chasm
65 "Ready, ___!"
66 Animal house

DOWN

1 Molls and dolls
2 Tiler's measurement
3 Queen's place, in fiction
4 See 38-Across
5 Pitching stats
6 What prisoners do
7 "What's the ___?"
8 Yellow Pages listing
9 It's a knockout
10 Needed to be kneaded, maybe
11 Ready to go into overtime
12 Lioness of book and film
13 Part of CBS: Abbr.
19 "___ good time . . ."
21 Give strokes
25 Inamorata, say
26 With whom Moses went to Egypt
27 Semi section
28 Jack
29 Mixed up
30 Smartens (up)
31 Queens's place
32 Farewell
33 "Don't let those fellas escape!"
36 Filthy rich
39 Select, with "for"
45 Counter positions
46 Not quite a majority
47 Piles on
48 Finalize, as a cartoon
50 Aussie greeting
51 Singer McEntire
52 "Don't have ___, man!"
53 Whence the line "It is more blessed to give than to receive"
54 Sig Chi, e.g.
55 "Gotcha!"
56 Sport with masks
57 Tailor-made
59 "Chances ___"

by Manny Nosowsky

28

ACROSS

1 Blind trio in a children's rhyme
5 Cripples
10 Hindu prince
14 On the ocean
15 Eve of "Our Miss Brooks"
16 "Be it __ so humble . . ."
17 Tenant's monthly check
18 Embroidery, e.g.
20 Crosses (out)
21 Wrote fraudulently, as a check
22 Armored vehicles
23 Chicago-based TV talk show
25 Actor Bert in a lion's suit
27 Lantern usable during storms
31 Snaky curves
32 Activist Brockovich
33 Mauna __ (Hawaiian volcano)
36 Like arson evidence
37 Bread for breakfast
39 Bucket
40 Prefix with cycle
41 Closed
42 Refuse a request
43 Hanukkah food
47 Dramatist Simon who wrote "Plaza Suite"
48 Rewords
49 Tolerate
52 Fable writer
54 Olympic gold-medal runner Sebastian
57 Some makeup
59 Alluring
60 Actor Baldwin
61 Hackneyed
62 Leg's midpoint
63 Hazard
64 Without the help of written music
65 Hankerings

DOWN

1 Karl who philosophized about class struggle
2 "Aha!"
3 Government suppression of the press
4 Have dinner
5 Nutcase
6 Franklin known as the Queen of Soul
7 __ fixe (obsession)
8 Busybodies
9 Weekend NBC hit, for short
10 Put on the stove again
11 The Bard's river
12 Bozo
13 Torah holders
19 Wharton's "__ Frome"
21 __ Kringle
24 Hunter's target
26 Landed (on)
27 Summer oppressiveness
28 SALT I signer
29 "Cool!"
30 Do some acting
34 Sty sound
35 __ vera
37 Spicy Asian cuisine
38 Criminal activity
39 Treaty
41 Precipitous
42 Small scissor cut
44 Next up
45 Pre-euro Spanish coin
46 Worshipful one
49 Way, way off
50 "__ Ha'i" ("South Pacific" song)
51 Frosty desserts
53 __ Britt on "Desperate Housewives"
55 Yoked beasts
56 What the starts of 18-, 27-, 43- and 57-Across all have
58 Wagering loc.
59 Heavens

by Lynn Lempel

ACROSS

1 Maître d's offering
5 Name on planes, once
10 Storyline
14 Drug dealer's customer
15 TV antenna of old
17 Lee of Marvel Comics
18 Hirsute Himalayan beast
19 Rug rat
20 Vintner's prefix
21 RR stop
22 Tourist attraction near Giza
24 Pacino danced it in "Scent of a Woman"
29 Neural network
31 Stein contents
32 PC monitor part
33 Exotic jelly flavor
36 "The Soup ___" (classic "Seinfeld" episode)
38 ___ Tzu (toy dog)
39 Appropriate comment for this puzzle
42 Jockey strap
43 Asia's ___ Sea
44 Pinker in the middle
45 La-la lead-in
46 An ex of Frank
47 Coal-rich German region
49 Mets contest at Shea, e.g.
52 Go from pub to pub
56 "Lord, is ___?"
57 Cash holder
59 G.P. grp.
60 Project's conclusion
64 Bikini parts
65 Is compliant

66 "___ it a pity?"
67 Smoke or salt, maybe
68 Day one
69 ___ Pet

DOWN

1 They're required
2 Bar, legally
3 Not o'er
4 Large coffee container
5 Composition's original form
6 Spahn teammate Johnny
7 Monk's superior
8 "Can ___ dreaming?"
9 Slower, in mus.
10 Tetra- plus one
11 Secure oneself in port
12 ". . . man ___ mouse?"
13 Sound of rebuke
16 Have a sample of
20 Tatum of "Paper Moon"
23 Former Nascar driver Ernie
25 Filberts
26 Wiesel who wrote "Night"
27 Dirt
28 Catchall category
30 Memory trace
33 Waist size
34 In ___ (not yet born)
35 Turkey's locale
37 Celestial altar
38 Reporter Brenda of the comics
40 Magma, after surfacing

41 Rural village in South Africa
46 Nimble
48 Most up to the task
50 Marchers' camp
51 Les ___-Unis
53 Hard on the ears
54 Muscat native
55 Fusilli or rotini
58 "Ah so!"
60 TV regulatory grp.
61 Marker letters
62 Old hand
63 ___ Solo of "Star Wars"
64 Inexpensive pen

by James R. Leeds

ACROSS

1 Related
5 Acted like
9 ___-Detoo of "Star Wars"
14 Glass piece
15 Olympic rings, for one
16 Heinz canful
17 1981 Paul Newman/Sally Field film
20 Loving murmur
21 9-Across, e.g., informally
22 Vain
23 Hidden asset
26 Oppressor
28 Part of E.M.T.: Abbr.
29 Strident complaint
31 Place for a buzzer
32 AOL, e.g.: Abbr.
35 Catch red-handed
37 Cooler
38 Hose site
42 It can give you a sinking feeling
43 About
44 Where to find sweaters
45 Mayberry souse
47 Some basketball players: Abbr.
49 Diamond protector
53 Separate
55 Most-used key
58 Like a sunny room
60 Dander
61 Oklahoma native
62 What 17-, 23-, 38- and 55-Across have
65 Four for four, say
66 French abstraction
67 Touch
68 Rooney and Roddick
69 Crossing point
70 This, to Teodoro

DOWN

1 Army helicopter
2 Not just a bang
3 Loafer liner
4 Name part in some alumni directories
5 Maker of Reynolds Wrap
6 Bookstore section
7 Conceit
8 Tip politely
9 Taper off
10 Find yummy
11 Meineke stock item
12 Quick look
13 Sugar suffix
18 Original "Bonanza" airer
19 Chocolaty desserts
24 Rock's Clapton
25 "American Bandstand" extras
27 Jack's inferior
30 Retail store opening?
33 ___ generis (unique)
34 Start the workday, maybe
36 Big lead in a race
38 Defeat democratically
39 Worked up
40 "The A-Team" actor
41 "Big" kid in the comics
42 Physique, informally
46 Catchphrase for Willie Mays
48 Actor Brent of "Star Trek: T.N.G."
50 Causes of Bikini blasts
51 Tell on
52 Immediately
54 Film teasers
56 Like most football passes
57 Corp. V.I.P.
59 End-of-the-week cheer
62 Secret org.
63 Union agreement?
64 Fannie ___

by Lee Glickstein and Nancy Salomon

ACROSS

1 Comedian Foxworthy
5 Tiff
9 Manhandle
14 Early TV role for Ron Howard
15 Author Victor
16 Comment to the audience
17 1960's series about a boy and his bear
19 Outsides of lemons and limes
20 12th-grader
21 Swiss-based relief group
23 Johnny of "Pirates of the Caribbean"
25 Itsy-bitsy
26 Choose
29 Greeting with a hug and a kiss, say
35 Cawing birds
37 Go bankrupt
38 Ever and ___
39 Kind of lamp at a luau
40 Composer Franz
41 Give temporarily
42 Genesis garden
43 ___ Major
44 Popeye's burly foe
45 Feature of the Christian God
48 Cathedral seat
49 Dernier ___ (the latest thing)
50 Cold and damp, as a basement
52 Home of a hypothetical monster
57 "I haven't the foggiest"
61 Miss ___ of TV's "Dallas"
62 Compliment
64 Grabs (onto)
65 Object of devotion
66 Mailed
67 "Full House" actor Bob
68 Being nothing more than
69 "The Bridge on the River ___"

DOWN

1 Runs for exercise
2 Sporting sword
3 Huckleberry ___
4 Offensive-smelling
5 Mountain climber's guide
6 Place to play darts
7 Chemical used by document forgers
8 Dial ___
9 Package
10 "If memory serves . . ."
11 Overindulger of the grape
12 Throws in
13 ___ Trueheart of "Dick Tracy"
18 Big name in movie theaters
22 Lived (in)
24 Employer of flacks
26 Santa's reindeer, minus Rudolph
27 Egotist's sin
28 Subway coin
30 En ___ (as a group)
31 Harry Potter, for one
32 Outdo by a little
33 Three-card scam
34 Furnish with a fund
36 Porch music maker
40 Alison who won a Pulitzer for "Foreign Affairs"
44 Previously, up to this point
46 Polar explorer Shackleton
47 Wick holder
51 Newsstand
52 Chicken drumsticks
53 Earthenware pot
54 Job for a drain cleaner
55 Read over hurriedly
56 Pro or con
58 Provoked, as enemy fire
59 Poet ___ St. Vincent Millay
60 Wine-producing region of Italy
63 Neither hide ___ hair

by Dave Tuller

ACROSS

1 Cube creator Erno
6 Rudely ignore
10 Computer graphics file format
14 "Saturday Night Live" alum Cheri
15 Green Hornet's sidekick
16 Push for
17 Two-time Oscar winner Dianne
18 Asia's __ Sea
19 Roseanne, formerly and again
20 Camera type, briefly
21 See 33-Down
24 Points a finger at
26 Leases again
27 Nogales nap
29 Oliver's request
30 Indianapolis gridder
31 Be slack-jawed
34 Pool measurement
38 Hole-making tool
39 Is a member
41 "Yes, madame"
42 "You never know . . ."
44 Decorative case
45 Barely manages, with "out"
46 Narrow inlets
48 S.F. Giants' div.
50 Map feature
53 Less complicated
55 See 33-Down
57 Aunt Polly's nephew, in a Twain classic
60 Yugoslavia's Josip __ Tito
61 Heart of the matter
62 Throw with effort
64 Boxer's prefight attire
65 "Able was I __ . . ."
66 Kindergartners
67 They sometimes "have it"
68 Telemarketer's aim
69 Tea leaf readers, e.g.

DOWN

1 Seating sections
2 Gas, e.g.: Abbr.
3 See 33-Down
4 Form 1040 org.
5 Popular Hershey bar
6 Do lutzes, e.g.
7 Pushers' pursuers
8 Six-sided state
9 Ravel classic
10 On fire, as some desserts
11 Ramble on
12 White-plumed wader
13 Listerine targets
22 Spin doctor's concern
23 The out crowd
25 D-Day craft
27 Shell game
28 Corn Belt state
29 List of options
32 Drinks with heads
33 Word that defines 21- and 55-Across and 3- and 35-Down
35 See 33-Down
36 Mardi Gras, e.g.: Abbr.
37 H.S. subject
39 It's alive
40 Kind of knife advertised on TV
43 Summer coolers
45 Farm female
47 "Let sleeping dogs lie" and others
49 Start of a director's directive
50 Virgo's follower
51 Jetson boy
52 Shakespeare's theater
53 1950's automotive embarrassment
54 Clarinetist Shaw
56 The euro replaced it
58 All done
59 Military meal
63 Artist's asset

by Allan E. Parrish

ACROSS

1 "The Family Circus" cartoonist Keane
4 Undoer of "ritardando"
10 Early late-night name
14 Big bird
15 Big bow
16 Avatar of Vishnu
17 Very cool 1970's N.F.L.er?
19 Painter Nolde
20 Medical facility
21 Some nods
23 Feverish
24 Nobel or Oscar
25 Watch readout, for short
27 Dwight beat him twice
29 Wipe out
30 Girl rescued by Don Juan
32 "Fiddler on the Roof" matchmaker
33 Like Beethoven
35 Menu words
36 Strapped
37 Fresh-squeezed ex-football star/pitchman?
40 Pill variety
43 Set of wedges?
44 Doesn't shut up
48 Hoagy Carmichael's "Star Dust," e.g.
49 Was sweet (on)
51 Turn
52 Blair's predecessor
53 "___ calls?"
54 Course coup
56 Alley org.
57 Sample
59 ___-faire
60 Novelist Janowitz
62 Novelist/poet not playing the field?

65 Harbinger
66 In the least
67 Prefix with -lithic
68 Illustrator Thomas
69 Musically connected
70 Both Begleys

DOWN

1 Like some whales
2 Company in the Martha Stewart stock trading scandal
3 Country singer Williams
4 Eddying
5 Rash response?
6 Judge in I Samuel
7 Word on both sides of "to" and "for"
8 Gong site

9 City in SW Russia
10 Opposite of post-
11 Children's author trying to dry out?
12 Tardy person's question
13 Came from behind
18 "The fifth Beatle"
22 Decline
25 Leslie Caron musical
26 Fasten firmly, as to a bench
28 1960's Detroit Tigers star McLain
31 Right on the map
34 Leaf
36 Shrink's statement
38 Boos
39 Compassion

40 City SE of downtown Los Angeles
41 Auburn foe
42 Mystery writer with a badge?
45 W.W. I battle locale
46 Maintained order over
47 Sound systems
49 Nymph loved by Apollo
50 Loved by
55 "___, Caesar!"
58 "American ___"
59 Loretta of "M*A*S*H"
61 Colony member
63 Stilt's place
64 Litigator's org.

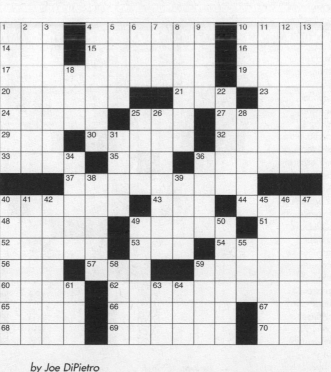

by Joe DiPietro

ACROSS

1 Word repeated before "black sheep, have you any wool?"
4 Semester
8 Seizes (from)
14 Building add-on
15 Downwind, on a ship
16 Kitt who played Catwoman on "Batman"
17 Avg., sizewise
18 Aromatherapy liquid
20 Cereal named for two ingredients it doesn't have
22 ___ of Cleves, English queen
23 Back of a boat
24 Emergency PC key
25 SSW's reverse
26 The "I" in T.G.I.F.
28 Jacuzzi
31 Jacuzzis
34 Maxima maker
38 "Put ___ Happy Face"
39 Really tired
42 Small bed
43 Followed the leader
44 Shady giants
45 Becomes a parent not by childbirth
47 Slangy assent
49 "Once upon a midnight dreary" writer
50 Veneration
53 Numbskull
57 No. on a baseball card
59 Gary Cooper film of 1928
61 Overwrought writing
64 Architect I. M. ___

65 Removes, as a knot
66 Sporting sword
67 Nest item
68 Turns back to zero
69 Lifeless
70 "Nope"

DOWN

1 Floaters in northern seas
2 Vigilant
3 Tiny pond plants
4 Aptitude
5 Pizazz
6 Variety show
7 Swim competitions
8 Said "I do" together
9 Norma ___, Sally Field role
10 On the wrong course

11 Paleolithic hammer or ax
12 Skinny
13 Realtor's aim
19 President's foreign policy grp.
21 Light refractor
25 All's opposite
27 Rebuffs rudely
28 Robust
29 E pluribus ___
30 Upside-down sleepers
31 Org. offering creature comforts?
32 Trudge
33 Fenders, taillights, etc.
35 Swelling reducer
36 Where a telescope is aimed
37 "Get it?"
40 Lug

41 Train stop
46 Baked entree with a crust
48 Controlled the mike
50 Austrian peak
51 Sent by bank transfer
52 Get hitched hastily
54 Turn red, as an apple
55 End of the Greek alphabet
56 Whinny
57 Cowboy boot part
58 Ditty
60 Between ports
62 Permit
63 Twisty turn

by Lynn Lempel

ACROSS

1 Old-fashioned phono
5 "No problemo"
10 Smoky European peak
14 ___ Islands of Galway Bay
15 More like a wallflower
16 After that . . .
17 The art of masonry, in Boston?
19 Pucker-producing
20 Adams who photographed Yosemite
21 Electronic music pioneer Robert
22 Comprehensive
23 Bar total
25 "My bad!"
27 Recipe amt.
30 Most revered person in the land, in Boston?
36 Computer woe
38 Pendulum paths
39 Hang around
40 La Scala highlight
41 Cubs' homes
43 Fuel that's shoveled
44 Less desirable turkey parts
46 Signature part: Abbr.
47 "Cómo ___?"
48 Saying hi to some food fish, in Boston?
51 D.C. V.I.P.
52 F.B.I. agent
53 Director Craven
55 Skipper's cry
57 Skipper's direction
61 Calculus calculation
65 Eardrum-busting
66 Finishing school for models, in Boston?
68 "Animal House" party attire
69 For crying out loud, e.g.
70 Andy's sidekick, in old radio
71 ___-dokey
72 Most driver's ed students
73 Database command

DOWN

1 LOL, spoken
2 Unwrinkle
3 The twist, once, and others
4 Miniature map
5 TV drama with multiple spinoffs
6 "Um, pardon me . . ."
7 Spanish boy
8 Like Erté's style
9 Salem's home
10 Sundance Kid's girlfriend
11 "Yuck!"
12 Detective Wolfe of fiction
13 Animated bug movie of 1998
18 Extended family
24 Jezebel's idol
26 Feedbag morsel
27 Country singer's sound
28 More ticked off
29 Earn windfall profits, perhaps
31 Wabash Cannonball, e.g.
32 Cake topper
33 "Hamlet" courtier
34 Use a soapbox
35 Bob who sang "A Hard Rain's A-Gonna Fall"
37 Challenge from Dirty Harry
42 Tuck away
45 B&O stop: Abbr.
49 Soon
50 Compaq competitor
54 "___ Marner"
55 Voice below soprano
56 End of a wooden arm
58 Prospector's discovery
59 Falco of "The Sopranos"
60 Supply-and-demand subj.
62 Office reminder
63 Assistant with a hunch?
64 Midterm, e.g.
67 Sounds of meditation

by Randall J. Hartman

36

ACROSS

1 Appropriate-sounding papal name
5 Word on a headstone
9 Gulped bar drinks
14 Waffle brand
15 "East of Eden" director Kazan
16 Kind of typing
17 They have a chilling effect
19 Exterior
20 Skating great Yamaguchi
21 Doubting Thomas, for one
23 Top guns
26 Ancient
27 Not imaginary
31 Gun
32 "___ directed"
33 Unswerving
35 Popular brand of lingerie
39 Excellent, slangily
40 Word that can follow the starts of 17- and 61-Across and 10- and 30-Down
41 "One Tree Hill" target viewer
42 Jack-tar
43 X ___ xylophone
44 Gave up
45 Cut (off)
47 Port of Japan
49 Scam
52 Rod and reel, e.g.
53 Harvesting team
55 Subdued
60 Departmental opening?
61 1983 Burt Lancaster film
64 "Keep your ___ the ball"
65 Surefooted goat
66 In the thick of
67 ___ of time
68 Runtish
69 "___ Lisa"

DOWN

1 Pickled peppers measure
2 Famed lab assistant
3 Wrinkled fruit
4 Landscapers' supplies
5 "No nasty comments!"
6 Commercial suffix with Rock
7 Abbr. on a headstone
8 G-suit acronym
9 Laughingstock
10 Congressional Record info
11 ___ lunch
12 Kind of count in a blood test
13 Bit, as of evidence
18 General's display
22 Whittles (down)
24 Singer James and others
25 "The Twilight Zone" host
27 Recipe measures
28 Hazmat regulator
29 "Hud" Oscar winner
30 Rancher's equipment
34 Ones touching elbows
36 Spartan queen
37 Techie, stereotypically
38 Me, myself ___
40 Escapade
44 Song often sung outdoors
46 Where the buoys are?
48 Astronomical study
49 Alternative to onion rings
50 Actress Lotte
51 Ingested
54 Skirt feature
56 "Pow!"
57 ___ sabe
58 Land o' blarney
59 "Star Wars" sage
62 Part of a geisha's attire
63 100 yrs.

by Elizabeth C. Gorski

ACROSS

1 "Mutiny on the Bounty" captain
6 Half a McDonald's logo
10 Blend
14 Anouk of "La Dolce Vita"
15 Mineral in transparent sheets
16 "Told you I could do it!"
17 1944 Judy Garland movie
20 Feathery scarves
21 Magazine revenue source
22 Soda can opener
23 Gets on the nerves of
25 Mideast leaders
27 Marsh plant
29 Facing trouble
33 With 15-Across, 1993 Tom Hanks/Meg Ryan movie
37 Aerosol
38 Krazy ___ of the comics
39 Jamboree participant
41 Going way back, as friends
42 Dog collar attachment
45 See 33-Across
48 Hits the roof
50 Morales of "NYPD Blue"
51 Pointed, as a gun
53 Mild aftershock
57 "Oh my heavens!"
60 Luau instrument, informally
62 Nickelodeon's ___ the Explorer

63 2000 Richard Gere/Winona Ryder movie
66 Russia's ___ Mountains
67 Early Bond foe
68 Spine-chilling
69 Portend
70 Twist, as findings
71 Utopias

DOWN

1 "La ___," 1959 hit
2 Rest atop
3 "To put it another way . . ."
4 Become peeved
5 Skirt edge
6 Surrounded by
7 Step after shampooing
8 Syringe amts.
9 Millinery accessory
10 Clogs, as a drain
11 Drawn tight
12 Prefix with -syncratic
13 Hoarse voice
18 Flip chart holders
19 The ___ Prayer
24 "You betcha!"
26 Apply incorrectly
28 Make up one's mind
30 Gait between walk and canter
31 Ring up
32 Jekyll's bad side
33 Slaloms
34 Stow, as cargo
35 Suffix with cigar
36 Prince, to a king
40 Exam taker
43 Generally speaking

44 Brother with a fairy tale
46 Swiss river to the Rhine
47 Like some Grateful Dead fans' attire
49 Corrects
52 Irene of "I Remember Mama"
54 Poet Clement C. ___
55 Sen. Hatch
56 Does fall yard work
57 Apply carelessly, as paint
58 Continental coin
59 Not much
61 Have down pat
64 Vex
65 Minuscule

by Harvey Estes

ACROSS

1 Blast maker, informally
6 Basketball position
11 Opening word usually skipped in alphabetizing
14 Interstate interchange establishment
15 Zhou ___
16 Squeal (on)
17 Former Portuguese territory in China
18 "Hasta la vista, baby!," e.g.
20 Tivoli's Villa ___
22 ___-car
23 Boar's mate
26 Bad economic situation
29 Gleeful laugh
31 Cup part
32 Jibe
33 "Oh yeah? ___ who?"
34 "Get outta here!"
38 Description of 14-, 18-, 26-, 29-, 46-, 48-, 57- or 66-Across
42 Ice cream brand
43 Lad
44 Grandmothers, affectionately
45 Strong and healthy
46 Citrus fruit
48 Seat-of-the-pants figure
53 ID for the I.R.S.
54 Dark
55 "Aunt ___ Cope Book"
57 Home movie maker
60 Unfreezes
64 U.S.N. noncom
65 Stop for a second
66 Big, tough cat
67 "For what ___ worth . . ."
68 Amphetamines, slangily
69 Belgian city in W.W. I fighting

DOWN

1 "Well, let me think . . ."
2 Wrapper that's hard to remove?
3 Like some stocks, briefly
4 Honeyed drink
5 Prairie grass used for forage
6 Res ___ (deeds)
7 Release to float, as a currency price
8 Pie ___ mode
9 Did a marathon
10 Two-letter combination
11 Singer Lopez
12 Must
13 Actor Hawke
19 Tennis official's call
21 The Cardinals, on a scoreboard
23 Outdoor scene in a painting
24 George Burns film
25 Fret
27 Gratis
28 Oscar winner Minnelli
30 Soaks, as flax
33 Place to wallow in mud
34 Loot
35 Sharpens, as a knife
36 Tests for Ph.D. candidates
37 Takes way too much, briefly
39 Somewhat
40 Answer to the Little Red Hen
41 Sloppily
45 Lens settings
46 Blackened
47 Place to enter a PIN
48 Haute couture name
49 Not suitable
50 St. ___ fire
51 [Not my mistake]
52 Reagan cabinet member Edwin
56 She, at sea
58 Popular music category
59 Owed
61 Cabinet post: Abbr.
62 "___ Willie Winkie"
63 H.S. prom attendees

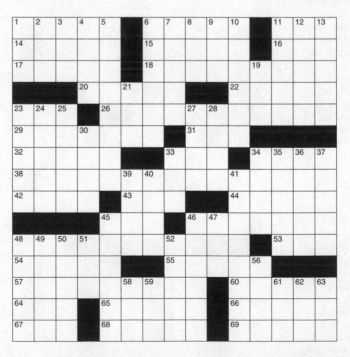

by Ed Stein

ACROSS

1 ___ Strip
5 Fight off
10 Magic charm
14 Wows
15 Slip away, as support
16 Go up against
17 Headline?
18 Thumb, e.g.
19 "Little ___ in Slumberland" (early comic)
20 Breakup line from a data inputter?
23 Scottish river
24 Canal locale
25 Breakup line from an astronaut?
33 Mountain lakes
34 Tarzan's transportation
35 Pick, with "for"
37 Afr. or Eur.
38 Ice hockey game interruption
39 Noted tower site
40 Initials on the high seas
41 Less sportsmanlike
42 Round dance
43 Breakup line from a grammarian?
46 Steno's need
47 Modern navigation aid, for short
48 Breakup line from a farmer?
56 "Anything ___?"
57 What "audio" means in Latin
58 Curse
60 In
61 Dusk to dawn
62 "___ walks into a bar . . ."
63 ___ Music of 1970's–80's rock
64 Stimulate
65 ___ v. United States, 1967 decision limiting wiretapping

DOWN

1 Breach
2 "Shoo!"
3 Complete drip
4 Candidate for valedictorian
5 Turn in
6 Actress Moran of "Happy Days"
7 "We have met the enemy and he is us" speaker
8 Tweak, say
9 "Hmmm . . ."
10 Oft-repeated phrase
11 Word removed from many modern wedding vows
12 Parachutist's act
13 Cornhusker State tribe
21 Cold war side
22 Sounds in pounds
25 Wanderlust, e.g.
26 One of the Judds
27 Surrealist Max
28 Manifest
29 "Home-Folks" poet
30 First page of a calendario
31 Mattress layer
32 ___ salts
36 Wiretapping evidence
38 1970's fad item
39 Man of letters?
41 Unforeseen difficulty
42 Notre Dame footballer coached by Rockne
44 Express
45 Lorre's "Casablanca" character
48 Sport
49 "Redhead" on "Sesame Street"
50 Midsize motor
51 Miami River's outlet
52 "___ Together" (song from "Grease")
53 Casual denials
54 Baltic capital
55 Letter-shaped hardware item
59 End of kindergarten?

by Adam Cohen

40

ACROSS

1 The life of Riley
5 Blessings
10 "How about ___?!"
14 Voting group
15 AM/FM device
16 Rabbit moves
17 When one might wear a hat
19 Singer India.___
20 Binary code digit
21 Presidential advisers
23 Done permanently, as writing
26 The first "T" of TNT
28 Smart ___ (wiseacres)
29 Neighbor of Vietnam
30 Gidget player in "Gidget"
32 "___ Abner"
33 Popular soap
35 Son of, in Arabic names
36 Motto of New Hampshire
41 Western treaty grp.
42 Rick's love in "Casablanca"
43 Bit of hair cream, say
45 Generic modeling "clay" for tots
49 Bull in a bullfight
50 Airs, in Latin
51 ___ Beta Kappa
52 "A right ___ old elf" (Santa)
53 Three-letter combo
55 Mooer
56 Ascent
57 Stamp on an envelope without enough stamps
63 Verb type: Abbr.
64 ___ Park, Colo.
65 Late civil rights activist Parks
66 "What ___!" ("How cool!")
67 Fashion
68 Headliner

DOWN

1 Flow's partner
2 Chicken ___ king
3 Lawn makeup
4 Sounds in an empty hall
5 Cheese from France
6 Boater's blade
7 Like 1, 3, 5, 7 . . .
8 An essential vitamin
9 Kind of bean
10 It was once Siam
11 Like bulls' heads
12 Each
13 Sleeping sickness carrier
18 Raggedy ___
22 Singer Streisand
23 Running a temperature, say
24 Hammer's target
25 ___ sci (college major, informally)
26 Pre-1917 Russian ruler
27 North Carolina's capital
31 "Vaya con ___" ("Go with God")
33 More tired
34 Assuming that's true
37 Travelers
38 Relating to grades 1–12
39 British rocker Billy
40 Countess's husband
44 "Whew!"
45 Homeland, to Horace
46 Tempting
47 Record label for many rappers
48 Highest
49 TV transmission sites
52 Morning run, perhaps
54 "Planet of the ___"
55 24 cans of beer
58 Hog haven
59 No. with an area code
60 Period
61 Land north of Mex.
62 End point for an iPod cord

by Sarah Keller

ACROSS

1 Auto amenities, for short
4 Baseball and football star Sanders
9 Having one's jaw dropped
14 Wish undone
15 ___-Detoo
16 Was rude at a dance
17 Oar
20 Black cats and dark clouds, e.g.
21 Reverse of post-
22 Doesn't just ask
23 Or
27 Bubkes
28 Craft over Niagara Falls?
31 45, for one
35 Nine-to-five activity
37 Chance to get on base
39 O'er
43 One often leaving his initial behind
44 Lao-tzu principle
45 Trading org.
46 Hereditary ruler
49 Josh
51 Orr
57 Way, way off
60 Friend of Morpheus in "The Matrix"
61 Some sports commentary
62 Ore
66 Of base 8
67 Theater employee
68 Where S.F. is
69 Busts
70 Shows its age, as wallpaper
71 Quaker possessive

DOWN

1 Traffic director
2 Former New York 53-Down
3 Rats' milieu
4 Ted of "Becker"
5 Piece of work?
6 "Is ___, Lord?"
7 Pizazz
8 Easy
9 Stuff in trays
10 Start of a David Letterman countdown
11 Done to ___
12 Building extension
13 Warring Tolkien creatures
18 Not Dem. or Rep.
19 Luke's sister, in "Star Wars"
24 Golfer Vijay Singh's homeland
25 Thrombosis cause
26 Start of some juice blend names
29 Online flea market
30 Back muscles, for short
31 Baker's no.
32 Device with a Nano model
33 Pretty agile for one's age
34 Southern treat
36 "Wanna ___?"
38 Not just "a"
40 Fly high
41 Acorn sites
42 Straight man, for a comedian
47 Phoenix five
48 Busy
50 Room treatments
52 Bing, bang or boom
53 Statehouse V.I.P.
54 President-___
55 Grammy winner Jones
56 How deadpan jokes are delivered
57 Love, in Lima
58 Kind of tax that funds Soc. Sec.
59 Prefix with body
63 "Kidnapped" monogram
64 Word for half of hurricanes
65 Cartoon film art

by Tyler Hinman

ACROSS

1 Makes lace
5 It may do your bidding
9 One played for a fool
14 Impulse
15 Capital of Togo
16 Gossip
17 Minute amount
18 Rich earth
19 Lacking spice
20 Hint for identifying a mystery man's shirts?
23 50 minutes past the hour
24 Oslo's land: Abbr.
25 Tint
28 Exterminator's job, maybe?
33 Cosmo or Natl. Geographic
36 Lollapalooza
37 Next-to-last round
38 Healing balm
40 Fix again, as masts
43 Remove, as text
44 Like a designated driver, presumably
46 Volume of Horace
48 Paneled room, maybe
49 Vestiges of skin blemishes?
53 Perched
54 Cry of annoyance
55 Sensations before migraines
59 Cautionary sign at a dog park?
64 Fred's dancing sister
66 Toss of the dice
67 Scheme
68 Hostile response
69 Space
70 Space between dotted lines, maybe
71 Stamp sheets
72 Las Vegas light
73 Gives a gander

DOWN

1 In the middle of, quaintly
2 "Oh, give me ___ . . ."
3 Cronus or Oceanus
4 Gray matter
5 Room extensions
6 Italy's outline
7 Indian nurse
8 Aden citizen
9 Sci-fi beings
10 It may be hired
11 Showing no remorse
12 Quite a hgt.
13 Bottom of a paw
21 1980's–90's chancellor Helmut
22 Big load
26 Serviceable
27 City on the Ruhr
29 Shirley Temple's "___ Little Girl"
30 Arena cry
31 "Presumed Innocent" author
32 Bloodshot
33 Spars
34 "Yo, Ho!"
35 Liaison
39 It's slippery when wet
41 Panhandle state: Abbr.
42 Neth. neighbor
45 Places for retired basketball jerseys
47 Guide for the Magi
50 Error denoter
51 1943 conference site
52 Lithe
56 Connection maker/breaker
57 Make amends
58 Bass-baritone Simon ___
60 Out of the wind
61 Times past
62 Promise to a cook?
63 ___ Bator, Mongolia
64 Nile reptile
65 Kind of sample

by Jack McInturff

ACROSS
1 With: Fr.
5 Milkshake item
10 In ___ (together)
14 Hawaiian port
15 "The Devil Wears ___"
16 Get better, as a cut
17 State with conviction
18 Drive away
19 Artist Bonheur
20 Historic Boston neighborhood
22 Wiggle room
24 Loads and loads
25 Gush
26 Totaling
29 Comedian who created the character Jose Jimenez
33 Manipulate
34 Burden of proof
35 Half a sch. year
36 Toll unit on a toll road
37 What "yo mama" is
39 Cover for a wound
40 Plop oneself down
41 "Are you ___ out?"
42 Gem of an oyster
43 Ailment that may cause sneezing
45 Go by, as time
46 Wolf's sound
47 Jump named for a skater
48 Empty, as a lot
51 Auxiliary wager
55 Composer Stravinsky
56 Some Apples
59 Say yea or nay
60 Line of stitches
61 Modern assembly line worker

62 Love god
63 "The Thin Man" dog
64 Les ___-Unis
65 Mardi Gras follower

DOWN
1 Melville captain
2 Start of a Spanish cheer
3 Util. bill
4 Sound-absorbing flooring
5 Helped bust out, as from prison
6 Cards above deuces
7 Séance sound
8 Juice drink
9 Where to get juice for a household appliance
10 Astute
11 "Man, that hurts!"
12 Astronaut's insignia
13 Potter's medium
21 007
23 Slithery fishes
25 Ireland's ___ Fein
26 Covered with water
27 The South
28 River mouth feature
29 Word that can follow the first words of 20-, 29-, 43- and 51-Across and 4-, 9-, 37- and 39-Down
30 BMI rival
31 Draws nigh
32 Mosey (along)
37 Winter traction provider
38 Lounge
39 Death Valley is below it
41 Computer image
42 Appealed earnestly
44 Greg's sitcom partner
45 Is
47 English race place
48 Document checked at a border
49 Matures
50 Jacket
52 Bloviator, often
53 Princely prep school
54 Exam
57 Bon ___ (witticism)
58 Lawyer's org.

by Paula Gamache

ACROSS

1 ___-Seltzer
5 Serb or Pole
9 Botanical gardens display
14 "Metropolis" director Fritz
15 Astronomical effect
16 Car that spends too much time in the shop
17 Brain passage
18 Bygone award?
20 Star
22 Plenty
23 Ring decision, briefly
24 Schwarzenegger, today?
28 What a handkerchief may wipe away
29 Turnstile locale
33 Former train station attendants?
38 Bridgestones or Michelins
39 So-so grade
40 Sam who was a three-time Masters champ
42 Dander
43 Wee hour
46 Farm equipment that's been put to another use?
49 Italian automaker since 1906
51 Architect Saarinen
52 Old customs?
58 Court figures, briefly
61 Pennsylvania port
62 Unlikely race winner
63 Executive at American Motors or Enron, e.g.?
67 One of the Aleutians

68 Actor Reeves
69 Author ___ Neale Hurston
70 Nerd
71 Bar, legally
72 Mongolian tent
73 Gaelic

DOWN

1 One of TV's "honeymooners"
2 Kind of paint
3 Prepared to pray, say
4 Accept
5 Ursula Andress film
6 West Coast air hub
7 ___ Highway (old 1,500-mile route)
8 "There you have it!"
9 Complete and direct, as a denial
10 Rent
11 Skip
12 Knight's neighbor
13 Part of A.D.
19 Little ones
21 ___ Rabbit
25 Gym floor covers
26 Singer Cara
27 Diamond stat.
30 Legal order
31 Prefix with -naut
32 Belgian river
33 Area of E.P.A. purview: Abbr.
34 TV's warrior princess
35 Round end of a hammer
36 Alternative to Rover
37 Full and happy

41 Eins + zwei
44 Big name in hardware stores
45 Befuddles
47 Crafts' partner
48 Just-made-up word
50 Longfellow's bell town
53 Posh
54 English quintet
55 Cowboy film
56 Popular footwear
57 Quench
58 Hockey feint
59 Fires
60 Public scene cause
64 John Lennon's adopted middle name
65 Bruin legend
66 Turner of note

by Alan Arbesfeld

ACROSS

1 "Back in Black" rock band
5 Tablelands
10 Diner cuppa
14 Yowl
15 Hail
16 Plowers
17 Jacob's brother
18 Pace
19 Proceeded
20 *Title fellow in a 1971 #1 McCartney hit
22 *Amorous alcoholic in "The Philadelphia Story"
24 Was a parasite
27 County north of Limerick
31 P, to Plato
32 Egg
36 ___ studies (modern college major)
38 Blood type syst.
40 Has ___ with
42 1960's TV hit . . . whose last word completes the answers to the nine starred clues
45 "Jungle Book" star, 1942
46 Online chortle
47 "To a Waterfowl" poet
48 High-flier's org.?
50 Cabernet, e.g.
52 Displays 1-Down
53 1941 Stanwyck/Fonda comedy, with "The"
56 *Mr. Television
60 *One of TV's Addams family
64 Locale of 1869's Golden Spike
65 Polio vaccine developer
68 Garden party?
70 Big rig
71 Incessantly
72 12-point type
73 Feds
74 Some conifers
75 Brood (over)

DOWN

1 Wonder
2 Hombre's home
3 Radio part
4 Driver, e.g.
5 About a yard, at Scotland Yard
6 Phillips ___ Academy
7 *Figure in a star-spangled hat
8 High point of a European trip?
9 Vermont ski town
10 It hangs under the chin
11 Rink move
12 Part of a boast of Caesar
13 Put (up)
21 "Paride ed ___" (Gluck opera)
23 Punch line to "What's the longest sentence in the English language?"
25 *"My Three Sons" housekeeper
26 Vagabond
27 100-lb. units
28 Actress Lindsay
29 Bio 101 subject
30 *Brer Rabbit taleteller
33 *Chekhov title character
34 Open, as a toothpaste tube
35 Christopher Robin's creator
37 Weekend TV staple since '75
39 White House fiscal grp.
41 Brings home
43 Major employer in Detroit
44 Yens
49 Boxer Laila
51 Practice lexicography
54 "The Boy Who Cried Wolf" writer
55 Sells
56 Essential
57 Any thing
58 Inadequate
59 Dilute
61 Lights-out signal
62 Blue-pencil
63 Tour de France, e.g.
66 Young Darth Vader's nickname
67 *Old Texas rice grower of note
69 Big mouth

by John Farmer

46

ACROSS

1 End place for many a car accident
6 Mire
9 "Shhh!"
14 Novelist Calvino
15 Bother
16 The "U" of UHF
17 Astronaut's attire
18 Fluffy scarf
19 Go into
20 Not the real Charlie of StarKist ads?
23 Born: Fr.
24 Big part of an elephant
25 Ambulance worker, for short
26 Tetley product
29 Vintage French wines?
32 Rabble-rouse
34 Inexperienced in
35 Italian volcano
36 Assistant in a con game
39 Nix by Nixon, e.g.
40 Mire
42 Peanuts
44 1960's sitcom ghoul on the terrace?
47 1976 and 2001, e.g.: Abbr.
48 Sunbather's shade
49 Founded: Abbr.
50 Korean automaker
53 What 20-, 29-, 44- and 53-Across are of each other
56 Actress Sarandon
59 "Exodus" hero
60 Muscat native
61 Prank
62 Lower, as the lights

63 Stirred up
64 With feigned shyness
65 Reverse of WNW
66 Trap

DOWN

1 "Start eating!"
2 Reply to "Who's there?"
3 Brownish gray
4 Annual award named for a Muse
5 Stressful spot
6 The Sultan of Swat
7 Smell
8 Uncle Sam facial feature
9 Director Tarantino
10 Arm bone
11 Major defense contractor
12 "But I heard him exclaim, ___ he . . ."
13 Driveway surface
21 Bye-byes
22 Referee
26 Pisa landmark
27 French political divisions
28 Regarding
29 City on Biscayne Bay
30 Have the throne
31 Emphatic no
32 In armed conflict
33 Pesky swarm
35 Catch sight of
37 Lollygag
38 "___ luck!"
41 Effectiveness
43 Racetrack habitués
45 Deface

46 Like beds before housekeeping
50 Australian "bear"
51 Word before tube or circle
52 Off the direct course
53 Bucket
54 "Exodus" author
55 Poker player's declaration
56 Anatomical pouch
57 Tres – dos
58 Muddy enclosure

by John Calvin Williams

ACROSS
1 Proofer's mark
5 Hinged fastener
9 "Fiddlesticks!"
14 In person
15 Gen. Bradley
16 Get in touch with
17 Flooring measure
18 Like some pizza orders
19 Skylit lobbies
20 Desktop container
23 Banned insecticide
24 Place to rehearse
25 Wine bottle datum
27 Get-up-and-go
28 Take step one
32 Army one-striper: Abbr.
35 Trash receptacle
37 Dairy case buy
38 Belgrade native
40 Subject of a cigarette rating
41 Think ahead
42 Ocular woe
43 Fast-food dispenser items
46 Norm: Abbr.
47 Exhaust tube
49 Small battery size
51 It may be filed
52 Premier Khrushchev
55 Unit of work
57 Software flaw
61 Mustard choice
63 Sites for studs
64 Bit of dust
65 Pong maker
66 What's more
67 In a bit, to bards
68 Mandrake's forte
69 New driver, typically
70 Hatchling's home

DOWN
1 Prelude to a duel
2 Runs out of steam
3 Media attraction
4 It sits in a saucer
5 Nickname on "M*A*S*H"
6 Oil company that merged with BP
7 It's a long story
8 Cowherd's tool
9 Bedtime appeal
10 Good to go
11 Crusty bakery buys
12 Battery fluid
13 "Come again?"
21 Think tank nugget
22 Cannon of Hollywood
26 On the peak of
28 Close call
29 The O'Hara estate
30 Heroic deed
31 Sweet on, with "of"
32 Low-key "Hey!"
33 Cheese in salads
34 Blubberer's binge
36 Letters before ://www
39 Composer Bartók
43 Feed holder
44 Serves at a restaurant
45 Sushi go-with
48 Ant attractor
50 Barnstormer, e.g.
52 Clara Barton, for one
53 Steakhouse selection
54 Ends of 20- and 57-Across and 11- and 34-Down
55 Cheese in a ball
56 Meter maid of song
58 Spam, e.g.
59 Hardly tanned
60 Mannerly sort
62 ". . . __ quit!"

by Gail Grabowski

48

ACROSS

1 Kind of pit at a rock club
5 Locks up
10 Epsilon follower
14 On the subject of
15 Make sense
16 U2's Bono, e.g.
17 Start of a quip from a returning vacationer
20 Animal with a snout
21 Rumble, e.g.
22 Some hosp. cases
23 Mai ___
25 New Haven student
27 Quip, part 2
36 Site of tiny orbits
37 Norwegian saint
38 1960 Everly Brothers hit
39 Ferdinand, e.g.
40 Whines
42 Hospital room staples
43 Ending with aero-
45 Lifesaver, maybe
46 "Spare me!", e.g.
47 Quip, part 3
50 Sound during shearing
51 Smog control grp.
52 Scenery
55 London institution since 1785, with "The"
59 Egypt's Sadat
63 End of the quip
66 Competent
67 Poly- follower
68 1950's British P.M.
69 Stag party attendee
70 It's not good to do this at the sun
71 Bottom

DOWN

1 Longtime name on "Today"
2 Workers' protection org.
3 Rung
4 Brisk seller
5 Part of a dinosaur find
6 Sugary drinks
7 Lay off
8 Libertine's feeling
9 Gets back at angrily
10 Promgoer's woe
11 Repeat
12 Kenneth Grahame's ___ Hall
13 Marchers in single file
18 Kind of tradition
19 "Good riddance"
24 Lottery player's happy shout
26 Nigerian language
27 Croc's head or tail?
28 New Mexico county
29 "What's it ___?"
30 Root of diplomacy
31 Four-star reviews
32 Turn inside out
33 Carpet fiber
34 It may be within a judge's grasp
35 Start of hazarding a guess
40 Put under
41 Ear part
44 Diamond org.
46 Gambols
48 Common Spanish boys' names
49 Give ___ on the back
52 Ripoff
53 Isle of exile
54 Usage fee
56 Faddish 1990s computer game
57 "Cómo ___ usted?"
58 Litigant
60 Hall-of-Famer Boggs
61 Sailing
62 Monthly check
64 "Understand?"
65 Wrath

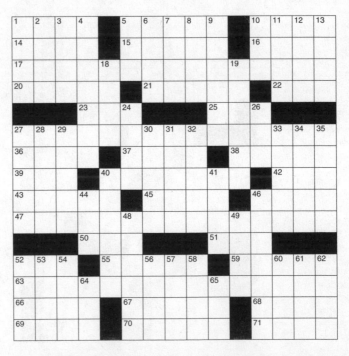

by Adam G. Perl

ACROSS

1 Soaking site
5 Cry like a baby
9 Early Peruvian
13 Jai ___
14 Category
15 Sweetheart
16 Window ledge
17 Jason's sorceress wife
18 Long and lean
19 Comment upon bumping into an old friend, #1
22 Russian refusal
23 Soul singer James
24 San Francisco/ Oakland separator
27 Comment #2
31 John, Paul and George: Abbr.
34 Hi-___ monitor
35 Wordsworth works
36 Pistol, e.g.
39 "Forget about it!"
41 Bubbling on the stove
42 Like sushi
43 Militant 60's campus org.
44 Comment #3
49 Absorb, with "up"
50 Word that's an example of itself
51 Klutz's cry
54 Comment #4
59 "Let's get crackin'!"
61 Forearm bones
62 "Agreed!"
63 Wolf's cry
64 ___ Rizzo of "Midnight Cowboy"
65 Peaceful period
66 ___-bitsy
67 Deuces
68 Häagen-Dazs alternative

DOWN

1 Wingding
2 Visitor from another planet
3 Running total
4 Jewish campus group
5 Borscht ingredient
6 Julie who played Mary Poppins
7 Christmas garland
8 Makeshift shelter
9 Run in place
10 Not-so-potent potables
11 Campbell's container
12 Biblical boat
14 Baseball bigwigs: Abbr.
20 Plains Indian
21 Responses of shock
25 Carrying a weapon
26 Go-aheads
28 Sch. named for a televangelist
29 Author Kesey
30 ___ polloi
31 Persian potentates
32 Just not done
33 Blizzard battlers
37 Opposite of multiplication: Abbr.
38 First American to orbit Earth
39 Arrest
40 Have bills
42 Meet unexpectedly
45 Dannon product
46 Wanted felon
47 Ages and ages
48 Pasta bit
52 Nom de plume: Abbr.
53 Serta competitor
55 Nothing but
56 The "m" of E = mc²
57 "___ Beso" (Paul Anka song)
58 Building additions
59 "The Sweetheart of Sigma ___"
60 Bon ___ (witticism)

by Nancy Salomon

50

ACROSS

1 Clear of stale odors, maybe
7 Early Ford
13 Catastrophic
15 Genetic shapes
16 Dracula's least favorite citations?
18 Asian occasion
19 Tiny bit
20 "Well, ___ had it!"
21 Swedish-based furniture chain
23 Cozy inn, briefly
25 Puts to work
26 Historian Thomas who wrote "The French Revolution"
28 Drifting
30 1950 film noir classic
31 ___-X
32 Dracula's least favorite sporting event?
41 Grand Cherokee, e.g.: Abbr.
42 Ink dispenser?
43 Night school subj.
44 Sound at a salon
46 Lascivious sort
47 Longtime Magic 8 Ball maker
48 "Pale" drinks
50 Actress Sorvino
51 Staggering
52 Maple product
55 Director Kurosawa
57 Dracula's least favorite time?
60 Unreturnable serve
61 Golf reservation
62 Elephant grp.
63 Kind of school
64 Doesn't fold
65 Aves.

DOWN

1 Frigid
2 California's motto
3 One who's revolting?
4 Reply to a ques.
5 How-___ (handy books)
6 Prefix with Asian
7 French sea
8 Rousing cheer
9 Kipling's "Gunga ___"
10 Cut out
11 "Frasier" actress Jane
12 Size up
14 Hairs on a caterpillar
15 Ibsen's "___ Gabler"
17 Idol follower
22 Robert of Broadway's "Guys and Dolls"
23 White wines
24 Sequel to Kerouac's "On the Road"
25 One out on a limb?
27 John left Cynthia for her
29 "Miracle" team of 1969
32 Ltr. additions
33 Compete in track
34 Having a mean, mean look
35 Pilot's prediction: Abbr.
36 Tosspot
37 007, for one
38 Janitor's belt attachments
39 Snail at Chez Jacques
40 Warning in a school zone
45 Stage after a sunburn
47 Disneyland's Enchanted ___ Room
49 Narrow cuts
50 Whiz
51 Comic Sandler
52 Home to the 29-Down
53 Trial fig.
54 Trident-shaped letters
56 Nile snakes
58 Pick up
59 French friend

by Patrick Blindauer

ACROSS

1 Take ___ at (try)
6 Wield, as influence
11 Lens holder, for short
14 Statesman known popularly as Panditji, or "Scholar"
15 Mister abroad
16 Draft choice?
17 Kind of acid
18 Place to see a Goya
19 Cookie holder
20 Show hospitality at the door
22 *Coin collector's purchase
24 Tom, at birth
26 Game pieces
27 Splitsville?
28 *It has "E pluribus unum" on it
30 Broker's quarry
31 Setting for many a joke
32 Peccadilloes
33 Donnybrooks
34 *Has a clear conscience
36 Small military craft
39 Release
40 Side in checkers
43 Butler at Tara
44 *"Friends" was once part of it
46 Cosmetics maker ___ Laszlo
47 It may not be easy to shoot
48 Fixed, as a loose lace
49 *"Dig in!"
51 Menace to society
52 Suffix with Moon
53 Rockne of Notre Dame fame

55 "A Faust Symphony" composer
58 G.I. chow
59 Spine-tingling
60 Wiesel and namesakes
61 One form of ID
62 Was out
63 Soprano Fleming

DOWN

1 It begins with enero
2 Partner of poivre
3 Play ground?
4 Record label founded by Clive Davis
5 *Sports car feature
6 Disney-owned channel
7 Gen ___
8 Nail polish
9 "The Gates of Hell" sculptor
10 Pioneering 1982 sci-fi film
11 *Colorful marble
12 Property receiver
13 Gurus
21 Not give an inch
23 In fact
24 Org. in which Putin was once an officer
25 Roth ___
26 Rubber
29 Suffix with differ
30 *What a writer hopes to write
33 Teacher at an école
34 Old newspaper sections
35 Grp. gotten by dialing 911
36 Tourney starters
37 Education fundamentals
38 *1988 vice presidential candidate
40 Restrains
41 When the French fry?
42 Movie format
44 Adultlike
45 Prima ballerina
47 Jury
50 Squeezes (out)
51 Pedal pushers
54 Show instability
56 Last of 26
57 Literary monogram found in the answers to the nine asterisked clues

by Paula Gamache

ACROSS

1 PC alternatives
5 Big name in pest control
10 Resident of 29-Down
14 "Shake ___" (1981 song by the Cars)
15 "Me, too!"
16 Get the wrinkles out of
17 Dickens's "little" girl
18 Showed interest in, as at a bar
19 This, in Madrid
20 Jakarta
23 Poet's Muse
24 Common Web site section, for short
25 O, Us or GQ
28 Cats' prey
32 TWA competitor
34 "___ Poetica"
37 Nickname for Namath
40 Certain carpet or hairdo
42 Skylit courts
43 What a casting director tries to fill
44 Employee benefit
47 Free from, with "of"
48 Madison Avenue worker
49 Japanese wrestling
50 Take care of a bill
51 Helpers for profs
54 Singer ___ Khan
59 Fuddy-duddy
64 Sites of monkey business?
66 Closet wood
67 Calf-length skirt
68 Rick's love in "Casablanca"
69 Squiggly mark in "señor"
70 Nuclear energy source
71 Peelable fruit
72 Proceed on tiptoe
73 NASDAQ alternative

DOWN

1 Cut into tiny bits
2 "Don't shed ___"
3 "Mea ___"
4 Challenging bowling pin arrangement
5 Agency with workplace regs.
6 Agitate
7 The Green Hornet's valet
8 Cry at a leave-taking
9 "Teenage Mutant ___ Turtles"
10 Chicken ___
11 Big Dipper's locale
12 Decompose
13 Genetic stuff
21 ___ of the Unknowns
22 Blue hue
26 Garlicky mayonnaise
27 King Midas's downfall
29 Mideast land
30 Big maker of perfumes
31 Famous family of Western lawmen
33 Damascus's land: Abbr.
34 BMI rival
35 "The Mary Tyler Moore Show" spinoff
36 1998 National League M.V.P.
38 God, in Paris
39 In the 70s or so
41 3.5, e.g., for a student
45 Prefix with lock
46 1970s–80s Big Apple mayor
52 Bank holdings: Abbr.
53 Coil of yarn
55 Muscly fellow
56 Friendship
57 Praise
58 Stop on ___
60 Ivan the Terrible, e.g.
61 Not in use
62 It means nothing to Juan
63 Long, long walk
64 12345, in Schenectady, N.Y.
65 Corrida shout

by Christina Houlihan Kelly

ACROSS

1 Pool sites
5 Certain turns
10 It might be found, appropriately, in a newspaper morgue
14 Nonclerical
15 Dickens's Heep
16 Lose support, as at campaign's end
17 Red state
19 Twerp
20 Where the river meets the sea
21 Corp. top dog
22 Intentionally vague statement
23 Tyrants
25 Hindu princess
26 Home of the NCAA Spartans
27 Kind of alert
29 Quick refresher
32 Speed
35 What an ogler gives
37 Prefix with friendly
38 Smeltery input
40 Unfairly outnumbers, with "on"
42 Little beauty
43 Former Saudi king
45 Nasty vipers
46 Uncle ___
47 Taj Mahal site
48 ___ Taylor, the Tool Man, on "Home Improvement"
50 Press, as to vote
52 Rappers and poets, say
56 One who needs to be rubbed out?
58 Fannie ___
59 Campfire remains

61 "Metamorphoses" author
62 Blue state
64 Effect of yeast on dough
65 Actor Christopher
66 Till compartment
67 Elegant shade trees
68 Shooting game
69 Part of the country where polls close later

DOWN

1 Dropped, as in the polls
2 Having separate glass segments
3 Divider in the House of Representatives
4 Rob Roy and kin
5 Hon, in Hampshire
6 Put up
7 Nifty bridge play
8 South-of-the-border order
9 Timid
10 Frequently
11 Blue state
12 Beatnik's "Gotcha"
13 French head
18 Swimmers may do them
22 Actress Uta
24 Red state
25 Blue state
28 Start of something big?
30 Small bra part
31 Daddy-o
32 Gluttons
33 District
34 Red state
36 Successor

39 Eligible, as to vote
41 Daytime TV staple
44 Chicago-based food giant
49 Apple variety
51 Election Day freebies from party workers
53 Throw with great effort
54 French wine region
55 Tennis's Monica
56 Clinton's number two
57 The dark side
58 Docile
60 Part of CBS: Abbr.
62 "___ Doubtfire"
63 Butterfly catcher

by Bruce P. Douglas

54

ACROSS

1 Army cops, for short
4 "On the Record" host Van Susteren
9 Ruth's mother-in-law
14 __ straw
15 Get connected to the Web
16 Kind of planner
17 "I'll be right there!"
19 Origins
20 First name in bicycling
21 Bard's "before"
23 Nimitz, for one: Abbr.
24 Lover boy?
25 Unsatisfying boxing result
29 Loses it
31 Took the cake
32 Dallas-to-Memphis dir.
33 Was a busybody
35 Sectioned, as windows
37 Upbeat, outgoing sort
41 "Later"
42 Thick smoke?
43 Vegas opening?
44 Graffiti artist's "signature"
47 Surrender, as arms
51 Square-dealing
54 Puccini piece
55 Minute
56 Carrier to Karachi
57 Titles are often written in them, briefly
58 Prolific writer's output
60 Hair challenge . . . or a hint to the last words of 17-, 25-, 37- and 51-Across

63 Borden bovine
64 Parka parts
65 "Imagine that!"
66 Ray __, 1980s–90s Boston mayor
67 __-craftsy
68 Miss a beat, perhaps

DOWN

1 Cabbage
2 Hat made of jipijapa
3 People in a pool
4 Much merriment
5 Taiwan, initially
6 Pride part
7 Muscularly defined
8 First name of two U.S. presidents
9 Greek letters
10 Specialties
11 Fetching?
12 Impulse buyer's means
13 Electees
18 Not afraid to mix things up
22 Green: Prefix
25 Film category
26 Has an outstanding figure?
27 Live, as a football
28 Composer Rorem
30 Dream up
34 Med school grad
36 Show time
37 Have good intentions
38 "Have no fear"
39 4,100-mile-long river
40 "I've Got __ in Kalamazoo"

41 __-mo
45 Swiss peak
46 Gentleman's companion
48 California county
49 "Our Town" playwright
50 Lake __, on the 39-Down
52 Surround
53 Something in the air
57 Teeny, for short
58 Whistler, at times
59 One of 100: Abbr.
61 Fate
62 Barkeeps' requests

by Lee Glickstein and Nancy Salomon

ACROSS

1 Practice boxing
5 Setting for "Hansel and Gretel"
10 Like very early education, for short
14 Brand of blocks
15 ___ Hoffman of the Chicago Seven
16 Education by memorization
17 Region
18 Religious belief
19 Super-duper
20 One-L lama
23 Rational
24 "___ Misérables"
25 Cutting up, as logs
28 Housekeeper
30 Crow's call
33 "___ goeth before a fall"
34 Building with a loft
35 Sulk
36 Two-L llama
39 Architect ___ van der Rohe
40 Some Keats poems
41 Put into law
42 Upper chamber member: Abbr.
43 War god on Olympus
44 Speakers' spots
45 No. of ft. above sea level
46 . . . .
47 Three-L Illama?
55 Toward the rising sun
56 Ricochet
57 4, on a sundial
58 Nick at ___
59 Express a thought
60 Lease
61 ___ the Red

62 Stuffed
63 Actions on heartstrings and pant legs

DOWN

1 Hunk of marble, e.g.
2 Where Lima is
3 Elderly
4 Locales for rest stops
5 Using the kiddie pool, say
6 More than fat
7 Sad news item
8 Gossip, slangily
9 Wheat product used in making pasta
10 Bows one's head in church
11 Kitchen or bath
12 Sicilian spouter
13 Eager
21 Fruit of the Loom competitor
22 Conducted
25 Bombards with unwanted e-mail
26 Golfer Palmer, to pals
27 Expand, as a highway
28 Old battle clubs
29 Torah holders
30 Unconscious states
31 Quickly
32 Whip marks
34 Wished
35 Attire covering little of the legs
37 Temple entrances
38 "Groovy!"
43 Drink often labeled XXX in the comics
44 Heading to a bad end
45 Indian conquered by the conquistadors
46 Hum
47 The "B" of N.B.
48 Hideout
49 ___ Spumante (wine)
50 Auto parts giant
51 Londoner, e.g., informally
52 In ___ of (replacing)
53 ___ Yang Twins (rap duo)
54 Things to pick

by Peter A. Collins

56

ACROSS
1 Flubs
6 Order's partner
9 X-rated
14 Dickens title starter
15 16-Across residue
16 Havana, e.g.
17 Coup ___
18 Nike product
20 Genes govern them
22 Bearer of town news, once
23 Sphere at the Olympics
25 Kindergarten basics
29 Withered
30 Stay out of sight
32 Cardinal letters?
35 Poetic foot
38 Quench
39 What 18-, 23-, 52- and 61-Across have in common
43 Made public
44 Margarita glass rim coater
45 Language suffix
46 ___ Pointe, Mich.
48 Kiltie's gal
51 "Grand" ice cream brand
52 Prom beverage
58 Bullion unit
60 Madrid madam
61 Unhippielike characteristic
65 John on the Mayflower
66 Lost on purpose
67 Crafty
68 Falsified, as a check
69 Quickie ghost costume
70 Links prop
71 Heeds a roadblock

DOWN
1 Fox comedy show
2 In ___ (unborn)
3 Causing ruin
4 Thrashes about
5 Small sofa
6 ___ Palmas
7 Pet protection org.
8 Thumbprint feature
9 Entr'___
10 British P.M. before Gladstone
11 "Yuck!"
12 Southeast Asian tongue
13 Uno + due
19 Streamlet
21 Half of the United Arab Republic
24 Pintos, e.g.

26 Pianist Eubie
27 Drinks with the old slogan "Refresh yourself"
28 Jenny Lind, e.g.
31 Enabler of WWW access
32 Oater transport
33 Bronze medalist's place
34 Sports artist Neiman
36 C.E.O.'s deg.
37 Melvin, the King of Torts
40 "You betcha!"
41 Music store mdse.
42 ESPN figures
47 Run after D
49 Sounds off
50 Like some bright rooms
53 Friars fete

54 Serving a purpose
55 Acknowledge, in a way
56 Sleazeball
57 Ranch crew
59 Food label abbr.
61 Ave. crossers
62 L.B.J.'s veep
63 It needs refining
64 Deli loaf

by Sarah Keller

ACROSS
1 Bulova alternative
6 Hunt and peck, e.g.
10 Grabs 40 winks
14 Manicurist's expertise
15 Film vault holding
16 Relative of butterine
17 Appeal to caprice
19 When tripled, a war movie
20 Gave the O.K.
21 Highway headache
22 On the open deck
25 Ponzi scheme, e.g.
27 You might put some money in it, briefly
28 Viking Ericson
30 Kind of house
34 Military jets' mission
36 Show that inspired "30 Rock": Abbr.
37 Roundabout
38 Perch
40 Perch
42 Musical Mel
43 Draw in
45 Calder Trophy org.
47 Something usually eaten with sauce
48 Penetrate slowly
49 Cedar alternative
51 "__ luck?"
52 Each
54 Not caught
56 Pentagonal part of a diamond
59 High regard
61 Native Rwandan
62 Go all out for a party, say
66 __ a secret

67 "Don't Tell __" ("Cabaret" song)
68 Fed. bill
69 Site associated with this puzzle's theme
70 Kind of sch.
71 Comparatively peculiar

DOWN
1 Picketing, perhaps
2 Chinese revolutionary
3 German "a"
4 Sharon of "Cagney & Lacey"
5 Attack violently
6 Parts of some car deals
7 Aches (for)
8 Zane Grey's "West of the __"
9 Ron who played Tarzan
10 "Hurry!"
11 Soothing plant
12 Indiana town where Cole Porter was born
13 Halloween prankster's aid
18 Bona __
21 The Sun, The Moon or The Emperor
22 Popes' headgear
23 National rival
24 Conditional release
26 E.M.T. specialty
29 Longtime Buick plant site
31 __, Straus and Giroux
32 Turning plowshares into swords?
33 "Ta-ta!"
35 Begins to play
39 Claptrap
41 1980s TV show with a stenciled logo
44 Musician Brian
46 Glove material
50 Compulsive lifter
53 Kind of colony
55 Alter
56 TV's Dr. __
57 Roman moon goddess
58 Gobs
60 Not all
62 "Enough already!"
63 Wink's partner
64 Canonized mlle.
65 Suffix with auction

by David Benkof

ACROSS

1 Rock outcropping
5 Dive among coral reefs, say
10 Sheep cries
14 Gossipy Barrett
15 Artist's stand
16 Break in the action
17 Wading bird
18 Tear away (from)
19 Airport for Air France
20 FLOP
23 Power for Robert Fulton
24 Razor sharpener
25 Stare (at)
28 Smother
32 Serving of corn
35 Civil rights org.
38 Game move
39 FLAP
43 Kind of lily
44 Royal headpiece
45 Tues. follower
46 Texas city named for a city in Ukraine
49 Keep ___ on (watch)
51 Continental money
54 Marina sights
58 FLIP
62 Pseudonym of H. H. Munro
63 Borden cow
64 Ivy, for one
65 Landed (on)
66 Wasps' homes
67 Part that's sharp
68 ___ club (singers' group)
69 Lovers' get together
70 Burn the outside of

DOWN

1 Baby holders
2 Mechanical man
3 Japanese cartoon art
4 One who talks, talks, talks
5 In stitches
6 Low-___ diet
7 People before rehab
8 Intoxicate
9 Places for wedding vows
10 Tube on a welding tool
11 Special glow
12 Friend in war
13 Foxlike
21 Native of Muscat
22 "i" topper
26 Washed-out in complexion
27 Actor William of "The Greatest American Hero"
29 Piloted
30 Spend half the afternoon in a hammock, e.g.
31 Got a good look at
32 Exxon, formerly
33 Wowed
34 Fury
36 Greek X
37 Fuel from a bog
40 California national park
41 Victoria's Secret item
42 Jewish leader
47 Take to court
48 Hot-blooded
50 Does crosswords, say
52 Ship from the Mideast
53 Impudent
55 Off the direct path
56 South Seas kingdom
57 Look with a twisted lip
58 Ring up
59 Dust Bowl refugee
60 Tiny complaints
61 Toward sunset
62 Droop

by Bernice Gordon

ACROSS

1 Entreaty to a subscriber
6 TV watcher's seat
10 Assignment
14 Stood
15 Linda of "Jekyll & Hyde"
16 Sad
17 ___ code
18 Nereid, in myth
20 Generals and such
22 See red?
24 Shoe's end
25 Take part in an auction
26 St. Louis player
27 Lasted longer than
30 Figure to shoot for
33 Ridiculed
35 Harem room
36 Waiter's handout
37 Song in Disney's "Pinocchio"
41 Architect Saarinen
42 Actor/humorist Shriner
43 Rusty Staub or Darryl Strawberry
44 Typical G.R.E. takers
45 Loads and loads of cereal
48 Monopolist's portion
49 One working on the margin, briefly?
50 Prefix with con
51 Not, to a Scot
52 Hot, dry weather phenomenon
58 Musical group, or a hint to the ends of 20-, 37- and 52-Across
59 Formed for a specific purpose
62 "Later, dude"

63 Pitcher
64 Some have big heads
65 Bush adviser Rove
66 Command to Fido
67 Aggressive, personalitywise

DOWN

1 Emulate Eminem
2 It comes before long
3 Outsiders to the club
4 Morales of "NYPD Blue"
5 Rich
6 Sonnet part
7 Old music halls
8 Shake in one's boots
9 Certain well-traveled child
10 Car in a Beach Boys song
11 Hawkeye's portrayer
12 Doesn't sit still for mistreatment, maybe
13 Some male dolls
19 "Irish Rose" lover
21 Letters on a chit
22 Unrestrained revelries
23 Legal release
28 Author of "Mrs. Dalloway"
29 Has too much, for short
30 What doctors aren't known for
31 German chancellor Merkel
32 Steal some steers

34 It can ruin team spirit
36 Stir
38 What a double is worth on the diamond
39 Veto
40 Strong, as a voice
45 Scottish hillside
46 Not careful
47 Hawaiian Airlines freebie
49 Playwright Fugard
52 Punch
53 Musical solo
54 Neighbor of Va.
55 Abbr. on a food container
56 Field of study
57 W.W. II turning point
60 Bullfight cheer
61 Gen. Lee's side

by Stella Daily and Bruce Venzke

ACROSS

1 Secluded area
5 Austrian's "Alas!"
8 Bistro name starter
12 16-Across for Groucho in "Duck Soup"
14 La __ Tar Pits
16 See 12-Across
17 Author Segal
18 *Target for some bowlers
20 *Emmy-winning NBC comedy
22 Tractor name
23 Row C abbr., maybe
24 Water holder
27 Fable writer
30 Cooperstown's __ Lake
32 Klinger player on "M*A*S*H"
35 Bring (out)
37 Not shy
38 From the top
39 Ratty place
41 Bound along
42 Acquired relation
44 Withered
45 Some roll-call calls
46 Bejeweled toppers
48 Bill add-on
50 Witch's work
51 "__ bin ein Berliner"
53 Prefix with red
56 *"Saturday Night Fever" sequel
60 *Something with gates and gaits
63 Mob honchos
64 Newton or tesla
65 Pack away
66 "Les __ Mousquetaires"

67 Soccer __
68 Blaster's need
69 Prefix with skeleton

DOWN

1 Shot up
2 Like tabloid headlines
3 Cyber-send to the I.R.S.
4 *Topic for a doomsayer
5 Children's song start
6 Mountain goat's perch
7 Artist __ de Toulouse-Lautrec
8 Native Canadian
9 Quick trip
10 N.F.L.'er Manning
11 Meditative sect
13 Not hog

15 Hersey novel town
19 High-definition tube, for short
21 Places to roost
24 Tricker
25 Clearly stunned
26 Some spies
28 They need refinement
29 Word that can follow the starts of the answers to the six starred clues
31 *Cause of problems in radio communication
32 Islam or Buddhism
33 Sandy's mistress
34 Chill out
36 Actress Polo

40 Make even deeper
43 Ralph of "The Waltons"
47 Marks for life
49 Put on the books
52 Hilton competitor
54 Wisconsin college town
55 Steer clear of
56 Retired fleet
57 Representation
58 Politico Gingrich
59 Gas brand in Canada
60 Run smoothly
61 Lennon's love
62 Volcano feature

by Edward Alch

ACROSS

1 Family
5 Winter neckwear
10 Conclusions
14 Harvard rival
15 ___ Slobbovia (remote locale)
16 Vista
17 Store safely
18 Cockamamie
19 Ancient Peruvian
20 Start of a quote by Bertrand Russell relevant to crossword solvers
23 Roy Orbison's "___ the Lonely"
24 Rots
25 How to divide things to be fair
28 Revolutionary pamphleteer Thomas
30 Supersmart grp.
31 Atmosphere
32 Back talk
36 Ltd.
37 Middle of the quote
40 Chairman with a Little Red Book
41 In ___ of (standing in for)
43 Actor Tim of "WKRP in Cincinnati"
44 Adhesive
46 Pie nut
48 Quenches
49 Simoleons
52 Swizzle
53 Conclusion of the quote
59 Mission-to-Mars org.
60 Cognizant
61 One with adoring fans
62 Squeezed (out)
63 Hayseed
64 Capone fighter Eliot ___

65 Cry from Charlie Brown
66 Pivots
67 Way to get out of a field

DOWN

1 Anatomical sac
2 Strip of wood in homebuilding
3 ___ vera
4 Eponymous units of force
5 By a narrow margin
6 Brooklyn's ___ Island
7 Not at home
8 Gambling mecca
9 Revealing kind of slip
10 Demonstrates clearly
11 Old Japanese assassin
12 Wooden duck, say
13 Persuades
21 Member of an extended family
22 Poetic time after dusk
25 Disney's "___ and the Detectives"
26 "___, vidi, vici" (Caesar's boast)
27 Suffix with differ
28 Vladimir of the Kremlin
29 Like most of west Texas
31 Between ports
33 One way to run
34 ___-Coburg (part of historic Germany)

35 High-protein beans
38 Sites for grand entrances
39 Icy cold
42 Transfers files to a computer, maybe
45 It's "such sweet sorrow"
47 Have supper
48 Braces (oneself)
49 Worker with a light and a pick
50 Japanese port
51 Beginning
52 Spread, as seed
54 Dicey G.I. status
55 Drink with sushi
56 Notion
57 Maximum
58 ". . . or ___!" (threat)

by Marlon R. Howell

ACROSS

1 Clear away
6 Japanese beer brand
11 Huck Finn's raftmate
14 Canon competitor
15 Some Poe works
16 ___, amas, amat . . .
17 "The Joy of Sex" author
19 PC's "brain"
20 Rapper ___ Def
21 Underdog's win
22 Many a backpacker
24 Chicago-to-D.C. dir.
25 Common prop in close-up magic
26 So-called "King of Vibes"
32 A deadly sin
33 Lecherous goat-men
34 Suffix with novel
37 Canine woe
39 Sale item, maybe: Abbr.
40 Good news for a job applicant
42 Road crew's supply
43 To the rear, at sea
46 Houston hockey player
47 "Lady Sings the Blues" autobiographer
50 Cup holder
52 Realm of 3-Down
53 Start of a toast
54 At full speed
57 Bake sale org.
60 Give a boost to
61 Possible title for this puzzle
64 Caviar
65 Garlicky sauce
66 Like "Twilight Zone" episodes
67 What 61-Across contains
68 An inert gas
69 Some picker-uppers

DOWN

1 Oral, e.g.
2 Move, to a Realtor
3 Mars, to the Greeks
4 Either of two A.L. nines
5 "The dog ate my homework," e.g.
6 PIN takers
7 Out of harm's way
8 Jillions
9 Yon maiden
10 "Really?!"
11 Like many a disabled semi
12 Louvre pyramid architect
13 Express grief
18 Some German autos
23 Wall St. opening
24 Singer with an Oscar-nominated song in "The Lord of the Rings"
25 "All Things Considered" airer
26 Headed out
27 "To Live and Die ___"
28 Pile too much on
29 Half of Hispaniola
30 Cornered, after "up"
31 A gift of the Magi
35 Hospital fluids
36 "Iliad" city
38 Invoice add-on
41 Worth a C
44 Camera type, briefly
45 Like a hopeless situation
48 Clinch
49 Surgeon's tool
50 Mentally acute
51 Grade school quintet
54 Interminable time
55 Actor O'Shea
56 Have ___ (be connected)
57 X-rated stuff
58 Bit of kindling
59 Fruity drinks
62 Rush
63 Auto co. whose name was its founder's initials

by Alan Arbesfeld

ACROSS
1 Classified ___
4 Part of a U.R.L.
7 What a famous woman may play in a movie
14 Depress, with "out"
15 "Gotcha!"
16 Pigged out
17 Bowlegged comic of classic films
19 See 27-Down
20 Talk with an Irish brogue, e.g.
21 Bamboo muncher
22 Unwanted mail
24 Ostrich cousins
26 Height: Prefix
30 Some cartridges
31 Not agin
32 Lament
34 Classroom missile
36 Caron of "An American in Paris"
37 Suffix with west
38 Canadian Thanksgiving mo.
39 Wide's partner
40 Orthodontist's deg.
41 Matthew of "Full Metal Jacket"
43 Carom
45 Ran sandpaper over
46 Mork's planet
47 Prefix with magnetic
48 Composer Rorem and others
49 0-star movie
50 Not speak clearly
51 Cooking pots
54 At any time
56 See 3-Down
59 One who knows the score?
62 Friendly

63 "We ___ the World"
64 Wrap up
65 Walks the beat
66 They're burned on purpose
67 Mom's mate

DOWN
1 "Dynasty" airer
2 "Isn't that obvious?!"
3 Petty creature of the Rockies, with 56-Across?
4 Bulwark
5 Pallid pirate, with 32-Down?
6 Pallid
7 Laughter
8 Prince's school
9 Abbr. after many a general's name

10 Bows
11 Whitney who invented the cotton gin
12 Cut (off)
13 Mil. installations
18 Gas stove light
21 Knitter's stitch
22 Diamond figures
23 Be on the mend
25 Sandwich from the oven
27 Merciless "M*A*S*H" medic, with 19-Across?
28 Indiana Jones's entourage
29 Convenient kind of shopping
32 See 5-Down
33 Architect Saarinen
35 Study (up on)

39 Not budging
42 To the extent that, with "as"
43 Little kangas
44 Gives a hoot
49 Creepy motel of filmdom
52 Gray wolf
53 Lie around
55 Churchillian gestures
56 Protestant denom.
57 "___ little teapot . . ."
58 "Scram!"
59 Bucko
60 Biology class abbr.
61 Otherworldly

by Barbara Olson

ACROSS

1 Actor Baldwin
5 Go a mile a minute, say
10 Canaanite god
14 Length between mini and maxi
15 Uptight person
16 Peter ___, classic cartoonist for The New Yorker
17 One's equal
18 Dances at Jewish weddings
19 Alliance since '49
20 1852 book
23 Old Italian money
24 Long, long time
25 1944 play
31 Trap
32 Low-cal
33 Miner's find
35 Egyptian fertility goddess
36 Takes a turn on "Wheel of Fortune"
38 Unadulterated
39 "Queen of denial" for Queen of the Nile
40 Ollie's partner in old comedy
41 Wild
42 1992 movie
46 Actor Chaney
47 Classical paintings
48 1970's TV show with a literal hint to 20-, 25- and 42-Across
55 Feeling that makes you say "Ow!"
56 Biblical spy
57 When repeated, a court cry
59 For men only
60 The Little Mermaid

61 The "N" of N.B.
62 "Dear God!"
63 Pee Wee who was nicknamed The Little Colonel
64 Quick cut

DOWN

1 Unit of current, informally
2 In ___ of (instead of)
3 Home for Adam and Eve
4 Vultures, at times
5 Globe
6 For the time being
7 Currency that replaced 23-Across
8 Dutch cheese
9 Puddings and pies, e.g.

10 Snack for a monkey
11 Saudi, e.g.
12 Not for
13 Crazy as a ___
21 Fertilizer ingredient
22 Arrive
25 "To recap . . ."
26 Wet, weatherwise
27 Thin pancakes
28 "Ich bin ___ Berliner"
29 Grieve
30 Lineup
31 Taste, as wine
34 Sushi fish
36 Vehicle that does crazy tricks
37 ___ de deux
38 Funds for retirees
40 Shortly
41 What soap may leave

43 Tight, as clothes
44 Bank's ad come-on
45 Practical, as a plan
48 Lhasa ___ (dog)
49 Homebuilder's strip
50 Actor Neeson
51 Long-eared leaper
52 Nobelist Wiesel
53 City on the Rhone
54 Abominable Snowman
58 Microwave

by Linda Schechet Tucker

ACROSS

1 Serf's oppressor
5 Pirate Laffite
9 Joe ___ (average guy)
14 Numbered work
15 Competent
16 Butter maker
17 Drink for Vanna?
19 Funny O'Donnell
20 Augusta National members
21 Rob ___ (drink with Scotch)
22 Caught some Z's
24 Novelist Lurie
26 Regulation for Natalie?
29 Cold place?
30 Barbarian of the comics
31 Potato feature
32 Wilts
33 Critique harshly
34 Fools around (with)
36 Dessert for Edith?
39 Roundup rope
42 Form 1040 org.
43 Shade providers
47 Prez on a fiver
48 Sharp-tasting
50 Enough
51 Family for Pearl?
53 Appreciative diner
54 Diarist Nin
55 Kipling hero
56 Sales worker, for short
57 Give the O.K.
59 Sound quality for George?
62 River's end, sometimes
63 Soothing gel ingredient
64 Place to broil
65 Scaredy-cat
66 Pen points
67 Plain writing

DOWN

1 Catholic rite that lacks singing
2 Tragic figure in "Hamlet"
3 Spoiling
4 P.M. brightener
5 Chief Argonaut
6 Auction site
7 Entirely
8 "Schindler's List" star
9 Airport anti-terrorism worker
10 Cuts (up)
11 Disco dances
12 Certain hosp. test
13 Solitary
18 Cupid, to the Greeks
23 Andes climbers
25 Kind of bar
26 Hand over, as for sale
27 Senate vote
28 General Clark, to friends
30 Knave
33 Former New York governor
35 Step (on)
37 Erodes
38 Attempt
39 Family dog, for short
40 Baghdad's ___ Ghraib prison
41 Consumer safety measures
44 Give the go-ahead
45 Sniffler's supply
46 Garden of Eden inhabitant
49 Sentra maker
50 Prepares to shoot
52 Comb stoppers
53 Moon-related phenomena
55 Radio dial
57 Madison Ave. output
58 Oahu memento
60 ___ Baba
61 Young 'un

by Lynn Lempel

ACROSS

1 DNA half
6 Went over like __ of bricks
10 Plunder
14 Hold forth
15 Curb
16 Ninth in a series
17 Geographical combo #1
20 Series finale
21 Catchall category: Abbr.
22 Lock
23 Goddess with cow's horns
25 Way back when
27 Geographical combo #2
34 "Family Ties" mother
35 CD follower
36 Went kaput
37 Island chain?
38 Easy run
42 M. : France :: __ : Italy
43 Diving raptors
45 Luau serving
46 Barely ahead
48 Geographical combo #3
52 Snitched
53 "A Book of Verses Underneath the Bough" poet
54 Optometrist's field
57 Part of a casa
59 Pro's rival
63 Classic novel, following "A," with a literal hint to 17-, 27- and 48-Across
66 Food thickener
67 Swabbies
68 Stick-on
69 Portend
70 Prohibitionists
71 Fred's dancing sister

DOWN

1 Firefighter's need
2 Middle of Q.E.D.
3 Yuri's love, in "Doctor Zhivago"
4 Slanted writing
5 Illiterates' signatures
6 Drawer
7 Waiter's after-dinner offerings
8 6-Down purchase
9 Dir. from Columbus, Ga., to Columbus, Ohio
10 "Listen" without hearing
11 Opposite of gush
12 "Miss __ Regrets"
13 Plates
18 Bypass
19 Result of an insect bite
24 Courted . . . or used the courts
26 Nautilus captain
27 V.I.P.
28 Olds offering
29 Perjury
30 Bandleader Shaw
31 Golfer's wear
32 Isabella, por ejemplo
33 Barely beat
39 Australian export
40 Kindergarten commendation
41 Bluefin or yellowfin
44 "What'd I tell ya?!"
47 Like many family flicks
49 Fictional dog from Kansas
50 "I didn't care about that anyway"
51 Apple of many colors
54 Wild guess
55 Moor's betrayer
56 Bag brand
58 Haywire
60 "Way to go!"
61 Blue hue
62 Tropical stop
64 Bouquet business
65 Cider girl of song

by John Minarcik and Nancy Salomon

ACROSS

1 Freighter or whaler
5 Read cursorily
9 Chick's cries
14 Window section
15 Prefix with sphere
16 Uncredited actor
17 Rocketeer
19 Writer Joyce Carol ___
20 Cheerleader's cheer
21 Novelty dance spawned by a 1962 #1 hit
23 CD player
25 Freudian ___
26 Reach by foot
29 Certain fir
33 "I love," in France
35 "___ perpetua" (Idaho's motto)
37 Raison d'___
38 Holder of funerary ashes
39 What the ends of 21- and 57-Across and 3- and 30-Down all name
42 Leading pitcher
43 Close by, in poetry
45 Words of enlightenment
46 Goose egg
48 Less difficult
50 Have high hopes
52 Nickname for Dallas
54 Fiats
57 Party bowlful
62 "___ la la!"
63 Lenin's middle name
64 Big business-related
66 Small recess
67 "What is to be done?!"
68 Kind of tea
69 "___ With Love" (1967 hit)
70 Wild hog
71 Units of resistance

DOWN

1 Poles on a 1-Across
2 Attacks
3 Waiting just out of sight
4 The "p" of m.p.h.
5 Dope
6 New Jersey's ___ University
7 Former talk-radio host Don
8 Hands, in slang
9 Central Illinois city
10 Case in point
11 Blues singer ___ James
12 F.D.R. or J.F.K.
13 Window frame
18 Dish often served with home fries
22 Rudely poke
24 St. Louis gridder
27 "___ of the D'Urbervilles"
28 Actor Milo
30 Old West transport
31 St. Louis landmark
32 Get together
33 Beaver's mom on "Leave It to Beaver"
34 Opera highlight
36 "Little piggies"
40 Sign of late summer
41 Declared
44 Small patio grill
47 Mentalist Geller
49 A choice word
51 Jalapeño, to name one
53 1983 Mr T flick
55 Pole carving
56 Outbuildings
57 Blood donation, maybe
58 Mishmash
59 Tiny spasms
60 Popular cream-filled cake
61 "My Friend ___" of old radio/TV
65 Brazilian getaway

by Allan E. Parrish

68

ACROSS

1 Basics
5 Raft wood
10 Goes (for)
14 Christine ___ (29-Down's love)
15 Leave stranded by a winter storm
16 One who says "I say, old chap"
17 See 11-Down
18 It crashes in 29-Down/ 60-Across
20 Seethes
22 Reverse of WNW
23 Site of Margaret Mead studies
24 With 40- and 51-Across, composer of 29-Down/ 60-Across, as well as 63-Across
26 Position
27 End a suit
30 Oboist's need
31 ___ Stadium, home of the U.S. Open
32 Theater areas
36 Old spy org.
39 Addict
40 See 24-Across
41 Aware of
42 Slice (off)
43 Toy gun ammo
44 Condo, e.g.
45 When repeated, words of agreement
47 Communion tables
49 Famed fireman Red
51 See 24-Across
54 Buddhist temple sights
55 "___ had it!"
56 Persistently worry
60 See 29-Down
63 Second-longest-running show in Broadway history

64 Cheer (for)
65 Painter Matisse
66 Real name of 29-Down
67 West Point team
68 Hot, blue spectral type
69 Salon supplies

DOWN

1 Attaches
2 Can of worms?
3 Spelunking site
4 Brine
5 Pen name
6 One who's sore
7 Place for a renter's signature
8 Tendon
9 Now ___ then
10 Flattened at the poles
11 Carlotta, in 29-Down/60-Across

12 Fasten, as a ribbon
13 Costly strings
19 Twisty curves
21 NBC fixture since '75
25 Casino worker
27 Fellow named Bellow
28 Petrol provider
29 With 60-Across, longest-running show in Broadway history
30 Levi's jeans brand
33 Indisposed
34 Peruvian money
35 Soap ingredient
37 Cookbook direction
38 Tipplers
41 Went faster than
43 Examine grammatically

46 You might get a ticket for doing this
48 Novelist Deighton
49 Old marketplace
50 Help with
51 Wetnaps, e.g.
52 Happening
53 Quotable Yogi
57 Indiana city near Chicago
58 Play to ___
59 Sounds of disapproval
61 "So there you are!"
62 Put on TV

by David J. Kahn

ACROSS

1 Dismay
6 Like flags
10 Rap sheet letters
13 Ragú rival
14 Native Canadian
15 Hasty escape
16 Tchaikovsky overture
19 Carrier to Europe
20 S __ sugar
21 Former Georgia senator Sam
22 Frost-covered
24 Boiling point of water on the Celsius scale
28 Noted painter of flowers
30 Opposite end of the point
31 Composer Franck
32 Best Picture of 1958
33 Number of plays attributed to William Shakespeare
38 "Rats!"
39 Decorative pitchers
42 "__ Mucho"
45 Can't-miss proposition
47 Heinz tally of flavors
49 "Star Trek" helmsman
50 Fuji film competitor
51 "What __ can I say?"
53 Test site
54 Sum of 16-, 24-, 33- and 47-Across
59 Plane domain
60 Brewer's kiln
61 Staring intently
62 Growing fig.?
63 Squeaks (out)
64 Flying Pan

DOWN

1 Boorish
2 Most stiffly proper
3 Good baseball throw
4 Turkish title
5 Much
6 Locale
7 Directional suffix
8 Freshly painted
9 Fresh
10 Fascination
11 Julie known as the voice of Marge Simpson
12 Fix
17 Article in Die Zeit
18 Extremes
19 Former McDonald's head Ray
23 "Woo-hoo!"
25 "__ an Englishman" ("H.M.S. Pinafore" song)
26 Impel
27 Less worldly
29 Islamic Sabbath
32 Ob-__
34 Butts
35 Koala's hangout
36 Pasture parents
37 Convert to a fine spray
40 Salon treatment
41 One-inch pencil, for example
42 V.I.P.
43 Physical exertion
44 Photo repro
45 Ward of "The Fugitive," 1993
46 Open with a pop
47 Political party in Palestine
48 Sleeveless garments
52 Barely beat
55 Make a bed?
56 Furniture wood
57 Homonym for 36-Down
58 Convened

by Mel Rosen

ACROSS

1 Persistent annoyer
5 Upper or lower bed
9 Monastery head
14 Author Wiesel
15 Geometry calculation
16 Does a prelaundry chore
17 Leader of an 1831 slave rebellion
19 "___ or treat?"
20 Rejects, as a lover
21 "That's ___" (Dean Martin classic)
23 1960s-70s singer Hayes
24 Bottom line, businesswise
28 Dobbin's doc
29 Actresses Graff and Kristen
31 "___ number one!" (stadium chant)
32 Suffix with Brooklyn
33 Meat that's often served piccata
34 Tête topper
35 Faultfinder extraordinaire
38 1988 Summer Olympics city
41 It may be kicked in anger
42 Alt. spelling
45 Jai ___
46 Duds
48 Opposite WSW
49 "Slow down!"
51 Ban rival
53 African language
54 "Relax, soldier!"
55 Makes, as a salary
57 Müeslix alternative
60 "The final frontier"

61 Meadowlands pace
62 ___ fixe (obsession)
63 Belief
64 Trig function
65 Boys

DOWN

1 Deep in thought
2 Goes by, as time
3 Put in place
4 Prefix with -hedron
5 Jail cell parts
6 Vase
7 Maiden name preceder
8 Activity with chops and kicks
9 Early fur trader John Jacob ___
10 Person using a library card

11 Less wordy
12 Stock page heading: Abbr.
13 "For shame!"
18 Rude
22 Brit. legislators
24 Semimonthly tide
25 Joins up
26 Rage
27 Lunar New Year
30 Tennis court call
34 Under
35 Pain in the neck
36 IOU
37 White wine cocktail
38 ___ Juan, P.R.
39 "Roll Over Beethoven" grp.
40 Healthful cereal grain
42 Front porch
43 Liqueur flavoring
44 Overnight flights

46 Back, at sea
47 Teases
50 Beginning
52 Lubricate again
54 Pot starter
55 N.Y.C. winter clock setting
56 King Kong, e.g.
58 Spoonbender Geller
59 Coal unit

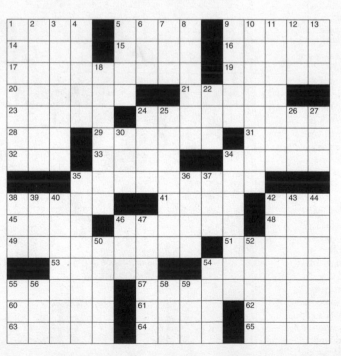

by Sarah Keller

ACROSS

1 Round after the quarters
6 Sweetheart
10 Music staff symbol
14 Frank who directed "It's a Wonderful Life"
15 Noisy quarrels
16 Come-on
17 [ ]
20 Stranded motorist's need
21 Bump off
22 [ ]
28 Stridex target
29 Bank take-back, briefly
30 #1 Oak Ridge Boys hit
32 Swelling shrinker
35 Star's part
39 Nasdaq unit. Abbr.
40 [ ]
42 Bamboozle
43 Attack
45 Number on either side of a +
47 Time-honored
49 "Othello" villain
50 Paycheck abbr.
52 [ ]
55 Penetrated
57 Mattel card game
58 Answers to 17-, 22-, 40- and 52-Across, literally
65 Gofer: Abbr.
66 Letters
67 Bridal path
68 Flower fanciers
69 C & W mecca, with "the"
70 Band with the 1984 hit "Legs"

DOWN

1 "Nova" subj.
2 Grab a bite
3 AWOL trackers
4 Nest-egg investment, briefly
5 Sleigh driver
6 Look without buying
7 Geological span
8 Sense of wonder
9 Cold war initials
10 Amtrak amenity
11 Rest atop
12 Come after
13 Celebratory suffix
18 Hither's opposite
19 Watched over
22 Slap target, sometimes
23 "Wag the Dog" actress Anne
24 La Scala production
25 Corn holder
26 In sum
27 "Z" actor Montand
31 Paul Simon's "___ Rock"
33 First name of the second first lady
34 Chromosome constituent
36 Bounding main
37 Vowel sound in "phone" and "home"
38 Fund, as a university chair
41 Yours, in Ypres
44 Scams
46 "Hägar the Horrible" cartoonist Browne
48 In a gloomy way
50 Answer choice on a test
51 Employed
53 Austin-to-Dallas dir.
54 November birthstone
55 Wound protector
56 Jules Verne captain
59 Easy mark
60 Madam's mate
61 Designer Claiborne
62 Suffix with solo
63 "Strange Magic" grp.
64 Autumn mo.

by Nancy Salomon

ACROSS

1 In years past
5 Throws on
9 Took steps
14 ___ of faith
15 Mirror-conscious
16 Halt
17 Supermarket section
18 "What ___?"
19 Film reviewers' showings
20 Shame a star of "Singin' in the Rain"?
23 Well-developed area?
24 Words said while holding hands
25 It may be brought out during a blackout
28 Israeli legislature
32 Netzero.com service
33 Radio's "___ & Anthony Show"
35 Corrida call
36 Pay no attention to a vampire?
40 Santa ___
41 Essential for an investigator
42 Sad sack
43 Softens
46 Rising stars
47 "Yes, ___!"
48 Rugby formation
50 Send a president out?
55 Vanishes
56 Kind of horse
57 Actor Wyle
59 Gladiator's venue
60 Facility
61 Spoil, with "on"
62 Tripmeter feature
63 Tore
64 Brain part

DOWN

1 Antediluvian
2 Impecuniosity
3 Cartel city
4 Like a soap opera
5 Against, with "to"
6 ___ Lama
7 Some are slipped
8 Snick and ___
9 Give in
10 Big strings
11 Caboose, e.g.
12 Glimpse
13 ___ Plaines, Ill.
21 Big name in California wines
22 Former Pirates slugger Ralph
25 Chest material
26 Nitrogen compound
27 Sounding like one has a cold, say
28 N.B.A. star Jason
29 Lush
30 Aunt ___ of "Oklahoma!"
31 A sad thing to be in
33 Wallet fillers
34 School grp.
37 Prefix with sound
38 Not silently
39 Is in charge
44 Ancient ascetic
45 Barely catches, as the heels
46 Stretched in order to see
48 Deep-six
49 Selected
50 Bell the cat
51 Fateful date
52 Lashes
53 ___ court, law student's exercise
54 Make full
55 Distant
58 Bottom line?

by Sheldon Benardo

ACROSS

1 Martini garnish
6 Mrs. Dithers in "Blondie"
10 Colonel or captain
14 1976 Olympic gymnastics gold medalist ___ Comaneci
15 Assert
16 Away from the wind
17 OVALS
20 Words before roll or whim
21 Murder
22 "You're ___ talk!"
23 Affix one's John Hancock
24 On one's rocker?
26 K
32 Ship's crane
33 Needle parts
34 Évian, par exemple
35 Pizazz
36 Jazz instruments
38 ___ Strauss jeans
39 Be sick
40 Elisabeth of "Leaving Las Vegas"
41 Add a lane to, perhaps
42 STORY
46 "Lovely" Beatles girl
47 Bad news for a dieter
48 Assassinated
51 Atlantic Coast area, with "the"
52 Thrilla in Manila victor
55 X
59 Reverse, as an action
60 Commedia dell'___
61 Fit for a king
62 Gripe

63 Many a teenager's room
64 Alibi

DOWN

1 Aware of
2 Croquet area
3 Conception
4 Beaujolais, e.g.
5 Grovel
6 Checking out, as a joint
7 Kitchen hot spot
8 Gun, as an engine
9 "___ you kidding?"
10 Gilda of the early "S.N.L."
11 Soothing agent
12 Brilliantly colored salamander
13 Gambling game with numbers
18 Indian mystic

19 They're taboo
23 "Wheel of Fortune" turn
24 Eye sore
25 11s in blackjack
26 Actress Shire
27 Picture frames lacking corners
28 Under a spell
29 Must-haves
30 Icicle holders
31 Destroy
32 It may be new, raw or big
36 Gun blast
37 Mystique
38 Circus animal with a tamer
40 Hogs
41 Novelists
43 Son of Poseidon
44 Playing marbles
45 Alternative to check or charge

48 Pond gunk
49 Jay of late-night
50 Wing ___ prayer
51 Young 12-Downs
52 Jason's ship
53 Fibber
54 Without doing anything
56 Ewe's mate
57 Mine find
58 "___ lost!"

by Mark T. Milhet

ACROSS

1 It may be played in elevators
6 MGM co-founder
10 Soldier who's nowhere to be found
14 Entree served with a ladle
15 Pro's opposite
16 Waiter's offering
17 Psychologist sweethearts?
19 Sea dog
20 These can be vital
21 "___ Angel" (1960 #1 hit)
23 Deli loaf
24 Manila ___
25 Ring of frangipani blossoms
27 Lender terms: Abbr.
29 How a psychologist might start over?
34 Mustard city
37 Sleigh pullers
38 10 C-notes
39 Anthem with both English and French lyrics
41 Preordain
43 Manage without assistance
44 Jacob's twin
46 Hosiery brand
47 Psychologist's fast-food order?
50 Grope
51 Actor Stephen
52 "Now I see!"
55 ___, amas, amat . . .
57 The Tower of London was one
59 "Laughing" animals
62 Atticful
64 What a psychologist does at midnight in a motel pool?
66 Helper
67 Compos mentis
68 Struck forcefully
69 Kind of vision
70 Spotted
71 San Rafael's county

DOWN

1 Not the most rewarding work
2 Communications officer on "Star Trek"
3 Sharply piquant
4 Pond organism
5 Glazier's oven
6 W.C.
7 Erstwhile
8 "To be," in Tours
9 Smart aleck
10 Wake-up times, for short
11 Gets tiresome
12 Sole
13 Accompaniment for a madrigal
18 1952 Olympics site
22 "Morning Edition" airer
26 Punctuation used for stress
28 Wicker material
29 Melted-cheese dish
30 Genetic strand
31 Win over
32 New Year's Eve party hat, essentially
33 Shades
34 Remove, as a hat
35 Cake decorator
36 Best-selling "Workout" video maker
40 Far from elite
42 H. Rider Haggard novel
45 American or Swiss
48 M.D., e.g.
49 E. J. ___ Jr., longtime writer for The New Yorker
52 Choice words
53 Half of Hispaniola
54 Poplar tree
55 "Cleans like a white tornado" brand
56 1960's TV's "The Ghost and Mrs. ___"
58 "Fine by me"
60 Polite response from a ranch hand
61 Humorist Bombeck
63 Critical
65 Composer Rorem

by David Sullivan

ACROSS

1 Composer Satie
5 Progeny
10 Doorway part
14 Math sets
15 Sure-footed mountain animal
16 Village Voice award
17 Record label with many collections
18 Actor Paul of "American Graffiti"
19 Proceed
20 *Disney's ___ McDuck
22 *Mr. Television
24 Muffed
27 ___ vez (again): Sp.
30 Manfred Mann's "___ La La"
31 Ex of the Donald
36 Plot
38 Like
40 Elvis ___ Presley
41 Hit 1960's TV show with a hint to the nine starred clues in this puzzle
44 Karachi tongue
45 Actress Dolores ___ Rio
46 All the same
47 Monster
49 Journey part
51 Is profitable
52 Mount ___ (oldest of the Seven Sisters)
55 *"Highly charged" character on "The Addams Family"
59 *Gentleman rabbit of children's lit
64 Melville novel
65 Hubbub
68 "Got Milk?" ad partner
69 John Lennon's "Happy ___ (War Is Over)"
70 Explanatory phrase
71 Anorexic
72 Gabs
73 Camp sights
74 "___ Thin Air" (1997 best seller)

DOWN

1 Colorado Rockies game?
2 Campus program, initially
3 Hockey skater, informally
4 Smuggler's amount
5 Volunteer's offer
6 Cold showers?
7 *Man in a star-spangled suit
8 Thurman of "Pulp Fiction"
9 Wonderland cake words
10 It may get a nip on "Nip/Tuck"
11 Help in crime
12 Smaller than compact
13 "Adam ___"
21 Senator who wrote "Dreams from My Father"
23 Uganda's Amin
25 *"My Three Sons" housekeeper
26 Nimbus
27 Earth tone
28 Silents star Bara
29 *Brer Rabbit tale teller
32 *Chekhov title character
33 Cockroach of literature
34 Some court pleas, slangily
35 From the start
36 It's ripped off at the movies
37 Close
39 Docs' org.
42 Hew
43 Let float, as a currency
48 Café alternative
50 1940 Marx Brothers movie
53 Elliptical path
54 Highland attire
55 Cunning
56 Madame Bovary
57 Good, long bath
58 Turn's partner
60 Asian desert
61 Flattener
62 Fast time?
63 It can go around the world
66 Drink suffix
67 *Onetime Texas rice grower of note

by John Farmer

76

ACROSS

1 Madam's counterpart
4 Resort island near Venice
8 Voodoo charms
13 Poem of praise
14 Stove part
15 Inventor's goal
16 Slangy negative
17 Renowned bandleader at the Cotton Club
19 "I have an idea!"
20 Go before
21 Androids
23 By way of
24 24-hr. banking convenience
27 Dernier ___ (latest thing)
28 Raisin ___ (cereal)
30 Suffix with buck
31 Belief
33 Beats a hasty retreat
34 Emilia's husband, in "Othello"
35 Chinese province
36 They're "easy" to find in 17- and 53-Across and 3- and 24-Down
37 Rural's opposite
38 High: Prefix
39 Muskogee native
40 Walks like an expectant father
41 Noticed
42 Stoop
43 With 45-Across, for the time being
44 Mess up
45 See 43-Across
46 Monkeylike animals
49 Tends, as a patient
52 Butterfly catcher's tool
53 Seize power
56 Road goo
57 Reap
58 Arnaz of "I Love Lucy"
59 Hwy.
60 Dizzy-making drawings
61 Ooze
62 Big fat mouth

DOWN

1 Submarine-detecting system
2 Just 45 miles of it borders Canada
3 Place to get clean
4 When said three times, a real estate mantra
5 Several Russian czars
6 Bankruptcy cause
7 "___ upon a time . . ."
8 Island country south of Sicily
9 15-Down tribe
10 Synagogue attender
11 Keep ___ short leash
12 Hog's home
15 Where the buffalo roamed
18 Like Calculus II
22 Confer holy orders on
24 Jordan or Iraq
25 Ancient Roman robes
26 Mars has two
28 Train stoppers
29 Apply, as cream
30 Military branch with planes
31 Pursue
32 12" stick
37 Mustache site
39 Fairy king, in Shakespeare
45 Silently understood
46 Not tied down
47 Rodeo rope
48 ___ throat
49 "Good buddy"
50 Regulations: Abbr.
51 Not tied down
53 Sporty Pontiac
54 Grandmaster Flash's music genre
55 Alias, for short

by Adam G. Perl

ACROSS

1 Cheese choice
6 It's no free ride
9 Gangster gals
14 Like a Hitchcock audience, typically
15 Grant opponent
16 Poet T.S. ___
17 Hitchhikers' needs
18 Turkish chief
19 Not completely white anymore
20 "Where did ___ wrong?"
21 Testing, as one's patience
24 S-shaped molding
25 Fear
27 Scant
29 Like 90 proof liquor
30 Non-Rx
31 Four Monopoly properties: Abbr.
34 European carrier
35 Bad winner's behavior
37 "Who's the ___?"
40 Peking or Siam suffix
41 Direction for a wagon train
42 Large turnip
45 ___ good clip
47 Valuable rock
48 Spying device
49 Reviewer
53 Outsiders may not get it
56 Put a new handle on
57 Ticklish Muppet
59 Thick-skinned critters
61 33⅓ r.p.m. spinners
62 Many a pope
64 Before, in poetry
65 California team [and 18 letters in the grid to circle . . . and then connect using three lines]
67 Lightly burn
68 N.Y.C. ave. between Park and Third
69 Red Square notable
70 Gang's slanguage
71 Allow
72 Newsboy's shout of old

DOWN

1 Comic page offerings
2 Scale reading
3 Not outside
4 Memphis-to-Mobile dir.
5 Troubadour's six-stanza verse
6 Pot composition
7 Sponsorship
8 Gardener's vine support
9 Dr.'s field
10 Stews
11 Common Valentine's Day gift
12 Theater section
13 Eye ailment
22 Lively piano pieces
23 Córdoba cat
26 ___ nova (1960's dance)
28 Zenith competitor
32 Surgical assts.
33 ___ Snorkel
35 Fed. purchasing org.
36 Wit who wrote "When in doubt, tell the truth"
37 Sis's sib
38 Your and my
39 Hot under the collar
40 Shade of white
43 U.K. radio and TV inits.
44 Violinist Leopold
45 Prefix with 25-Across
46 Railroad support
50 Skill
51 Damage
52 Business jet maker
54 Zaire, now
55 "Yes ___, Bob!"
57 She, in Roma
58 Bandit's refuge
60 Call in a bakery
63 Holiday in Vietnam
66 Bewitch

by Patrick Merrell

78

ACROSS

1 Nightclub light
5 Jorge's eight
9 Ace taker
14 Sailor's patron saint
15 Pearl Buck heroine
16 Beethoven's "___ Joy"
17 Penthouse feature
18 6-Down's subj.
19 Overseas assembly
20 Cowboy toppers
23 Sports facilities
24 Spills the beans
28 A Guthrie
30 Snookums
31 French/English conflict that started in 1337
36 Crime lab evidence
37 Home mortgage stats
38 Moviegoer's reprimand
39 A message may be left after it
40 "What a relief!"
41 Resort area on the U.S./Canada border
45 Annual carrier of toys
47 Push
48 Like George Carlin
51 Time for a 52-Down wake-up call?
55 Natalie Merchant's old group
57 Under
60 Chicago paper, for short
61 Raised
62 Christmas wish
63 Sight from Bern
64 Film director Petri
65 Noted 1999 hurricane
66 Flexible Flyer, for one
67 Aid and abet: Abbr.

DOWN

1 English-speaking Caribbean island
2 "Middlemarch" author
3 Watch word?
4 In these times
5 "Eet ees so nice!"
6 One of nine sisters in myth
7 Lacks
8 Words with go or cheap
9 Rude subway rider
10 Sight from the Black Sea
11 "Jeopardy!" supercontestant Jennings
12 In-flight info: Abbr.
13 Balderdash
21 Money with Garibaldi's picture
22 "Betsy's Wedding" star
25 Fifth Avenue spa
26 Like composition paper
27 Springs
29 Roughly
31 "No thanks!"
32 Seat of Marion County, Fla.
33 Census choice
34 Cinemax alternative: Abbr.
35 Taylor or Tyler
39 Uneasy feelings
41 "Oops!"
42 "What a mistake!"
43 Convertible
44 Reclined
46 Boneheadedness
49 Smidgens
50 Pinkish hue
52 See 51-Across
53 ___ the hole
54 PC program
56 Bog
57 Beach bottle letters
58 Daughter of Loki, in Norse myth
59 Altitudinous Ming

by Elizabeth C. Gorski

ACROSS

1. 1960s–'70s draft org.
4. Purse feature
9. Where hair roots grow
14. Photo
15. Singers Ochs and Collins
16. Causing goosebumps
17. Excitement
18. Pulitzer-winning biography of a Civil War general
19. Take in or let out
20. Modern fashion-conscious guys
23. Didn't participate in
24. Circular staples
25. Appropriate
28. Use a swizzle stick
30. Reception amenity
33. Clubs or hearts
36. Central point
38. Shinbone
39. Unlikely showing at a multiplex
43. Germ cell
44. Day-___ paint
45. "___ of the D'Urbervilles"
46. Item on a gunslinger's hip
49. Bangkok native
51. Perry Como's "___ Impossible"
52. Nectar collector
54. List at a meeting
58. Yanks vs. Mets matchup, e.g.
61. Olympics craft
64. "You ___ right!"
65. ___ Lilly and Company
66. Delight
67. Suddenly cut out, as an engine
68. Rogue
69. Nintendo products
70. Sprayed, as a sidewalk
71. Iris's place

DOWN

1. Sends unwanted e-mails
2. Most-played half of a 45
3. Willard of "Today"
4. Bamboo beginning
5. 1973 Newman/Redford movie
6. Annoy
7. Billy Joel's musical daughter
8. Prefix with intellectual
9. Circus performer with a ball
10. Disney collectibles
11. Paintings
12. Fail a polygraph
13. The "p" in r.p.m.
21. Lists
22. Dangerous hisser
25. Hoffman of 1960s–'70s radicalism
26. Buckets
27. Mine transports
29. Karel Capek classic
31. LAX posting
32. Cooler
33. Some Japanese cuisine
34. Prepare to transplant
35. Fan mail recipients
37. Morass
40. No longer working: Abbr.
41. Final: Abbr.
42. Easy, as a loan
47. Recede
48. Clean again
50. Ancient
53. Keep an ___ the ground
55. Nephew's sister
56. Holdup
57. In reserve
58. Fill up
59. Hawaiian strings, informally
60. "Pro" votes
61. Beer bust purchase
62. Like
63. Thanksgiving side dish

by Joy C. Frank

ACROSS

1 Computer character set, for short
6 Fruity alcoholic brand
10 Alternative to whole or 2%
14 Bombards with bogus offers, say
15 Land of Esau's descendants
16 Office missive
17 Booze
19 John, in Russia
20 Followers of appetizers
21 Comic's gimmick
23 Sport ___ (vehicle)
24 Chemistry Nobelist Otto
25 Hopalong Cassidy player William
28 Sparked, as curiosity
32 Vampire's form
35 Offshoot of the Winnebago tribe
36 Sandwich go-with
37 Princess' accessory
39 Ignores
41 Isn't anymore
42 How much music is sold nowadays
43 Stearns & Foster competitor
44 Mars' Greek counterpart
46 Horn sound
47 "___ you kidding?"
48 Suffered defeat at the hands of
50 Professor 'iggins
51 Ballerina's garb
53 Yalta conf. attendee
55 Church candle lighter
58 Some cowboys
62 Bearded animal
63 Czar's treasure
65 Yalta conf. locale
66 Airs
67 Not exactly a brainiac
68 Soul singer James
69 Preacher's reading
70 Uncool sorts

DOWN

1 Tennis's Arthur
2 Approximately 1,600 feet, for the Brooklyn Bridge
3 Skipper: Abbr.
4 Not wise
5 "The best ___ to come"
6 Chief Olympian
7 Mean Amin
8 Soft shoes, informally
9 Mustachioed Don of classic films
10 Most common U.S. surname
11 "Apollo 13" co-star
12 Colorful computer
13 "Monty Python and the Holy Grail" figure
18 Wranglers, e.g.
22 "It ___ Be You"
25 ___ nova
26 Not this or that
27 Comment to a goner
29 Offshoot of the Winnebagos
30 Milk purchase
31 In a lather
33 Fervency
34 Yummy
38 Serve as a mediator
40 Like most potato chips
45 Up to now
49 Costume
52 Hardly a moderate
54 Started eating
55 Malarial symptom
56 How much to pay
57 Life of Riley
58 Lady's escort
59 Crown prince, e.g.
60 Prayer start
61 Some NCO's
64 Go a few rounds

by Stella Daily and Bruce Venzke

ACROSS

1 Pentathlon need
5 Seasonal air
10 New England team, to fans
14 Mystery author Paretsky
15 Amtrak speedster
16 Speckled steed
17 Top line
19 Eclectic mix
20 Sam and Tom, e.g.
21 Yield to gravity
23 Fruity-smelling compound
24 Center line
28 Planter's place
30 Follows closely
31 Cacophonies
34 Operatic slave
37 Addled
38 Genetic letters
39 Bottom line
41 Small songbird
42 Viewpoint
44 Biblical fall site
45 Workers' ID's
46 Timbuktu's river
47 New Ager John
49 See 62-Across
53 It may start as a grain of sand
57 "Steady ___ goes"
58 "Oklahoma!" vehicle
59 Artist Miró
62 With 49-Across, where 17-, 24- and 39-Across are seen
64 It flows through Florence
65 Dean Martin song subject
66 Manicurist's tool
67 Small songbird
68 Bow over?
69 Come clean, with "up"

DOWN

1 Suffix with Kafka
2 One row on a chessboard
3 How we stand
4 Like harp seals
5 Low islands
6 Prefix with pressure
7 Actress Tara and others
8 Psalm starter
9 ___ luxury
10 Isaiah or Elijah
11 Popular I.S.P.
12 Mai ___
13 ___-Globe
18 Actress Polo
22 Old Irish alphabet
24 Mad Hatter's guest
25 Isn't serious
26 Last name in fashion
27 Exams for aspiring D.A.'s
29 Far from firm
31 Guzzled
32 Belly button type
33 Shrewish
35 Netflix mailing
36 Is an accomplice to
39 W.W. II Japanese fighter planes
40 New Orleans-to-Detroit dir.
43 Locale for Hezbollah
45 Nottingham villain
48 Urge (on)
50 "I'm gonna make you ___"
51 It's hard to do with "orange"
52 Redcap's workplace
54 An ex of Ava
55 Line holders
56 Ancient strings
58 ___' Pea
59 Shoot the breeze
60 Bruins legend
61 Hydrocarbon suffix
63 "___ tu che macchiavi quell'anima"

by David Kwong

82

ACROSS

1 "My Fair Lady" horse race
6 Wrigley Field team
10 Hinged fastener
14 Tiresome task
15 "Got it"
16 Germany's von Bismarck
17 Film director Frank
18 Sharp-toothed Atlantic swimmer
20 Ron of Tarzan fame
21 Record-setting miler Sebastian
23 Diner's bill
24 Actress Gardner
25 Overabundance
28 Washing site
30 Fuss
31 Toyota rival
34 Must-have
35 Holey cheese
37 Entice
39 Doohickey
43 Sir ___ Newton
44 Skin woes
47 Total flop
50 Evening up, as a score
53 Ice cream purchase
54 About 71% of the earth's surface
56 All-time winningest N.F.L. coach
58 The "I" in T.G.I.F.
59 Acorn producer
62 ___ and Coke
63 Seize
64 1978 Donna Summer hit . . . or a hint to 18-, 25-, 39- and 56-Across
67 Tennis's Agassi
69 Nights before holidays
70 Wines like Merlot
71 Prolonged attack
72 Office furniture
73 Annoyer
74 Jackrabbits, actually

DOWN

1 Takes, as an offer
2 Not deep
3 Tweak, as magazine text
4 Hockey legend Bobby
5 Class instructor, informally
6 Roman orator
7 Grp. putting on shows for troops
8 Not straight
9 Big video game maker
10 Opposite of vert.
11 Relaxed
12 Musical Wonder
13 Pope John Paul II's homeland
19 Diminish
22 Cry of wonder
26 Tokyo electronics giant
27 Heartburn reliever
29 Ohio college named for a biblical city
32 Rep.'s foe
33 Dr.'s advocate
36 Lisa, to Bart Simpson
38 Bedwear, briefly
40 ___ King Cole
41 Not straight
42 Alternative to a fly ball
45 Expand
46 Navy building crew
47 Heated, as water
48 "Do, re, mi, fa, sol, la, ti, do" range
49 Slobs' creations
51 What the weary get, in a saying
52 Horned beast
55 Silent O.K.
57 Huge hit
60 Org. for those 50+
61 Thigh/shin separator
65 "For shame!"
66 PC inserts
68 Vardalos of "My Big Fat Greek Wedding"

by Lynn Lempel

ACROSS

1 Scotch go-with
5 Each
9 Like an old Andean empire
14 Got 100 on
15 Gymnastics coach Karolyi
16 Bond before Dalton
17 Do-it-yourselfer
19 Attorney-___
20 Gets in the game
21 Prude
23 Like bookie joints, sometimes
25 Forever and a day
26 That, south of the border
27 Some pitches at baseball stadiums
28 Ja Rule's genre
30 Wealthy widow
33 Cold war side
35 Wee one
37 Vertical, at sea
38 Hardly a beauty queen
42 Debate topic
45 Tariff
46 Separate into lights and darks, say
50 Perpetual
53 Danger for a fly
55 Stephen of "Citizen X"
56 "Rope-a-dope" boxer
57 Cleanse (of)
59 Reversible fabric
61 Natty dresser
65 It may be at a tilt
66 "The Tempest" spirit
67 Sourpuss
69 Fan mags
70 Rick's love in "Casablanca"
71 Borscht need
72 3 on a par 5

73 Nikita's "no"
74 Exxon abroad

DOWN

1 Dry as a desert
2 Song words before "We stand on guard for thee"
3 Driller and filler
4 Threw in
5 Lawyers' org.
6 The Quakers of the Ivy League
7 Nostalgic number
8 What you may have to do for goods bought by mail order
9 "___ Old Cowhand" (1936 Bing Crosby hit)
10 One with a staff position?

11 Hall locale
12 Lake on the edge of Kazakhstan
13 Buffalo's home
18 Belgian river
22 Brian of early Roxy Music
24 Facts and figures
29 Luau fare
31 Pasty-faced
32 King Kong's kin
34 Concerto, e.g.
36 Blasting material
39 Tennis do-over
40 It may be cut by an uppercut
41 Took a bough?
42 Confused
43 Sunrooms
44 Taking potshots
47 Juicy fruits
48 Bails out
49 Learns easily

51 1960s–'70s Boston Garden hero
52 Hybrid language
54 Salve
58 Dawdle
60 Waffler's answer
62 Banana discard
63 "You're something ___!"
64 It smells
68 Stable staple

by Nancy Salomon and Harvey Estes

84

ACROSS

1 Own (up to)
5 Freezes
10 Hardly racy
14 Chichi
15 Old Intellivision rival
16 ___ Bator
17 Hoedown site
18 Recoiled
19 Place for studs
20 Hurricanes or Lightning
23 Suggest, as a price
25 Zip
26 Ship sent for breadfruit in 1787
27 Blasts of the past
29 "Out of the question"
31 Links obstacle
33 Valentine and others: Abbr.
36 Periodic table abbr.
37 Actor Kilmer
38 ___-Ball (arcade game)
39 Royale of old autodom
40 Device patented by Thomas Savery in 1698
44 Sharp-witted
45 You can take it with you
46 Pierce with a point
49 Horned Frogs' sch.
50 Opposite of great, to Burns
51 Put more pressure (on) . . . or a title for this puzzle?
55 Stuck, after "in"
56 Turner autobiography
57 "The Naked Maja" artist
60 Turner who was called the Sweater Girl
61 Off
62 Their milk is used to make Roquefort
63 Corrida cries
64 All in
65 Completely lose patience

DOWN

1 Terrif
2 Part of B.C.E.
3 Full-count cry
4 Harmony
5 Contents of some hookahs
6 Playwright Fugard
7 Of the flock
8 All-day hike
9 Court conference
10 Expression of annoyance
11 U.F.O. pilot
12 Charlotte Corday's victim
13 Other side
21 ___'acte
22 In the distance, poetically
23 Egypt's Sadat
24 Cabinet department
28 Spot for a scene
29 ___ Walton, author of "The Compleat Angler"
30 Like the eye of a hurricane
32 Picasso's "Colombe ___ fleurs"
33 Takes a powder
34 Pre-noon time
35 "Ciao"
38 Police rank: Abbr.
40 Original Enterprise navigator
41 Cravat adornments
42 Captivate
43 Modern, to Mahler
44 "The Spirit of Australia" sloganeer
46 Author Calvino
47 Diego Rivera work
48 Snip what's superfluous
49 Mortise's mate
52 Sunroof alternative
53 "The ___ Report," 1976 best seller
54 Matures
58 Roll call vote
59 Nile biter

by Paula Gamache

ACROSS

1 "Survivor" shelter
4 $$$ dispenser
7 Circumference
12 October birthstone
14 ___ Fox of Uncle Remus tales
16 "I love you," in Spanish
17 The year 1052
18 Be an omen of
19 Lady
20 007's introduction
23 Dustin's role in "Midnight Cowboy"
24 Sand holders at the beach
25 Slugger's stat
28 Mag. workers
29 Hip-hop doc?
31 Part of an ellipsis
32 Prominent part of a dachshund
33 Easy as ___
34 Except
35 Birthday dessert
36 Embroidered sampler phrase
40 Guns, as a motor
41 Cravat
42 Almost forever
43 Byron's "before"
44 "My gal" of song
45 Branch
46 Commercial suffix with Gator
49 Each
50 Map book
52 County on the Thames
54 Repeatedly
57 Soup eater's sound
59 Kitchen or bath
60 Aroma
61 Hearing-related
62 College digs
63 Traveled
64 Tableau
65 Airport screening org.
66 Snake's sound

DOWN

1 Man of La Mancha
2 Transfer to a mainframe, maybe
3 Contaminates
4 Alphabetically first pop group with a #1 hit
5 ___ l'oeil
6 Tragic woman in Greek drama
7 Maximally
8 Nasty
9 Nightmare
10 Britney Spears's "___ Slave 4 U"
11 Mr. Turkey
13 Jar tops
15 Ashes, e.g.
21 "Panic Room" actress Foster
22 Ink soaker-upper
26 Make a 35-Across
27 Anger
30 Say again just for the record, say
33 Afternoons, for short
34 Queen who might create quite a buzz?
35 Pro's opposite
36 Roll-call call
37 Orchestral intro
38 Weatherman Scott
39 "The Simpsons" dad
40 Agent, in brief
44 Just a taste
45 Noted family of financiers and philanthropists
46 Parenthetical comments
47 Fiends
48 Puts forth, as effort
51 In progress
53 Put away
55 Gulf land
56 Gwyneth Paltrow title role
57 Carrier to Stockholm
58 Capt. Jean-___ Picard of the U.S.S. Enterprise

by Andrea C. Michaels

86

ACROSS

1 ___ Island, Bahamas, boyhood home of 47-Across
4 Jack's partner
8 Brook sound
14 Egg cells
15 Cookie since 1912
16 Discomfort
17 With 64-Across, film for which 47-Across won an Oscar for Best Actor
19 President with an airport named after him
20 Shangri-la
21 Autobiography of 47-Across
23 Noisy to-dos
27 VCR button
28 Film starring 47-Across with a chart-topping title song
34 Squeeze (out)
35 Computer acronym about faulty data
36 Bygone U.S. gas brand
39 Broadway play (and later film) starring 47-Across
44 Bamako's land
45 Ripped
46 "All bets ___ off"
47 Actor born Feb. 20, 1927
52 Michael Stipe's band
53 Brontë heroine
54 Debut film for 47-Across, 1950
59 Relative of an ostrich
63 Kind of acid used in bleaches
64 See 17-Across
68 Fine wool
69 River to the Seine
70 ___-mo
71 Naval banner
72 Tampa/St. ___
73 Grp. that gave 47-Across a Life Achievement Award in 1999

DOWN

1 ___ slaw
2 Eager
3 Legend
4 Cup of ___
5 Apr. 15 check recipient
6 Preceder of Virgo
7 Gallery
8 Classic cigar brand
9 Intl. grp. for which 47-Across was named an ambassador
10 Sincere
11 Gift givers
12 Jet set?: Abbr.
13 Artist Magritte
18 Letters on a cross
22 Regal inits.
24 Grps.
25 1940s conflict, for short
26 Affix one's John Hancock
28 Nets or Jets
29 Gumbo ingredient
30 Closes tightly
31 Hoity-___
32 Neckline shape
33 Bit of French writing
37 "Certainly!"
38 Lollapalooza
40 Afternoon hour on a sundial
41 "Uh-uh"
42 King Priam's home
43 Prince, e.g.
48 Evaporating, with "up"
49 Reader of The Weekly Standard, perhaps
50 Relative of an ostrich
51 Actress Hatcher
54 Iditarod's finish
55 Plow pullers
56 Punic ___
57 Et ___ (and others)
58 Sporty car feature
60 Gas company with collectible toy trucks
61 Jazzy Fitzgerald
62 Work like ___
65 Make haste
66 Round fig.
67 Price of admission

by Jonathan Gersch

ACROSS

1 Meat loaf serving, e.g.
5 Preserve, as preserves
10 Possible college class pres.
14 El Cid, to Spaniards
15 "___ Foolish Things" (1930s hit)
16 Title girl in a 1986 Starship hit
17 ___ no.
18 Uncovered
19 Press
20 Slangy question from a benefactor, maybe
23 Prosperity
24 Style of shorthand, informally
27 Shocked
30 French possessive
32 Time, in Italian
33 Bullwinkle, for one
34 ___ of Leningrad, 1941–44
35 Hightail it
36 1964 party song by Manfred Mann
40 F.B.I. employee: Abbr.
41 "Gosh"
42 Cancellation
43 Wine and dine, say
44 Whips but good
45 Hangar contents
47 Higher-ranked
49 Author Sholem
50 Stuffy sort
56 Suffix with stink
58 Kind of artery
59 Numismatist's classification
60 Highly distasteful
61 Below, to a bard
62 Strikeout ace Nolan
63 Brokerage initialism
64 Parental units?
65 Cries during a bikini waxing?

DOWN

1 "Pygmalion" playwright
2 Solidarity's Walesa
3 Bowed, in music
4 Home of the Kalahari Desert
5 Craft for J.F.K.
6 Thing that doesn't go off without a hitch?
7 Oreg. or La., once
8 Did something with
9 Education
10 "Revolution," to "Hey Jude"
11 "The Company of Women" author, 1980
12 Old peso material
13 Give the ax
21 "Indubitably"
22 Like prunes
25 Soreness?
26 Some plasma TV's
27 Early in the morning
28 Baby talk
29 Do-it-yourselfer's collection
30 Seconds
31 Ancient dweller of modern Iran
34 Nod, maybe
37 In great disfavor
38 Towering over
39 Rushed
45 Excites, with "up"
46 Digital readout, initially
48 Earl ___, first African-American to play in the N.B.A.
49 "It's ___!" ("See you then!")
51 1997 Peter Fonda title role
52 Naturalist Fossey
53 Belafonte catchword
54 20-20, e.g.
55 Achings
56 German article
57 ___ Victor

by Elizabeth C. Gorski

88

ACROSS

1 Tempest
6 Cub Scout group
9 Singer Turner and others
14 Chili con ___
15 N.Y.C.'s Park or Lexington
16 "Dying / Is ___, like anything else": Sylvia Plath
17 E. M. Forster novel
20 Brooks of comedy
21 Old punch line?
22 Disreputable
23 Mia of women's soccer
24 To ___ (perfectly)
25 Car parker
32 One of the Astaires
33 Dictionary unit
34 Australian hopper, for short
35 Manner
36 Property encumbrances
38 "Cómo ___ usted?"
39 Hosp. scan
40 Cost of a cab
41 C-3PO, for one
42 Entities cited in the Penitential Rite
46 Tipplers
47 The Vatican's home
48 "La Nausée" novelist
51 "Star Wars" guru
52 Opposite of 'neath
55 What conspiracy theorists look for (as hinted at by 17-, 25- and 42-Across)
58 Colorado ski town
59 Dined
60 Spanish hero played by Charlton Heston
61 Louts
62 "Two clubs," e.g., in bridge
63 Cuts down on calories

DOWN

1 E-mail offer of $17,000,000.00, e.g.
2 Reel-to-reel ___
3 Spoken
4 I.C.U. helpers
5 Communiqué
6 Explorer Vasco ___
7 Even once
8 Ping-Pong table divider
9 Last part
10 Wanting
11 Zilch
12 Phoenix's home: Abbr.
13 Order to Fido
18 Peak
19 Some blenders
23 Robust
24 Lots
25 Letter after beta
26 Decorate
27 Excavate again
28 11- or 12-year-old
29 Crime sometimes done for the insurance
30 Untagged, in a game
31 Creatures said to cause warts
36 Remained
37 Gershwin and others
38 Cleveland's lake
40 Old gold coins
41 Requiring repair
43 Rolle who starred in "Good Times"
44 Spoke so as to put people to sleep
45 Ice cream drink
48 Dagger wound
49 "I see," facetiously
50 "___ Man," Emilio Estevez movie
51 Dubious sighting in the Himalayas
52 A single time
53 Blue-pencil
54 X-ray units
56 Small amount, as of hair cream
57 Inventor Whitney

by Peter A. Collins

ACROSS

1 "Thou ___ not . . ."
6 Conclude
11 Belly muscles
14 "Winning Bridge Made Easy" author
15 Bygone defense grp.
16 Well-dressed fellow
17 "The Razor's Edge" star, 1946
19 To and ___
20 "Avast!"
21 Engagement gift
22 Beau
24 Triangular house part
26 "Oh, my ___ back!"
27 1980s Scott Baio sitcom
31 At one's fingertips
32 Command to a police dog
33 Guinness Book suffix
34 Catcher's position
36 Comedian Margaret
39 1972 Olympics sensation Mark
41 Earth Day's month
43 Breakfast beverage
48 Lyndon's 1964 running mate
49 Intended
50 Big-budget films
51 Help with wrongdoing
53 Actress Ward
56 Pastor Haggard
57 Title for this puzzle
60 . . . due, ___, quattro . . .
61 Full
62 See 7-Down
63 Extra play periods, for short
64 Jeweled headwear
65 Twist in order to see better

DOWN

1 Some police dept. personnel
2 Baseball Hall-of-Famer Wilhelm
3 Haughty
4 Feline stalker
5 Spike TV's former name
6 Catches sight of
7 With 62-Across, nickname for former N.F.L. star Sanders
8 Hip-hop friend
9 Western tribe
10 Jaguar competitor
11 Amour
12 Yawn inducing
13 Moocher
18 Writer ___ Stanley Gardner
23 Kapow!
25 Adventurer Nellie
26 Part of I.R.A.: Abbr.
27 ___ Guevara
28 Keeps
29 Vehicle named for a Japanese river
30 Actress Vardalos
34 Search (through)
35 N.F.L. period: Abbr.
36 Standards
37 Hawaiian Punch competitor
38 Hooray, in Juárez
39 Mil. designation
40 Not give up
41 1977 Steely Dan album that spent 52 weeks in the top 40
42 Ogden Nash, notably
43 Run-down urban area
44 Media baron Murdoch
45 Dwells
46 Mrs. Marcos of the Philippines
47 Head, to Henri
51 "The Thin Man" dog
52 Ballpark buy
54 Feature of a dangerous circus act
55 Teen annoyance
58 Skater Babilonia
59 Public health agcy.

by Allan E. Parrish

ACROSS

1 ___ Willard, heavyweight champ dethroned by Jack Dempsey
5 Got together
10 Pot-au-feu
14 "Lord, it is good for ___ be here" (words of Peter to Jesus)
15 Wipe out
16 Two-handed sandwich
17 Check writer's record
18 More genuine
19 Sufficient, once
20 Establishment with spicy sauces
23 Brazilian-born bandleader Mendes
24 Cousin of reggae
25 Yang's counterpart
27 Table scrap
28 Harvest
31 Romanian composer Georges
33 Eaves dropping?
35 Prey for a hognose snake
36 Martial art
39 Sistine Chapel figure
41 Right triangle ratio
42 Country cuisine
45 Mid sixth-century year
46 Rapper Lil' ___
49 Yank's foe
50 Poodle's cry
52 Colorless gas
54 Finish the job
58 Sundance Kid's lady
59 One of the Marx brothers
60 Goddess depicted with a cow's horns
61 Wares encountered by Simple Simon
62 Wee hour
63 Risk
64 Vaulted area
65 "Ally McBeal" role
66 "Much" preceder

DOWN

1 Like this
2 Handel oratorio about a biblical woman
3 House of Charles I and II
4 Pulitzer-winning Ferber title
5 Sudden, swift and brilliant
6 Drops the ball
7 Like a trampoline's surface
8 "___ directed"
9 Powdered wig
10 Ballpark near La Guardia
11 "Locksley Hall" poet
12 "Delta of Venus" genre
13 "Holy Toledo!"
21 Perfumer Nina
22 Wasn't colorfast
26 Silent go-ahead
29 Phil who sang "Jim Dean of Indiana"
30 Employed busily
32 Virginie, e.g.
33 Neil Diamond's "___ Said"
34 Book after Proverbs: Abbr.
36 They're felt in mid-April
37 "Try it!"
38 Marry
39 It's south of Eur.
40 "Cut down on between-meal snacks," e.g.
43 Greenwich Village sch.
44 Draw (off)
46 Bob Dole, e.g.
47 One of the Gandhis
48 Camp meals
51 Smoother
53 Swiss miss
55 Allay
56 City south of Moscow
57 It's worn by some Libras
58 Air-testing org.

by Elizabeth C. Gorski

ACROSS
1 Digging tool
6 ___ McAn shoes
10 Felt remorse
14 Israel's Sharon
15 Lira's replacement
16 "Don't Tread ___"
   (old flag warning)
17 Planter without
   hired hands
19 Game-stopping
   call
20 "Zip-___-Doo-Dah"
21 "I didn't know
   that!"
22 Nervous giggle
24 Fabrics for towels,
   robes, etc.
26 Sukiyaki side dish
27 Auto mechanic
32 Nests, for birds
35 Fall site in Genesis
36 Eco-friendly org.
37 ___ Brothers, who
   sang "Rag Mop"
38 Fur tycoon
   John Jacob
40 Trickle out
41 A Bobbsey twin
42 Leave off
43 Storied engineer
   Casey
44 Any member
   of Nirvana or
   Pearl Jam
48 Java dispensers
49 Take back
53 Popular drink mix
56 Extra-wide,
   on a shoebox
57 Fitzgerald who
   knew how to scat
58 Eurasia's ___
   Mountains
59 Smear campaigner
62 Race that once had
   a four-minute
   barrier
63 Give off
64 Knight's mount
65 Borscht vegetable

66 D.C. nine, for short
67 Pig voiced by
   Mel Blanc

DOWN
1 Begin's co-Nobelist
2 Family of lions
3 Broadcaster
4 Cleanses
5 Keebler baker,
   in ads
6 Humanitarian
   Mother ___
7 Actor Cronyn
8 Smelter input
9 Edgar Bergen
   dummy ___ Snerd
10 Way past ripe
11 Condo or
   apartment
12 Noted plus-size
   model
13 ___ Xing (sign)

18 "The Morning
   Watch" writer James
23 Clickable screen
   symbol
25 E-file receiver
26 Change the décor of
28 Brief tussle
29 Like an eagle's
   vision
30 Blunted sword
31 Big fat mouths
32 Nail to the wall
33 Epps of TV's "House"
34 Chalkboard
   writing at a cafe
38 Emphatic words
   of agreement
39 Knighted ones
40 Bay of Naples
   tourist city
42 Hideous sort
43 Namath, for
   most of his career

45 Small seed
46 Blue jay toppers
47 It runs from
   stem to stern
50 "Ragged Dick"
   writer Horatio
51 One iron, in
   old golf lingo
52 Late, on a report
   card
53 Under the effects
   of Novocain
54 Lake named after
   an Indian tribe
55 Red-tag event
56 Trim, as text
60 Actress Thurman
61 AOL, e.g.: Abbr.

by Fred Piscop

ACROSS

1 Out-of-focus image, say
5 "Be ___ and help me"
10 Jets that boom
14 Cosmonaut Gagarin
15 Bamboo lover
16 Karate blow
17 Cassini of fashion
18 Following closely behind
19 Meter maid of song
20 *Lousy advice
22 Martini garnishes
24 Private eyes, for short
25 ___ Penh: Var.
26 Point the finger at
29 *Model behavior on the field
33 Elevator enclosure
34 From head ___
35 Announcement at Penn Sta.
36 Sport of horse racing, with "the"
37 Subject of the 2004 biopic "Beyond the Sea"
38 Teri of "Young Frankenstein"
39 Social finale?
40 "All for one and one for all," e.g.
41 Bagful on the pitcher's mound
42 *What the nouveau riche have
44 Commotions
45 Decorative pitcher
46 Dune material
47 "Finally!"
50 "You're on!" . . . and a hint to answering the seven starred clues
54 Boast
55 Laughs

57 First name in mystery writing
58 Spelunker's setting
59 Castaway's locale, maybe
60 Self centers
61 Warm up in the ring
62 Home on the range
63 "i" toppers

DOWN

1 Informal invitation letters
2 Humdinger
3 City NNW of Provo
4 *Things worth sweating, with "the"
5 Each
6 Owners of the Faeroe Islands
7 ___'acte
8 Hubbub
9 *Cutting it can bring tears to the eyes
10 Pinch pennies
11 Switchblade, slangily
12 Schlep
13 Health resorts
21 Quiz
23 Oral history
25 Barbecue site
26 Patty Duke's son Sean
27 Water park slide
28 Baseball Hall-of-Famer Rod
29 Number of winks in a nap
30 Tether
31 Places in the heart
32 Tall tales
34 Spud
37 *Words after "Been there"

38 *Samaritan's act
40 Tends to the lawn
41 Gossipy Barrett
43 Scanty
44 Pain in the behind
46 Like a day-old baguette
47 Rudiments
48 Police sting, e.g.
49 Source of basalt
50 Chain restaurant with a blue roof
51 As a result
52 Scads
53 Minus
56 "Thanks, but I already ___"

by Paula Gamache

ACROSS

1 Supersonic unit
5 Goalie's stat
10 Frizzy do
14 Old Greek theaters
15 One of the Horae
16 Speakeasy risk
17 Look-alike of a source of oil?
19 Concerned with
20 www address
21 Second ltr. addendum
22 Dugout V.I.P.
24 Place to play?
26 Overdo the T.L.C.
27 Spitting image of a children's storybook character?
33 Grills or pumps
36 Wine-and-cassis drink
37 School assignment
38 Devilfish
40 Microwave
42 Together
43 Self-interest doctrine
45 Easter preceder
47 Part of M.I.T.: Abbr.
48 Exact replica of six Northeastern states?
51 1813 battle site
52 Less assertive
56 Shoots down
60 In accordance with
61 Historic Virginian
62 Tandoor, e.g.
63 Carbon copy of a Cleveland ballpark?
66 Witty remark
67 Contents list
68 Drawn
69 Maybe more, maybe less
70 Loses it
71 "Handy" one

DOWN

1 Finish
2 Be nuts about
3 String quartet member
4 Lyricist David
5 Beer buy
6 Wall St. figures
7 Skein formation
8 Captivate
9 One serving a long term
10 Met highlight
11 Part of the mouth of a cottonmouth
12 Liturgy
13 Something in the air
18 ___ arms
23 Where Hercules slew the lion
25 Country
26 Send over the edge
28 Dick's mate, twice
29 Positive aspect
30 Crackpot
31 Buffet dispensers
32 Mark in the margin
33 Prayer period?
34 Learned
35 Have down cold
39 Beyond the pale?
41 Patronage purveyor, for short
44 Sells
46 One of 11 kings of Egypt
49 Stanza maker
50 ___ ball (spongy plaything)
53 Anne of fashion
54 Sniggled
55 Helen who sang "Angie Baby"
56 Self-defense school
57 At any point
58 Porgy's woman
59 Biblical preposition
60 Papermaking material
64 Group an atty. gen. might address
65 Give-go go-between

by Richard Silvestri

ACROSS

1 More eccentric
6 "Moby-Dick" captain
10 Reaction to a knee-slapper
14 Old pal
15 Food that may come in small cubes
16 Giant-screen film venue
17 Sign for a person in therapy?
20 ___, due, tre . . .
21 Abominable Snowman
22 Turtle's covering
23 Like college aptitude tests, for many students
26 Highway
28 Compete in a slalom
29 Moist
31 Lawyer: Abbr.
35 Together
38 "Well, then . . ."
40 By way of
41 Sign for a recovering alcoholic?
43 Annoy
44 Completely cover
46 "Hmmm . . ."
48 Japanese drink
49 Numbered hwys.
51 Faux ___
52 Perlman of "Cheers"
54 Comedian's gimmick
58 Candidate Stevenson of '52 and '56
61 Level
63 Rhetorical question, possibly
64 Sign for a gangster?
68 Fork prong
69 Washington daily

70 ___ Ste. Marie, Mich.
71 Went fast
72 Aussie jumpers
73 ___ Rose Lee

DOWN

1 Happen
2 Pilotless aircraft
3 Sign for a jury selector?
4 Suffix with differ
5 Seedy loaf
6 Eventgoer
7 Party thrower
8 Uphold
9 Prickly seed cover
10 Religious time
11 French girlfriend
12 Room connector
13 Skating jump
18 Science guy Bill
19 Cool ___ cucumber
24 Letters before an alias
25 Twists to be worked out
27 Eye-catching designs
30 Enough
32 Sign for a sunbather?
33 Went fast
34 Oxen connector
35 Currier and ___
36 Companion of the Pinta and Santa María
37 Plowmaker John
39 Pretty maiden of Greek myth
42 Mousse and mud pie
45 Exposed to oxygen
47 Consume
50 Skin art

53 Go quickly
55 ___-Magnon
56 They're stirred in the fire
57 Meower
58 Many urban homes: Abbr.
59 Annoyance from a faucet
60 "The ___ Ranger"
62 In that case
65 E.M.T.'s skill
66 "No ___" (Chinese menu notation)
67 It's pitched with a pitchfork

by Kevin Der

ACROSS

1 Poodle sounds
5 Aspirin target
9 Hymn accompanier
14 *Angler's float
15 Terrifying dino
16 *Bush's 2004 foe
17 Jazz singer Anita
18 Café au ___
19 Assists, three-pointers, turnovers, etc.
20 N.F.L. Hall-of-Famer Ford
21 Not systematic
23 ___ dixit
24 *1960s Richard Chamberlain TV role
27 Tease, with "on"
28 Nap under a sombrero
31 *Ava Gardner's co-star in "The Sun Also Rises"
37 Resistance unit
38 Wished otherwise
39 Will Smith biopic, 2001
40 Fateful March day
41 Little devil
42 *Deli request
46 Nursery rhyme opening
48 Miner's find
49 What the answers to the seven starred clues all are or contain
56 Persian sprite
58 Harangue
59 590, to Caesar
60 Partner of dangerous
62 Comic actor Jacques
63 Cry of fright
64 *Writer ___ Boothe Luce
65 Tucson-to-New Orleans route
66 *Quilt filling
67 It may be perfect
68 Actress Garr of "Mr. Mom"
69 Eye sore

DOWN

1 "It'll be ___ day in hell . . ."
2 Bull-riding event
3 Pre-euro money
4 Shade of blue
5 Not in custody
6 Model T feature
7 Storied Swiss miss
8 Praise highly
9 Approves
10 Quit for good, jobwise
11 Welch's product
12 Kennedy Center focus, with "the"
13 Wall Street inits.
21 Equine color
22 Store stock: Abbr.
25 Trampled
26 Publicize
29 ___ Might Be Giants (rock group)
30 Schoolyard retort
31 "Lou Grant" newspaper, with "the"
32 Arizona city
33 Tool kit carrier
34 Buddy
35 Bygone
36 Puns and such
40 "___ a traveler . . .": "Ozymandias"
42 "Bali ___"
43 Malt-drying kiln
44 Erich Weiss, on stage
45 Fish-eating eagle
47 Prickly plants
50 Cry to the band
51 Fruit-packing unit
52 Western flick
53 Birdbrain
54 Multilane rte.
55 Noisy public fight
56 Treaty
57 Author ___ Stanley Gardner
61 Actress Ruby
63 Football gains or losses: Abbr.

by Holden Baker

ACROSS

1 Enlighten
6 A couple of CBS spinoffs
10 1972 Broadway musical
14 Metal giant
15 Evict
16 Area
17 Surface again, as a road
18 Pirate or Padre, briefly
19 Camera feature
20 Barracks artwork, perhaps
22 River to the Ligurian Sea
23 Keg necessity
24 ". . . ___ he drove out of sight"
25 ___ St. Louis, Ill.
27 Preen
29 Greek peak
33 Vice president after Hubert
36 Patient wife of Sir Geraint
38 Action to an ante
39 Gain ___
40 French artist Odilon ___
42 Grape for winemaking
43 Single-dish meal
45 Broad valley
46 See 21-Down
47 Artery inserts
49 Offspring
51 Mexican mouse catcher
53 Medical procedure, in brief
54 "Wheel of Fortune" option
57 Animal with striped legs
60 Editorial
63 It gets bigger at night
64 "Hold your horses!"
65 Idiots
66 Europe/Asia border river
67 Suffix with launder
68 Leaning
69 Brownback and Obama, e.g.: Abbr.
70 Rick with the 1976 #1 hit "Disco Duck"
71 Yegg's targets

DOWN

1 Mastodon trap
2 "Mefistofele" soprano
3 Misbehave
4 Pen
5 More pleased
6 Treated with disdain
7 Enterprise crewman
8 Rhone feeder
9 Many a webcast
10 Mushroom, for one
11 Unfortunate
12 Nevada's state tree
13 Disney fish
21 Colonial figure with 46-Across
26 Poker champion Ungar
27 Self-medicating excessively
28 March 14, to mathematicians
30 Book part
31 Powder, e.g.
32 007 and others: Abbr.
33 Drains
34 Stove feature
35 Feet per second, e.g.
37 Italian range
41 Prefix with surgery
44 Captain's announcement, for short
48 Tucked away
50 Stealthy fighters
52 Sedative
54 Letter feature
55 Jam
56 Settles in
57 Symphony or sonata
58 Japanese city bombed in W.W. II
59 Beelike
61 Evening, in ads
62 Religious artwork

by Peter A. Collins

ACROSS

1 Like some committees
6 Designer Lauren
11 Lunch counter sandwich, for short
14 How most mail goes nowadays
15 Accustom to hardship
16 Whopper
17 Sinuous Mideast entertainer
19 Multivolume Brit. reference
20 Ballpark fig.
21 WWW addresses
22 Beaded counter
24 Basic course for a future M.D.
25 The "A" in DNA
26 Chance, at cards
31 Compass part
33 David Sedaris's comic sister
34 Springsteen's "Born in the ___"
35 Golfer Palmer, familiarly
36 Gives the green light
37 Pesto ingredient
39 Comic Caesar
40 New Year's ___
41 Yield
42 One way to fall in love
46 Goatee site
47 Blockheads
48 Dietetic
51 Novelist Ambler
52 "Without further ___ . . ."
55 ___ carte
56 Host of a Friars Club event
59 Chess pieces
60 ___ forth (et cetera)
61 Vibes

62 Word that may precede the beginning of 17-, 26-, 42- or 56-Across
63 Most common craps roll
64 Yahoo! or AOL offering

DOWN

1 French cleric
2 Colors, as Easter eggs
3 Sentry's command
4 Mideast export
5 Throw in the towel
6 Theater district
7 Raggedy ___ (dolls)
8 Film director Jean-___ Godard
9 Tediously didactic

10 Jazz's Hancock or Mann
11 Voting group
12 Stead
13 Senators Kennedy and Stevens
18 Explorer Sir Francis
23 Append
24 BMW competitor
25 Places to get quick money, quickly
26 ___ hand (help)
27 Fraud
28 Stratagems
29 Z ___ zebra
30 Poet Whitman
31 Poet Ogden
32 Shallowest of the Great Lakes
36 Pizzeria fixture
37 Muscle mag photos
38 Cure-___ (panaceas)
40 Satan, with "the"

41 Adjust one's sights
43 Roman 700
44 Tara plantation family
45 Dr. Seuss's "___ Hears a Who"
48 Genie's home
49 Butter alternative
50 Privation
51 To be, in old Rome
52 Gillette ___ Plus
53 Prefix with god
54 Said aloud
57 Really or truly, e.g.: Abbr.
58 Wal-Mart founder Walton

by Richard Chisholm

ACROSS

1 Flip (through)
5 Sugar amts.
9 Fire starter
14 Trucker's toll unit
15 Aesopian also-ran
16 Wore
17 Zig or zag
18 Toledo's lake
19 Gas in a layer
20 Gather sailors?
23 "Norma ___"
24 Half-witted
25 Genealogical diagram
27 Roofing pro
30 Stork delivery
33 Foul-line material
34 Rock's Green Day, e.g.
37 City north of Salt Lake City
38 Actress Thurman
39 Not really there
41 Traffic reg., e.g.
42 Doodad
44 Walkout defier
45 Sit for a shot
46 Like the B-2 bomber
48 Quaking in one's boots
50 "Diana" singer
51 Dote on
53 Big Blue
55 Dismay Reiser or Revere?
60 Whistle-blower's exposure
62 Pulitzer winner James
63 Out of kilter
64 Final authority
65 Sans ice
66 Slave away
67 Day one
68 Ferrara family name
69 Choice word

DOWN

1 Source of pumice
2 Many a Barron's reader, for short
3 A Waugh
4 Compound of iron
5 Where we are
6 Clear wrap
7 Sticker figure
8 Visionary
9 Dealership area
10 La ___, Bolivia
11 Love something offered at home improvement stores?
12 Gossipy Barrett
13 Joint that may jerk
21 A, in Ardennes
22 Hot time in Québec
26 E.S.L. part: Abbr.
27 Slimy creatures
28 One to a customer, e.g.
29 Wow Willie?
30 ___ bene
31 Far from windy
32 Broke off
35 Calamine lotion target
36 Business abbr.
39 Spot on a tie, perhaps
40 Like Betamax
43 "Geez, Louise!"
45 Examine by touching
47 Brewpub fixture
49 Org. in "The Good Shepherd"
51 Wise old heads
52 Fabric fold
53 "In that case . . ."
54 Fiber source
56 Plexiglas unit
57 M.P.'s quarry
58 "Topaz" author
59 Singer Lovett
61 Play for a sap

by Laura A. Halper

ACROSS

1 Solidarity leader
7 Gremlins, Pacers and others
11 "___ recall . . ."
14 Takes to excess
15 Blue matter
16 B & B
17 Start of a quote by 26- and 32-Down
20 Golfer Isao ___
21 Abu Dhabi's fed.
22 Intermission follower
23 Wherewithal
25 Fort Worth inst.
26 Shaped like a plum tomato
29 Relief measure of Elizabethan times
33 ___ Lanka
34 Bill killer
37 Java neighbor
38 Cramped space
40 Quote, part 2
41 Event before vacation, maybe
42 Author Seton
43 Slow-pot
45 Give a boost to
46 Plan for peace, in modern lingo
48 Andy of TV's "Andy's Gang"
50 Water on la Côte d'Azur
51 Musical with the song "On This Night of a Thousand Stars"
53 Go over
56 Tiny bit
57 Kemo ___
61 End of the quote
64 Track pick, informally
65 Complacency
66 More than pleases
67 Cries of regret
68 Some TV's
69 Attack from above

DOWN

1 Toddler's cry when thirsty
2 See 29-Down
3 Lie unobserved
4 Nunavut native
5 Twice tre
6 Mollify
7 Grateful?
8 Tussaud's title: Abbr.
9 Exhibition overseer
10 Exterior finish
11 "Is so!" retort
12 Pre-cable woe
13 Stats, e.g.
18 Spank but good
19 Pianist José
24 Green-eyed monster
26 See 17-Across
27 ___ Magli shoes
28 Tripoli's land
29 With 2-Down, toddler's game
30 Maui veranda
31 Actor Delon
32 See 17-Across
35 Sporty car roof
36 "Well, whaddya know?!"
39 Outlaws
41 Feature of some necks
43 Heart-related
44 They're fit to consume
47 Not so bold
49 Poughkeepsie college
51 Beats (out)
52 Oreck, e.g., in brief
53 Mystery author Buchanan
54 Inside look?
55 Smokes
58 "The Thin Man" dog
59 Bone to pick
60 Start of North Carolina's motto
62 Cryptologist's org.
63 PC key

by Ed Early

100

ACROSS

1 Cousins of mandolins
6 Marx with a manifesto
10 Not shallow
14 "Faust" or "Don Giovanni"
15 Hodgepodge
16 Neutral tone
17 Simple pleasure
20 Doctors' bags
21 Often-stained piece of attire
22 Manipulate
23 Drip from a pipe, e.g.
24 Leftover bit
28 Old Iran
30 Preordain
32 Daily allowance
35 Unruly head of hair
36 1978 Rolling Stones hit
40 Caribbean, e.g.
41 Worker in a stable
42 Humor that's often lost in an e-mail
45 Proverb
49 ___ B. Anthony dollar
50 Two of a kind
52 Word with neither
53 Four-alarm fire
56 Where 6-Down is
57 Sex appeal
61 Aria singer
62 ___ quilt (modern memorial)
63 Kind of pole
64 Plow pullers
65 Gait between walk and canter
66 Tickle

DOWN

1 Put in jail
2 Revolt
3 Be on the verge of falling
4 Periods in history
5 Day of the wk. . . . or an exam usually taken on that day
6 Seoul's home
7 Smart ___
8 Basketball coach Pitino
9 Stolen money
10 Flaw
11 Modern prefix with tourism
12 Blow it
13 Postpone, with "off"
18 Digs up
19 "Little ___ Sunshine"
23 Untruths
25 Coating of frost
26 In the near future
27 Get-up-and-go
29 Where you might get into hot water
30 Credit card bills, e.g.
31 Photographic film coating
33 Inevitable destruction
34 No ___, ands or buts
36 Boyfriend
37 Distinctive features of Mr. Spock
38 Backside
39 Empty, as a well
40 Radiator sound
43 Alligatorlike reptile
44 "The King and I" woman
46 Where originally found
47 Bump and thump
48 British weight
50 Home of many Velázquez paintings
51 Uneasy feeling
54 Kansaslike
55 Arab chieftain
56 ___ smasher
57 Hurly-burly
58 Veto
59 "If ___ told you once . . ."
60 When the pilot is due in, for short

by Eric Fischer

101

ACROSS

1 Mammoth
6 Like some mattresses
10 Doorframe part
14 Inuit home
15 Saint-Saëns song
16 Ike's alma mater: Abbr.
17 First sign of a highway headache
20 Peter, Paul and Mary, e.g.
21 U.K. heads
22 Damage
23 JFK and LAX overseer
25 On the foul line, ironically
26 Second sign of a highway headache
33 Nasser was its pres.
34 Back-to-back awards for Hanks
35 Like some ales
36 Shoulder bag feature
38 Dirt-dishing publication
39 Dame Nellie ___
40 Just managed, with "out"
41 Like petting-zoo animals
43 TV remote abbr.
44 Third sign of a highway headache
47 David Bowie's "___ Dance"
48 Nashville sch.
49 Keynote giver
52 Hammarskjöld of the U.N.
54 ___-to-order
58 Final sign of a highway headache
61 Love, personified
62 RC or Jolt
63 "I wanna!"
64 Big Apple ltrs.
65 Swarm
66 Alternative to avoid the headaches of 17-, 26-, 44- and 58-Across

DOWN

1 Encircled
2 Composer Stravinsky
3 Jai ___
4 Doze
5 Job for a wrecker
6 4-Her's home
7 Vexes
8 Kia model
9 Nut jobs
10 Kids' playground activity
11 Where Marco Polo explored
12 Mid 21st-century date
13 Entertainer Max or Max Jr.
18 Iridescent gems
19 Painter Nolde
24 Straddling
25 Prince Andrew's ex
26 Deli pancake
27 Slipped up
28 Down's opposite
29 Civil rights grp.
30 Battleship blast
31 Macaroni shape
32 TV word before and after "or no"
33 Rehab candidate
37 "The Scarlet Letter" subject
39 Rx items
41 Take away (from)
42 Set free
45 Corp. heads
46 Karaoke selection
49 In the blink ___ eye
50 Frost-covered
51 Ever's partner
52 Strike out
53 Comedian Sandler
55 ___ mater
56 Moore of "Striptease," 1996
57 Idyllic spot
59 ___ v. Wade
60 Final: Abbr.

by Lucy Gardner Anderson

ACROSS

1 Watermelon rind, e.g.
6 X-X-X part
9 Development units
14 Place to moor
15 Ex of Artie and Frank
16 Numbered works
17 Harvests more Anjous than needed?
20 Coastal flier
21 Quart halves: Sp.
22 ___ deer
23 Judges the crying of comic Johnson?
26 Landscaper's supply
27 Long or short measure
28 Cousin of a cassowary
31 Part of a voting machine
35 Australian mine find
39 Imposing look from an angry king?
43 Hawaiian coastal area
44 W. C. Fields persona
45 Long-distance letters
46 Kisser
49 Bracketed word
51 Tiny parasites spring from a Los Angeles newspaper?
60 Old Tokyo
61 Bum
62 Club of song
63 Freshest stories?
66 Poem division
67 M.D. specialty
68 ___ fixes (obsessions)
69 Either actress twin on "Full House"
70 Legal matter
71 Good April fool target

DOWN

1 Cable worker, at times
2 "It's the end of ___"
3 Diagonal
4 Conical abodes
5 Otherworldly ones, for short
6 Swinelike animal
7 Culturally advanced
8 Upscale eatery handout
9 Gets right on (it)
10 Unlock, to bards
11 Comic Anne
12 Faux pas
13 Submitters' encls.
18 James of "Boston Legal"
19 Bridge hand
24 Exclusive
25 Hydroxyl compound
28 Lodge member
29 1972 Nixon host
30 Ash holder
32 Member of a post
33 Something inflatable
34 Shoot the breeze
36 Skillet spray
37 Lob's path
38 Fragrant necklace
40 Soul's Marvin
41 Time-sharer, e.g.
42 Hardly rosy
47 Kutcher of "Punk'd"
48 Pair of nappies?
50 Summer buzzer
51 45-Across, e.g.
52 Old toy company that made Rubik's Cube
53 Kvetches
54 Bishop's topper
55 Foolheaded
56 Contests on horseback
57 Apartment sign
58 Modern pentathlon gear
59 Pert
64 ___ Jeanne d'Arc
65 15%–20%, usually

by Burton Clemans

ACROSS

1 With 71-Across,
   sort of person who
   might enjoy this
   puzzle?
6 Narrow cut
10 Like show horses'
   feet
14 Make up (for)
15 Comfort
16 Voice quality
17 Person in a
   polling booth
18 Good for
   what ___ you
19 Not written
20 Saying about
   the heart
23 One of the
   Kennedys
24 Hot to the tongue
25 ___ Four (Beatles)
28 Shuffles off this
   mortal coil
31 Bad-mouth
32 Wonder
33 Sonja Henie's
   Norwegian
   birthplace
35 Clamor
39 Crazy
43 Collect
44 It can sense scents
45 Pie ___ mode
46 Size above sm.
48 Campaign pros
50 Singer Rawls
   or Reed
51 Was patient for
55 Suffix with meteor
57 Outcast
63 Decorate again
64 Letter-shaped girder
65 Pertaining to
   warships
66 TV's
   "American ___"
67 Demolish
68 Songstress Baker
69 Instrument that's
   plucked

70 Elevator pioneer
   Elisha
71 See 1-Across

DOWN

1 Volcanic discharge
2 Part of a molecule
3 "The Wizard
   of Oz" dog
4 Unmoving
5 Strengthened
6 Actor Penn
7 Secular
8 Waterfront Long
   Island town
9 Tried out
10 Crushes with
   the feet
11 Lena who sang
   "Stormy Weather"
12 Walking ___ (happy)
13 What rain may
   cause

21 Expression
22 Think out loud
25 Werewolf's tooth
26 G.I. no-show
27 The "B" of N.B.
29 Channel for
   armchair
   athletes
30 Single-masted boat
34 ___ buco
36 Leaning, as type:
   Abbr.
37 Building beside a
   barn
38 Jacob's twin in
   the Bible
40 Woman's sheer
   undergarment
41 ___ a customer
42 Cantaloupe, e.g.
47 Robert of
   "Raging Bull"
49 Cue

51 First full month
   of spring
52 Overrun with
   dandelions and such
53 Passion
54 Touch lightly,
   as the corner
   of one's eye
56 Popular pipe
   cleaner
58 Ultra-authoritarian
59 Mined rocks
60 Tel ___
61 London museum
62 Wing-shaped

by Richard Hughes

104

ACROSS

1 Derby drink
6 Futile
10 Word with critical or Catholic
14 Tylenol competitor
15 Red resident of Sesame Street
16 Troubles
17 "Olympia" artist
18 Mies van der ___
19 Delete
20 Eddie Murphy/Nick Nolte double feature?
23 Indian honorific
24 Sales talk
25 "Come on in!"
29 Successor to Marshall on the Supreme Court
33 Part of a tuba's sound
34 Cheering loudly
37 [Oh . . . my . . . Lord!]
38 George Clooney/ Brad Pitt double feature?
42 Bankruptcy cause
43 The Creator, in the Koran
44 Contents of some pits
45 Poem part
48 Words below the Lincoln Memorial
50 Actor Davis
53 Archipelago part
54 Jessica Alba/Chris Evans double feature?
60 Race created by H. G. Wells
61 "Some busy and insinuating rogue," in Shakespeare
62 Long-billed game bird

64 Overflow (with)
65 Dog team's burden
66 Garden bulbs
67 Wheel turner
68 Banks on a runway
69 And those that follow: Lat.

DOWN

1 Stuff
2 ___ Bator
3 Director Riefenstahl
4 Still
5 Leader of the Lost Boys
6 Exceedingly
7 At ___ for words
8 Comment from a person who digs
9 Warning sign
10 Bar exam subject?
11 Baseball family name
12 Score connector, in music
13 Retired fliers
21 Layers
22 [snicker]
25 They can help you carry a tune
26 "Be silent," musically
27 Biblical queendom
28 ___ care in the world
30 Glossy alternative
31 Dam location
32 Wear
35 Hole puncher
36 Move, informally
39 Never
40 "Eraserhead" star Jack
41 A train may go down it

46 When doubled, a Gabor
47 Basketball statistic
49 Young swan
51 G8 member
52 "The ___ Sanction"
54 Greek salad ingredient
55 "Family Ties" son
56 Carol
57 Conclusion
58 Hastens
59 Hwy. with tolls
63 Title for a person with a J.D.

by David Quarfoot and Mike Nothnagel

ACROSS

1 Musical marks
5 Potentially offensive
9 Doll for boys
14 Shaping tool
15 "Quo Vadis" role
16 "___ Mio"
17 Manor man
18 Some folk acts
19 Some BlackBerry reading
20 Captain Renault player in "Casablanca"
23 Those against
24 Software pkg. item
25 Actor Epps
27 ___ corpus
30 Different
33 ___ Amin in "The Last King of Scotland"
34 Slangy assents
37 Nancy who married Ronald Reagan
38 Reuners: Abbr.
40 When clocks are changed back from D.S.T. in the fall
42 Fixes the time on, as a clock
43 ___ none
45 Like some checking accounts
47 "Citizen X" actor
48 "It's possible"
50 Like some stares
52 Dept. of Labor div.
53 From the top
55 Film lover's channel
57 Oscar nominee for "Pinky," 1949
62 Tuscany city
64 Zone
65 Island do
66 Studio sign
67 Decree
68 Jay Gould railroad
69 Slapped in court?
70 Revival setting
71 Partner of cones

DOWN

1 1 on the Mohs scale
2 One on a pedestal
3 Pound of verse
4 Break down and then draw in
5 Like Cousteau's work
6 Prefix with transmitter
7 Tourney for all
8 "___ fan tutte"
9 Loses it
10 Philosophy
11 "Enter Talking" autobiographer, 1986
12 Hodgepodge
13 They're caught in pots
21 Do-or-die time
22 NCO part
26 [sigh]
27 U. S. Grant's given first name
28 ___ Rogers St. Johns
29 Singer with the 1984 hit "Caribbean Queen"
30 B-52 org.
31 Symbols of highness
32 Op-ed piece
35 Au's is 79
36 Theme of this puzzle
39 Shows disconsolateness
41 Electrical power unit
44 Listened to again
46 He directed Marlon
49 Went nowhere
51 One in a rack
53 Mountain home
54 Reap
55 Starting on
56 Certain iPod
58 Sword handle
59 Mark's replacement
60 Bookie's worry
61 Hauls to court
63 Never, in Nuremberg

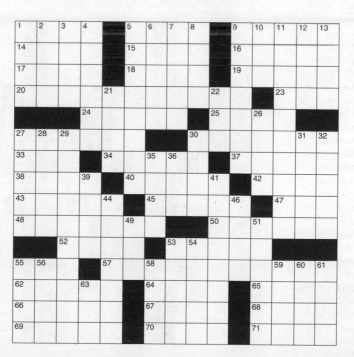

by Bette Sue Cohen

106

ACROSS

1 Lhasa ___ (dog)
5 High Hollywood honor
10 Ice hockey venue
14 "All ___ is divided into three parts"
15 Distress signal
16 First garden
17 German auto
18 *Park ranger's worry
20 Czech or Croat
21 Speak from a soapbox
22 Lab eggs
23 *Conifer exudation
26 Hopped to it
28 Pals
29 Come in last
31 ___ Doria (ill-fated ship)
34 Vagrant
38 Gossip queen Barrett
39 Like the starts of the answers to the six starred clues
41 Supply-and-demand subj.
42 Lively horses
44 Sudden
46 Mama ___ of the Mamas and the Papas
47 Command for Rover
48 Former Iranian leaders
51 *Metaphor for dense fog
55 Kernel holder
56 Sum
60 Adjust the pitch of
61 *Large seed of the alligator pear
64 Abbr. before the name of a memo recipient
65 ___ Strauss & Co.
66 1970s music fad
67 53, in old Rome
68 Not guilty, e.g.
69 Shuteye
70 Nifty

DOWN

1 Visibly horrified
2 Sainted eighth-century pope
3 Khartoum's land
4 *Peace offering
5 Popular insect repellent
6 Sailing vessels
7 Caleb who wrote "The Alienist"
8 Length × width, for a rectangle
9 Breather
10 Ump
11 Moron
12 Chutzpah
13 Work, as dough
19 Josh
24 Seek damages from
25 Proverbs
27 *Crunchy item at a salad bar
29 Gen. Meade's foe at Gettysburg
30 Rococo
31 Dadaist Jean
32 Neither's partner
33 Crime scene evidence
34 ___ Moines
35 Post-op location
36 Badge wearer
37 Explosive inits.
40 B. & O. and Reading: Abbr.
43 Words before spell, shadow or wide net
45 Sheep's cry
47 Put together, as film
48 Where hair roots grow
49 Shack
50 Superior to
52 Certain belly button
53 Loosen, as a knot
54 Enclose, as farm animals
57 Ten to one, e.g.
58 Hard work
59 Church recess
62 Spy org.
63 Blouse or shirt

by J. K. Hummel

ACROSS

1 Say "thay," e.g.
5 "Say good night, ___"
11 Land in la mer
14 Western edge of the Pacific Rim
15 A lot of summer TV
16 Buck's mate
17 Beatles girl "filling in a ticket in her little white book"
18 Rooster alternative?
20 Fantastic comics hero!
22 From ___ Z
23 Tennis do-over
24 Elevate
26 Marisa of "My Cousin Vinny"
28 Addict
31 Afternoon event
32 Items worn with shorts
35 Crafts' partner
36 Excellent novel title character!
38 Once-in-a-blue-moon
40 Smokey's tag
41 Blood-typing letters
42 Monopoly card
43 2006 Brad Pitt film that was a Best Picture nominee
47 Interest piquer
49 Horizontally: Abbr.
51 Like Chopin's "Tristesse" étude
52 Stupendous mentalist!
57 French vacation spot
58 Smokes
59 Crew need
60 "Later"
61 "This one's ___"
62 Parliament V.I.P.s
63 Golf course features
64 Spanish aunts

DOWN

1 Rodeo need
2 Likes
3 "Cheers," for one
4 Carson's predecessor
5 Steepness
6 Sparked anew
7 Elegant horse
8 See 12-Down
9 "By the power vested ___ . . ."
10 Dutch artist noted for optical illusions
11 Second Commandment prohibition
12 Small 8-Down of hair
13 Cry upon seeing a property tax bill, maybe
19 Unilever soap brand
21 Beethoven wrote for her
25 Profs' helpers
27 To be, in Brest
28 Goaded
29 Stick with a knife
30 Villa d'___
33 Abhor
34 Spillane's "___ Jury"
35 Magician's start
36 Show dog workers
37 Buffalo N.H.L.er
38 Mos Def's music
39 Patriarch of Judaism
42 Asleep for a while
44 Kind of wax
45 Riddle
46 Monocles, basically
48 Disfigure
49 Ohio city where Alcoholics Anonymous was founded
50 Animal stomachs
53 Actor Novello
54 Nick at ___
55 Trait carrier
56 Sean Connery, e.g.
57 Vertex

by Kevan Choset

108

ACROSS
1 Disney pup
6 Peaty places
10 Money in Pretoria
14 Neighbors of radii
15 Caen's river
16 Suffix with buck
17 Pre-wedding rituals
20 Speaks ill of
21 Hard-to-find object, perhaps
22 Vintage
24 Took off on
25 Parents' retirement place?
30 Actors Hale Sr. and Jr.
32 Puts on
33 Refrain syllable
34 Totally smitten
35 Musical John
36 Timid creature
37 Bush or Kerry, collegiately
38 Do a double-take
39 "A Girl Reading" painter
40 Classic Omar Sharif role
43 Village Voice award
44 Punny Bennett
45 "Let's go!"
48 Paddock sounds
52 Apt title for this puzzle
56 Hummus holder
57 Soft seat
58 Ostrich cousins
59 Alone, in a way
60 Asian nation suffix
61 It may be set in Paris

DOWN
1 Two-handed lunch orders
2 Silent sort
3 Utter conclusion?
4 School of Buddhism
5 Lady of rank
6 "No fair!"
7 Boston rink legend
8 Econ. yardstick
9 "Mystic River" co-star, 2003
10 Not for tender eyes
11 Like the Negev
12 Seasonal song
13 Two caplets, maybe
18 Aspiring J.D.'s exam
19 Orchestra section
23 Coat anew
24 Lacking life
25 Tricks
26 Toothed bar
27 Alamogordo's county
28 Snack with a cream center
29 Place to trade
30 Getting on in life
31 Composer Édouard
35 Quality of a ghost town
36 Ace versus ace
38 Bomb defuser, maybe
39 Education, law, etc.
41 Morgue ID
42 Peddle
45 Limits
46 Forget, maybe
47 ___ Hari
49 Writer from Zanesville
50 Make sound
51 Zaire's Mobutu ___ Seko
53 Go to seed
54 "Son ___ gun!"
55 Booster

by Bruce Adams

ACROSS

1 Gadabout
6 Dads' counterpart
10 Disconcert
14 January, in Juárez
15 Jai ___
16 Desertlike
17 Like folks cared for by former congressman Bob?
19 Telephone sound
20 Whichever
21 Book after Joel
22 Infuriate
24 Use a swizzle stick
25 Street urchin
26 Pollux's twin
29 Man of steel?
33 Wedding site
34 Quick job in a barbershop
35 Short-term worker
36 Max of "The Beverly Hillbillies"
37 "___ enough!"
38 Part of a judge's workload
39 Gen. Bradley
40 Sports "zebras"
41 Little Pigs' count
42 Boy genius of juvenile fiction
44 Holders of pirate treasures
45 Sword handle
46 Not single-sex, as a school
47 Naval affirmative
50 Complete flop
51 "Steady as ___ goes"
54 Angel's instrument
55 Like funds gathered by singer Vikki?
58 Writer Wiesel
59 Math class, in brief
60 Trap
61 Patch up
62 When Romeo meets Juliet
63 Dwarfs' count

DOWN

1 McEntire of country and western
2 ___ even keel
3 Extremely
4 Do something boneheaded
5 The spit in a spit roast, e.g.
6 Country estate
7 Bygone G.M. make
8 Screen siren West
9 Pistols and such
10 Like a ball retrieved by actor Jamie?
11 Diva's delivery
12 Get but good
13 Upper hand
18 Kuwaiti leader
23 "Delta of Venus" writer Anaïs
24 Like clay molded by drummer Ringo?
25 Does a garçon's job
26 Explorer Sebastian
27 Texas battle site of 1836
28 Geyser's emission
29 Knitting or beadwork
30 First, second, third and reverse
31 "No more, thanks"
32 Sporting blades
34 Larceny
37 Racetrack bet
41 Springsteen, to fans
43 Modus operandi
44 Freebie
46 Welsh dog
47 "Uh . . . excuse me"
48 Ivy League school
49 Land of leprechauns
50 Londoner or Liverpudlian, e.g.
51 Eastern European
52 "Kilroy was ___"
53 Genesis garden
56 Path of a javelin
57 White Monopoly bill

by Randall J. Hartman

ACROSS

1 Language of Libya
7 Food flavor enhancer, for short
10 Amo, ___, amat . . .
14 Number of feet between baseball bases
15 Mock, in a way
16 Streamlet
17 *Chicken
19 Sedgwick of Warhol films
20 Latin "behold"
21 Just about forever
22 Scout's quest
23 *Very good child
27 Tiny hill dweller
28 Tiebreakers, briefly
29 Not so sure
31 Guard
35 It lets things go
38 You might R.S.V.P. online to this
39 Contributed to
40 Celtic priest
41 Snugglers
43 Reddish-brown
44 "Die Lorelei" poet
45 Vietnam Memorial designer
46 World Series mo.
48 *Venus
54 Drastic sentence, with "the"
56 Judge pro ___
57 Cart puller
58 Parking meter filler
59 *Purple sandwich filler
62 Addresses starting http://
63 Peach center
64 ___ Mae (college money provider)
65 Pause
66 Part of a milit. address
67 Ethan and Woody

DOWN

1 Photographer Adams
2 Designer Nina
3 Put on ___ (fake it)
4 Special Forces headwear
5 Suffix with meteor
6 Charisse of "Singin' in the Rain"
7 City nicknamed "Heart of Georgia"
8 Sparkly
9 Play a good joke on
10 Region
11 *Short shadow caster
12 Make parallel
13 Street slickener
18 First half of a Senate vote
22 Obviously injured
24 More isolated
25 Airport info: Abbr.
26 Wriggler
30 Like an ivory-billed woodpecker
31 Hibernation spot
32 Noted apple eater
33 Has the rear end move side to side . . . or a hint to the five asterisked clues
34 Suffix with kitchen
35 ___ judicata
36 Germanic one
37 Cereal box fig.
39 Frequent flier's reward
42 Ltr. holder
43 Sloth, e.g.
45 Unfirm
46 Take place
47 Ironing, for one
49 "Keen!"
50 Stink
51 Veil material
52 Tuckered out
53 Spanish kings
55 Mass. ___ of Tech.
59 No. on a transcript
60 That one, in Tijuana
61 Major Asian carrier, for short

by Jennifer Nutt

ACROSS

1 Playground retort
6 Pre-bedtime ritual
10 Flower people?: Abbr.
13 Passes over
14 Made an overthrow, say
16 Milne baby
17 Rectory
19 Coastal bird
20 Super server
21 Multivolume refs.
22 Neckline?
24 Minor-league club, in baseball
26 Jumper alternative
28 Locked up
32 Make secure
33 Christopher of "Back to the Future"
34 Kinski title role
36 Look after
39 Delicacy that may be pickled
40 Worthless pile
43 Fish spawn
44 Speaker in the Hall of Fame
46 "__ were . . ."
47 Easy pace
49 Keep one's distance from
51 Glare blocker
53 Erudite sort
56 Foot specialist?
57 __ water
58 Part of A.A.R.P.: Abbr.
60 Autocrat of old
64 __ fault
65 Feast of Trumpets
68 Balance provider, for short
69 __-Detoo
70 Sounds to shop by
71 Hi-__ monitor
72 Harsh cry
73 Tickle

DOWN

1 L-__ (treatment for parkinsonism)
2 Apple variety
3 Desperate
4 Wok preparation
5 Bygone covert org.
6 Whales, elephants, etc.
7 Dominican-American major-league slugger, to fans
8 Tie up tightly
9 Cock and bull
10 Sprigs from the garden
11 Sculpted form
12 "__ disturb!" (and a hint for 17-, 40- and 65-Across and 10- and 30-Down)
15 American rival
18 __ de combat
23 Tel. message taker, maybe
25 1953 Loren title role
27 Mrs. Einstein
28 "Why should __ you?"
29 D-back, for one
30 Deli selections
31 Classic sodas
35 Go into business
37 Court plea, for short
38 They're game
41 Mideast capital
42 Cobble, for example
45 "Amscray!"
48 "The Night of the Hunter" star, 1955
50 To-the-max prefix
52 Hendryx of the group Labelle
53 "Norwegian Wood" instrument
54 Franklin's on it
55 Dreadlocked one
59 Keep an appointment
61 Bird in "The Lion King"
62 Literary olios
63 Croupier's tool
66 Suffix with direct
67 Little, to a lass

by Jim Page

112

ACROSS

1 Like some 1930s design, informally
5 Mafia biggie
9 Light from a lightning bug, e.g.
13 ___ Gay (W.W. II plane)
15 Worm's place on a fishing line
16 Make over
17 3" × 5" aids for speakers
19 Out of control
20 Take to court
21 Formerly, old-style
22 Sky-blue
23 Corporate office staffers
27 WNW's opposite
28 Elevator company
29 Shut loudly
32 Des Moines native
34 ET's craft
37 Identify exactly . . . or a hint to this puzzle's theme
41 Lumberjacking tool
42 Edgar ___ Poe
43 It might be slapped after a good joke
44 Writer ___ Stanley Gardner
45 New Year's ___
47 Fonzie's girl on "Happy Days"
54 Surrenders
55 Leo's symbol
56 Ph.D., e.g.: Abbr.
57 End-___ (ultimate buyer)
58 Head of a cabal
61 Doe's mate
62 Tehran's land
63 Add liquor to, as punch
64 Roly-___
65 Mishmash
66 "___ of the D'Urbervilles"

DOWN

1 Basic religious belief
2 Boredom
3 In secret language
4 Encouragement for a matador
5 Deep gap
6 Main artery
7 Pea holder
8 10-4's
9 Barely injures in passing
10 Cousin of a monkey
11 Stinks
12 Regained consciousness
14 Figure skating jumps
18 Indian of the northern Plains
22 Getting on in years
24 Record sent to a record producer

25 Hopeless, as a situation
26 ___ all-time high
29 Site of mineral waters
30 Illumination unit
31 Dined
32 Bit of land in the sea
33 Birds ___ feather
34 Vase
35 Enemy
36 Last number in a countdown
38 Drug agents: Var.
39 ___ May of "The Beverly Hillbillies"
40 Scraped (out)
44 Cabinet department since 1977
45 E.P.A. subj.
46 Barn toppers
47 Sauce in un ristorante

48 Perfect
49 Arm bones
50 Omens
51 Murphy who's heard in "Shrek"
52 Stinks
53 Meanies
54 Edge
58 Edge
59 Wrath
60 Fitting

by David Pringle

ACROSS

1 Rude sorts
6 Play a kazoo
9 Fix, as a photocopier
14 Naval convoy menace
15 Prefix with metric
16 Supercool
17 Pitcher of baseball's Gas House Gang
19 Speedpass-accepting gas company
20 Old codger
21 Exactly
23 Man of Steel's symbol
24 Says
27 Pass along, as an e-mail: Abbr.
30 Golf's 1984 U.S. Open winner
33 Dines
36 Top-shelf
37 Signs to heed
38 Sleep phase, for short
40 Cottage cheese, essentially
41 Ibuprofen target
42 Lunchtimes, typically
44 Patriarch on an MTV reality show
48 Born, on the society page
49 Skier's lodging
50 Draft org.
53 Like an eagle's vision
54 "Same goes for me"
57 With "cum" and 32-Down, a diploma phrase
60 The Fresh Prince's partner DJ
63 How the confident solve
64 Eggs, in labs
65 Really bother
66 Really bothers, with "at"
67 Equinox mo.
68 Girlie man

DOWN

1 Move a bit
2 Theater awards since 1956
3 Moves like molasses
4 Bronx cheer
5 Eyelid woe
6 Hotfoot it
7 ___ Today
8 Exotic dancer Lola
9 Fidgety feeling
10 Barber's call
11 The Jaguars, on scoreboards
12 ___ Z (the gamut)
13 Start of the work wk., for many
18 Syrian/Lebanese religious group
22 ___ y plata
25 Russian autocrat: Var.
26 Popular reliever of aches
27 Fauna's partner
28 "Peter Pan" heroine
29 Get decked out
30 Keister
31 Vocal stumbles
32 See 57-Across
33 Motorcyclist's invitation
34 Knock the socks off
35 Take forcibly
39 Pouty look
40 Anderson Cooper's channel
43 Baseball's David, nicknamed "Big Papi"
45 Vast amounts
46 That ship
47 Dixieland instruments
50 "Keep it in" notations
51 Love seats, e.g.
52 Kindhearted sort
53 Had down pat
55 Tattooist's supply
56 Town near Santa Barbara
57 Russian fighter
58 Cape ___, Mass.
59 4.0 is a great one
61 Forum greeting
62 Microwave

by Brendan Emmett Quigley

114

ACROSS
1 King who united England
7 Game period: Abbr.
10 Hinged closer
14 Friend
15 Laramie's state: Abbr.
16 They lean to the right: Abbr.
17 Teleologist's concern
20 Word on a Mexican stop sign
21 Bugged
22 French flower
23 1/100 of a euro
24 Vainglory
25 On the side of
26 Part of the verb "to be," to Popeye
28 Overlook
32 "September 1, 1939" poet
35 Old Asian ruler
37 Jaffa's land: Abbr.
38 Figuring something out
42 A hallucinogen
43 Hanging ___ a thread
44 August 15, 1945
45 Nosedive
47 Indent setter
48 Carrier with the in-flight magazine Scanorama
49 Actress Gardner
51 Cries during a paso doble
53 "It's not TV. It's ___"
56 Make worse
60 Clunker of a car
61 Part of a city code
63 Bring to naught
64 Give the coup de grâce
65 Lamebrain, in slang
66 ___ extra cost

67 Some ESPN highlights, for short
68 Oliver Twist and others

DOWN
1 Like two dimes and four nickels
2 Without much intelligence
3 Actress Naomi of "Mulholland Dr."
4 Sony co-founder Morita
5 Post-retirement activity?
6 Bureau part
7 Places to find the letters circled in the grid
8 Use 7-Down
9 Worker who makes rounds
10 Zoo heavyweights, informally
11 On
12 MS. enclosure
13 Argued (for)
18 10th anniversary gift
19 Scandal sheet
23 Neighbor of Gabon
25 Quagmire
27 Sounds leading up to a sneeze
29 Pirate captain of legend
30 La Española, e.g.
31 Hunted animals
32 "___ Lang Syne"
33 U.S. ally in W.W. II
34 One-named singer with the 2001 hit "Thank You"
36 Exploding stars
39 Meeting expectations

40 Cagers' grp.
41 Breakfast drinks, for short
46 "Scent of a Woman" Oscar winner
48 Going out with
50 Title for one on the way to sainthood: Abbr.
52 British "Inc."
53 Artist Matisse
54 Strips for breakfast
55 Some opinion pieces
56 Old Testament book
57 Eliminate
58 Have ___ with
59 It both precedes and follows James
60 Soccer star Mia
62 Actress Long

by John Farmer

ACROSS

1 King Kong's kin
5 Dry out
10 Aspen gear
14 N.Y.C. cultural center
15 Big name in can-making
16 Tight curl
17 Elastic holder
19 Opposed to
20 Depart's opposite
21 Lisa, to Bart
23 Actor Beatty
24 "Cheers" woman
25 Home of Notre Dame
28 Abbr. at the end of a company's name
29 1986 Indy 500 winner Bobby
31 Clear, as a chalkboard
32 S-shaped molding
34 Three Stooges laugh
35 Dreaded
36 Entrance, as through oratory
39 Macaroni and manicotti
42 Landon who ran for president in 1936
43 1978 hit with the lyric "You can get yourself clean, you can have a good meal"
47 Non-earthling
48 Win the first four games in a World Series, e.g.
50 Gear part
51 Ian Fleming creation
53 "Filthy" money
55 Stereo component
56 Deviation in a rocket's course
57 Actor Brando
58 Miniature plateau

60 1930s political group
63 Bustles
64 Filmmaker Coen
65 Neighborhood
66 Lost seaworthiness
67 Eccentric
68 Separators on badminton courts

DOWN

1 Medium for mostly news and talk these days
2 Raining cats and dogs
3 Hug
4 Polio vaccine developer
5 Whittle down
6 Priest's vestment
7 Color TV pioneer
8 Certain diplomat
9 "I've ___!" (cry of impatience)
10 Jamaican music
11 Greg of "You've Got Mail"
12 Strong, as emotions
13 Lost control of a car, say
18 At any time
22 Luster
25 Synagogue
26 Chicago suburb
27 Two-time Super Bowl M.V.P. Tom
30 Affirmative votes
33 ___ Lauder cosmetics
35 Flute in a march
37 Variety of violet
38 Ran in the wash
39 Nightclothes
40 Oakland's county
41 Bart or Lisa

44 Doug of "The Virginian"
45 Royal headgear
46 Lists for meetings
48 Part of Johannesburg
49 Schedule
52 Item on which to put lox
54 City-related
57 Quite a few
59 Query
61 Letter between pi and sigma
62 Rand McNally product

by Allan E. Parrish

ACROSS

1 Drink garnishes
6 Seizes
11 "How about that?!"
14 Broadcast workers' org.
15 Lash of bygone westerns
16 Former
17 Antic brother
19 Fish story
20 Stitched
21 Raw resource
22 Pack, to a pack animal
24 Sticking one's nose in
27 Canine line
28 Swan's mate, in myth
29 Order in the court
33 Brigitte's friends
36 Seattle-to-Phoenix dir.
37 Sci-fi invaders
38 Title of this puzzle
43 What Alabama cheerleaders say to "gimme" four times
44 Alley __
45 "Is there no __ this?"
46 Speaks when one should stay out
49 Tidy up topside
51 Inspiring sound
52 Like many Chas Addams characters
56 Dinner table item on a string
59 '07, '08 and '09
60 Onetime E.P.A. target
62 Chinese dynasty
63 Back
66 Non-Rx
67 Absurd
68 Coffee for bedtime
69 Play for a fool
70 Wild
71 Clifford who co-wrote "Sweet Smell of Success"

DOWN

1 Takes a sharp turn
2 Violinist Zimbalist
3 Vermont ski town
4 Rolled along
5 Animal pouch
6 Praise from a choir
7 Nagano noodles
8 Heavenly altar
9 Bedroom community, briefly
10 Like some relations
11 Place to pick up valuable nuggets
12 Peace Nobelist Wiesel
13 Heaven on earth
18 Phone button
23 School basics, initially?
25 Arnaz of '50s TV
26 Big cut
30 Author Harper
31 Leave in, in proofreading
32 Petrol brand
33 Quatrain rhyme scheme
34 PC pop-up
35 Mesmerized
36 Big inits. at Indy
39 "__ certainly do not!"
40 1970s TV's "The __ Show"
41 Down-to-earth
42 Without an agenda
47 Check
48 Zhivago portrayer
49 Equine color
50 Milquetoast
53 "Laughing" scavenger
54 Pizzeria order
55 Tore into
56 10 C-notes
57 Absorbs, as a loss
58 "The Match Game" host Rayburn
61 Makes calls
64 Alternative spelling: Abbr.
65 Tokyo, once

by Courtenay Crocker and Nancy Salomon

ACROSS

1 Rock's Green Day, for one
5 Worker during a walkout
9 First-stringers
14 Hebrides island
15 Manger visitors
16 Pulitzer Prize category
17 Closet pest
18 Concerning
19 Long-billed wader
20 Coin thrown for good luck?
23 Work started by London's Philological Soc.
24 Geeky guy
25 Grand Canyon beast
29 All lit up
31 Letterman letters
34 Kurds and Nepalis
36 My ___, Vietnam
37 Stones from the sky
38 Result of sitting on a court bench too long?
41 "The Morning Watch" author
42 River to the Rhine
43 Feed for livestock
44 Neurotic TV dog
45 Lusted after, visually
47 Palette choice
48 Scott Turow work set at Harvard
49 Sound of amazement
51 Bugged Bugs?
57 Edible shells
58 Neighbor of an Arkie
59 Projecting edge
61 Waters seen on Broadway
62 Creatures of habit?
63 Pinnacle
64 Shade of gray
65 Learned
66 Battery component

DOWN

1 The youngest Cratchit
2 It may be raised
3 Having as a hobby
4 Waikiki locale
5 Deal a mighty blow
6 Dudley Do-Right's home
7 Cultural beginning?
8 Like House elections
9 Stick
10 What a line on a chart may show
11 Be worthy of
12 Taiwan Strait city
13 Answer to the riddle of the Sphinx
21 Before Oedipus, who could answer the riddle of the Sphinx
22 Risks
25 Storybook elephant
26 Subject of Fowler's handbook
27 Up
28 Make copiously, with "in"
30 "Accident ahead" indicator
31 Alimentary ___
32 "You got it!"
33 Less straightforward
35 One putting on a show
37 Holy ring
39 Puffs out
40 Woman's shoulder wrap
45 Standing by
46 Plying with pills
48 Cousin of a mink
50 Much too big for one's britches?
51 "Haughty Juno's unrelenting ___": Dryden
52 Labor Dept. arm
53 Arctic bird
54 Well-executed
55 Mane site
56 The "Y" of Y.S.L.
57 Zing
60 Bus. phone line

by Richard Silvestri

ACROSS

1 Base on balls
5 Lowly chess piece
9 Afro-Brazilian dance
14 Nastase of tennis
15 Feel sore
16 "___ Gold" (1997 film)
17 See 18-Across
18 Grand ___ (annual French auto 17-Across)
19 "Carmen" composer
20 "The Breakfast Club" actor
23 Preceder of com or org
24 Desperately needing a map
25 Dangerous person
28 Donkey
29 Officer's honorific
30 '60s war site
31 More work than required
36 Lyricist Gershwin
37 "Um, excuse me"
38 "Foucault's Pendulum" author
39 The "A" in ABM
40 "My mama done ___ me"
41 It may come as a shock to a diver
45 Put to a purpose
46 Accomplished
47 French vacation time
48 Argentine grassland
50 Be wide-open
52 Salary
55 Domain ruled from Constantinople
58 Actor John of "The Addams Family"
60 ___ California
61 Pastel shade
62 Michaels of "S.N.L."
63 Brilliant display
64 Bath fixtures
65 Philadelphia N.H.L.er
66 Burden of proof
67 Radiator output

DOWN

1 Sent by telegraph
2 1836 battle site
3 Permissible
4 Part of a hull
5 Native American baby
6 Farm units
7 Early form of bridge
8 Cry at a motor vehicle bureau
9 Undermine
10 Green card holder
11 Floor between first and second
12 Spell-off
13 Winter hrs. in Bermuda
21 Ingrid's role in "Casablanca"
22 Ruler of Qatar
26 ___ blanche
27 Communication that may have an attachment
28 Sleeve filler
29 Chimney sweep's target
31 Devour hungrily
32 South African native
33 Rocket data
34 Nourish
35 TV watchdog: Abbr.
39 Good card to have "in the hole"
41 Lou Grant portrayer
42 Santa checks his twice, in song
43 Second airings
44 Topic of gossip
49 Thomas who wrote "Common Sense"
50 Corn or oat
51 Pear variety
52 Tickle, as one's interest
53 Dutch-speaking Caribbean island
54 It makes dough rise
56 Spanish river to the Mediterranean
57 Trail
58 TV extraterrestrial
59 Note between fa and la

by Janet Bender

ACROSS

1 French girlfriend
5 Karate strokes
10 Laugh uproariously
14 Suburban gathering place
15 Capital of Vietnam
16 Song for Dame Nellie Melba
17 One not taking just a few classes
20 Catholic prayer book
21 Avoid contact with
22 Lines of praise
23 401, in Roman times
25 Many a sword-and-sandals film
27 Magazine with the recurring heading "Onward and Upward With the Arts," with "The"
32 Comedian Fields
36 Eight: Sp.
37 Snakelike fish
38 Typo, e.g.
39 Large number
40 Polish receivers
43 El ___ (weather phenomenon)
44 Country/rock singer Steve
46 Noted Bronx locale
47 Wife of Geraint
48 Mill output
49 Kind of sale
51 Decorations on some rearview mirrors
53 Supped
54 Giant great Mel
57 "Gone With the Wind" setting
59 One of four in "America"
64 Starts of 17-, 27- and 49-Across
67 Bridge or foot feature
68 Emcee's delivery
69 It's a "terrible thing to waste"
70 Relative of a mandolin
71 Actor Davis of "Jungle Fever"
72 Lode stones

DOWN

1 Radio button
2 Lanai neighbor
3 Woes
4 Right angles
5 Offspring
6 Amateur radioer
7 Change for a five
8 More luxurious
9 Stomach strengthener
10 Bamboozled
11 Hydrox rival, once
12 Oboe, e.g.
13 Likely to miss the bus, say
18 Tex-Mex staple
19 Join forces
24 Retail furniture chain
26 Where ends meet
27 Beaks
28 Brilliance of performance
29 Info on an invitation
30 Cried out in pain
31 Doolittle of fiction
33 Singer Lopez
34 Column style
35 Wear away
41 Kinks hit with a spelled-out title
42 Quiet tap dancing
45 Type smaller than pica
49 Some long-legged birds
50 Townshend of the Who
52 Big name in calculators and digital watches
54 Translucent gem
55 No ___ Traffic
56 Diplomacy
58 Early p.m.'s
60 BB's, e.g.
61 Bet that's not rouge
62 District
63 &&&&
65 ___-wolf
66 Prefix with angle

by Sarah Keller

ACROSS
1 Churn
5 Tale with a point
10 Pre-Communist leader
14 It's a killer
15 Tubular instruments
16 Doing
17 Winston Churchill's description of a fanatic, part 1
19 Gymnastics apparatus, for short
20 Layout
21 Opposite of Mar. on a calendar
23 American Depression, e.g.
24 Part of A/C
25 Secured, as a fish on a line
27 Description, part 2
31 Suffer
32 Not the brainiest sort
33 December celebrations
36 Chooses
39 Dreadful
41 Rock's ___ Van Halen
42 Lug
43 "Lead ___ King Eternal" (hymn)
44 Description, part 3
49 How often federal elections are held
51 Science fiction author Stanislaw
52 "Well, ___ be!"
53 Free (of)
54 Formally speaks
58 Résumé addenda
60 Description's end
63 Rangy
64 Like a despot, typically
65 Western Indian
66 Pushing the envelope

67 Collars worn outside the lapels
68 Payment in Monopoly

DOWN
1 Part of the mouth
2 "Yes ___?"
3 Froster
4 Tin star wearer
5 Barber chair feature
6 "Dancing With the Stars" airer
7 It has some feathers around the neck
8 Contacts, e.g.
9 Revere
10 Margarine container
11 Leadfoot
12 Pong creator
13 Not italic
18 Alexander who said "I'm in control here"

22 "Elder" of ancient history
25 Tear (up)
26 Orbiting chimp of 1961
27 Legal assignment
28 Double-timed
29 From dawn till dusk
30 Owns
34 "Metropolis" director Fritz
35 Gin fruit
37 Bild article
38 Moth deterrent
39 Bldg. unit
40 Obscures
42 Indiscriminate amount
45 Squirm
46 Commonplace
47 Spearmint, e.g.
48 Key with three sharps

49 Oath taker's aid
50 Classic epic
55 Head, in an école
56 College course, briefly
57 Mark indicating "O.K. as is"
59 Heavens
61 Abbr. on W.W. II maps
62 Bayh or Biden: Abbr.

by Patrick Merrell

ACROSS

1 Some Apple computers
6 Fall behind
9 Milan's La ___
14 End of an Aesop fable
15 Eggs
16 Secret languages
17 *Mock rock band in a 1984 film
19 From the country
20 Hides the gray
21 Old-fashioned "Scram!"
22 "Dear" dispenser of advice
25 *Revealer of vowels, on TV
28 Hardly trim
30 Enclosure for grain or coal
31 "Cut it out!"
32 Hearing-related
33 Hawaiian veranda
35 *Part of a Valentine's Day bouquet
37 *Seasoned seaman
42 The mating game?
44 Rarin' to go
45 Citrus coolers
49 Parts of lbs.
50 Tie the knot
51 *Local place for making deposits or getting loans
54 ___ empty stomach
55 Garb
56 Long, long time
58 Around, as a year
59 Be logical . . . or what the last words of the answers to the five starred clues can do?
64 Parts of eyes
65 Nothing's opposite
66 Rub out
67 Oozes
68 "Affirmative"
69 Pub projectiles

DOWN

1 Quick online notes, for short
2 Clean the floor
3 ___ Onassis, Jackie Kennedy's #2
4 Butterfinger or 3 Musketeers
5 Smite
6 "___ luck!"
7 Gardner of "The Night of the Iguana"
8 Space between the teeth, e.g.
9 Fastener that turns
10 Robitussin suppresses them
11 Skillful
12 Crude shelter
13 Dozing
18 Impose, as a tax
21 Yawn-inspiring
22 From quite a distance
23 Azure
24 Poet
26 Org. with a 24-second shot clock
27 Bogotá boys
29 Voting coalition
33 Talk show host Gibbons
34 Notion
36 Ocean's edge
38 Tokyo "ta-ta!"
39 Not fer
40 Mother of Helen, in myth
41 1982 sci-fi film
43 Tax ID
45 You can always count on this
46 Latin case
47 Course before dessert
48 Headwear on the slopes
50 Place for a lawn mower
52 Military bigwigs
53 Phones
57 Was in debt
59 Stable diet?
60 Cheer for a matador
61 Road surface
62 Ballpark fig.
63 High-___ monitor

by Paula Gamache

ACROSS

1 Baseball's Rose
5 Struck, old-style
9 Violin master Zimbalist
14 Nike competitor
15 ___ Hari (infamous spy)
16 Native New Zealander
17 Super-easy decision
19 Carpet cleaner target
20 Tightwads
22 Dino whose body was more than 30 feet long
23 Vote in a legislative body
24 Official, informally
25 In ___ (as found)
27 Noted Charlton Heston role
29 Aunts' relatives
33 Reverent
36 Put too much pressure on
38 Gremlins and Pacers
39 Eyelid woes
40 "Dumb ___" (old comic strip)
41 Get the sniffles
43 Place with a "do or dye" situation?
44 Having an uninterrupted series of steps
45 Like 5:00 or 6:00 a.m., say
47 P.T.A. concern: Abbr.
49 Gray general
50 Full-bodied quaff
53 Electrical letters
56 Really, really dumb
59 Kitchen wrap
61 Recycled metal
62 Score with two balls
63 Body art, slangily
64 Singer Horne

65 "That's a lie!"
66 Accessory for Miss America
67 Places to tone bodies

DOWN

1 Garden bloom
2 Conjure up
3 Part of the lower body skeleton
4 Make, as a salary
5 Beams
6 Unabomber's writing, e.g.
7 Major Calif.-to-Fla. route
8 Fruity desserts
9 Grp. called after an accident
10 Big Easy bash
11 Surf sound
12 Buffalo's body of water

13 Flirt
18 Hairdos for Jimi Hendrix and others
21 Trig ratios
26 "My country, ___ of thee"
27 G.T.O.s, e.g.
28 Flair
30 Hip
31 Money since 2002
32 "South Park" boy who's always crying "Oh my God, they killed Kenny!"
33 Big donors to office seekers
34 G3 or G4 computer
35 Eight: Prefix
37 Enterprise warnings
39 Clean with elbow grease
42 Made a fool of
43 Get some shuteye

46 Same old stuff
48 Prices
50 One selling TV time, e.g.
51 Hotelier Helmsley
52 Author Ferber and others
53 Members' body: Abbr.
54 Mob boss
55 "Dagnabbit!"
57 Final Four org.
58 Suffers bodily woes
60 Hero of "The Matrix"

by John Halverson

ACROSS

1 Birthplace of Galileo
5 Up
10 Not much
14 Bad time for Caesar
15 Word with press or Marine
16 Broccoli ___ (leafy vegetable)
17 Thrill
19 Critical hosp. areas
20 Close communication?
21 Emmy winner for "Chicago Hope"
22 Couple
23 Part of a chemistry group
25 Conservatory graduate
28 Heartless one?
31 Companion of 28-Across
32 It merged with Mobil
36 Plane prefix
37 Seaport of New Guinea
38 Part of a coach's chalk-talk diagram
39 Start of a countdown
40 Baseball's Ed and Mel
42 ". . . like a ___ chocolates"
44 Tennis great Lacoste
45 Bernstein's "Trouble in ___"
47 Eye passionately
49 Jong who wrote "Fanny"
51 Boohoo
52 Roman septet
54 Flo Ziegfeld's specialty
59 Athens's setting

60 "Piece of cake!" (and a hint to the starts of 17-Across and 11- and 27-Down)
61 Musical Mitchell
62 One of Homer's in-laws
63 Maglie and Mineo
64 Diner sign
65 On pins and needles
66 Give out

DOWN

1 Willis's "Twelve Monkeys" co-star
2 Romeo's last words
3 Group of prayers
4 Didn't leave waiting at the door
5 Film overlay
6 Imbibed
7 One who watches the telly
8 Breathing problem
9 "Ba-a-a-ad!"
10 Huffington who wrote "Fanatics & Fools"
11 Part of a dash
12 Go up against
13 Half a classic sitcom couple
18 Places
21 Year before Trajan was born
24 Fuji, e.g.: Abbr.
25 Apportion
26 Rope with a slipknot
27 Do what is expected
29 Sporting site
30 Three trios
33 Kiss and hugs, in a love letter
34 Adults-only

35 Big name in kitchen gadgets
41 Certain cut
42 Certain razor
43 June 14
44 Medical setback
46 "___ a pity"
48 Mas with baas
50 Blanched
51 Soothers
52 Breakfast spot, briefly
53 Breakfast spot, briefly
55 Feature of the earth
56 Quahog, e.g.
57 Anklebones
58 Part of DOS: Abbr.
60 Gen. Lee's cause

by Patrick Blindauer

ACROSS

1 Late bridge columnist Truscott
5 Cry made with a flourish
9 ___ Park, Colo.
14 Of sound mind
15 Cheers for toreros
16 Seismic occurrence
17 Supreme Court justice known for a literalist interpretation of the Bill of Rights
19 Earthy pigment
20 Flub
21 Employee cards with photos, e.g.
22 Squad with red, white and blue uniforms
24 Deny
26 Three-card ___
27 Public square
29 Infer (from)
33 Analyze, as ore
36 Perry Mason's creator ___ Stanley Gardner
38 Eurasian duck
39 Cut, as a lawn
40 Los Angeles N.B.A.er
41 Yellowfin, e.g.
42 Jai ___
43 "Break ___!" ("Good luck!")
44 Violin bow application
45 Thrill-seeker's watercraft
47 Subject
49 Tom who played Forrest Gump
51 Former mayor who wrote "Mayor"
55 Emancipate
58 Show the effect of weight
59 Syllable repeated after "hot"
60 Napoleon on St. Helena, e.g.
61 Pie filling
64 Fracas
65 Winnie-the-___
66 Auto racer Yarborough
67 Religion of the Koran
68 Popular frozen dessert chain
69 Signs, as a contract

DOWN

1 Pale-faced
2 First lady after Hillary
3 Red-faced, maybe
4 Prefix with conservative
5 "What'd I say?!"
6 "___, poor Yorick! I knew him, Horatio"
7 Follower of Nov.
8 Provide an invitation for
9 Consider identical
10 Some theater productions
11 Perfume brand
12 Barely makes, with "out"
13 Antitoxins
18 Onion-flavored roll
23 Follower of rear or week
25 1966 Herb Alpert & the Tijuana Brass hit
26 What the last words of 17- and 61-Across and 10- and 25-Down are kinds of
28 Ardor
30 Don of morning radio
31 "___, vidi, vici"
32 Actor McGregor
33 Key related to F# minor: Abbr.
34 Only
35 Go for, as a fly
37 Toy block brand
40 Frankie who sang "Mule Train"
44 Chain of hills
46 Hoops great Abdul-Jabbar
48 A-O.K.
50 Well-groomed
52 Surfing spot
53 Writer on a slate
54 Loathes
55 Vehicle that can jackknife
56 Alimony receivers, e.g.
57 Cash register
58 Look-down-one's-nose type
62 Quadrennial games grp.
63 Sprint rival

by Allan E. Parrish

ACROSS

1 "Listen!"
5 Covered with water
10 Underwater growth
14 On deep water
15 Plan that stinks
17 Doe, in song
19 Art supporters?
20 Three-time U.S. Open champ
21 Pittsburgh product
22 Pickle juice
24 Tiny
27 Teeny-tiny distance
29 Greenish-blue
30 Computer program, for short
33 General Motors subsidiary
34 Light
36 Ray, in song
39 One of the Quad Cities, in Illinois
40 Stage assistant
41 Resort
42 "What's ___ for me?"
43 Money, slangily
45 Private eye, slangily
46 Nonsense
48 Charged particle
52 Spirit of a culture
54 Boxing combo
55 Me, in song
59 Modern computer feature
60 "Peter Pan" pirate
61 Queue
62 Muscat-eer?
63 Spanish direction

DOWN

1 Pluto's alias
2 "Have ___" (host's words)
3 Oscar-winning Witherspoon
4 N.B.A. first name that's Arabic for "noble" or "exalted"
5 Barks
6 Misery
7 Bill provider, for short
8 Red star?
9 Trojan captive
10 William the pirate
11 Alpine flower
12 Entertainer Pinky or Peggy
13 Average
16 Hawaiian goose
18 "___ Road," 1994 hit by the Gin Blossoms
22 Talk big
23 1987 sci-fi film set in near-future Detroit
25 Eagerly devour
26 Actress Verdugo
28 Rick's ___ Américain, "Casablanca" setting
29 Old cable inits.
30 Let in
31 Lying facedown
32 One dressed in blue
34 ___ fixe
35 1990 reunification site
37 Cockfight area
38 Bait
43 Drop one's weapon
44 Real
46 "Don't breathe a word of ___"
47 Golfer Mediate
49 Parts of a list
50 Little hooter
51 Lacking a charge
53 French noodle?
54 Prefix with potent
55 Gridiron org.
56 "The Greatest"
57 Meadow
58 Author Deighton

by Roger Wolff

ACROSS

1 Moisten, in a way
6 Q-tip, e.g.
10 In the sack
14 Really enjoyed
15 Sign of a saint
16 MS. accompanier
17 Junction points
18 Yemeni port
19 Part of a bird's gullet
20 Org. with a noted journal
21 Start of a quip from a hunter
24 Composer Rimsky-Korsakov
26 "__ hath an enemy called Ignorance": Ben Jonson
27 Quip, part 2
33 One putting out feelers?
34 Visa alternative, informally
35 "Little piggy"
36 Partner of trembling
39 Person with a code name, maybe
40 Fraction of a euro
41 Clumsy ox
42 Pump, e.g.
44 Federal property agcy.
46 Quip, part 3
52 Gal of song
53 Be fond of
54 End of the quip
59 Pa. nuclear plant site
60 Word repeated in a Doris Day song
61 Spring shape
62 Little laugh
64 Not of the cloth
65 Russian city on the Oka
66 Not pimply

67 Tram loads
68 Forms a union
69 Solving helpers

DOWN

1 Yogurt flavor
2 Like some energy
3 Neil who wrote "Stupid Cupid"
4 Calendar column: Abbr.
5 Delta follower
6 See 25-Down
7 Dry riverbed
8 Protected, in a way
9 Slave's state
10 Fancy neckwear
11 Stinging comment
12 Biblical "hairy one"
13 Like morning grass
22 Lacking slack
23 Fearsome dino

25 With 6-Down, Doctor Zhivago's portrayer
28 Boutonniere's place
29 "Little Women" sister
30 Western tribe
31 Cl⁻ or Na⁺
32 Lunar New Year
36 Watch spot
37 Évian, par exemple
38 Toward the stern
39 Mere pittance
40 Place to have a brioche
42 Do a cashier's job
43 "Geez Louise!"
44 Make a snarling sound
45 Pre-workout ritual
47 "Almost Paradise" author Susan
48 Some batteries

49 Kind of statement, to a programmer
50 Vegetarian's stipulation
51 Hotel bathroom amenities
54 Nobel city
55 Within a stone's throw
56 Great Lakes port
57 Sported
58 Got a move on
63 New Haven collegian

by Bruce Venzke and Stella Daily

ACROSS

1 Penny-pinch
6 Woes
10 Oats, to Trigger
14 "Deck the Halls," e.g.
15 Belle's gent
16 Auto shaft
17 Sex appeal
20 ___ judicata
21 Vintner's container
22 Some coffee orders
23 Amateur radioer
24 Initiation, e.g.
25 Where to grow carrots and spinach
33 Lycée, par exemple
34 Two cubed
35 Tool that's swung
36 It's typical
37 Anchor hoister
38 Scratch on a gem, e.g.
39 Bullring cheer
40 "Don't let these guys escape!"
41 Flinch or blink, say
42 Places to find some gems
45 "___ in China"
46 D-Day craft: Abbr.
47 Briny
50 & 52 Thomas Gainsborough portrait, with "The"
55 Game suggested by the first words of 17-, 25- and 42-Across
58 Super-duper
59 Continental coin
60 Go over, as lines
61 Latch (onto)
62 Aries or Libra
63 Flower with rays

DOWN

1 Memento of a knife fight
2 "Citizen ___"
3 Rainbow goddess
4 Soccer ___
5 Appease
6 Some early PCs
7 Unauthorized disclosure
8 Not keep up
9 Source of vitamin D
10 Not so slim
11 Sartre's "No ___"
12 If not
13 Clinton followers, for short
18 See 30-Down
19 Really bug
23 Place for a captain
24 Government in power
25 What a fang ejects
26 Worrisome food contamination
27 Charles who wrote "Winning Bridge Made Easy"
28 John, Paul, George or Ringo
29 Resided
30 With 18-Down, Tibetan V.I.P.
31 Meticulous
32 Brilliantly colored salamanders
37 Sharpshooters
38 Suffix with gab or song
40 Research money
41 ___ Stone (hieroglyphic key)
43 Rapper a k a Slim Shady
44 +
47 Men-only
48 Way off base?
49 Jay who does "Jaywalking"
50 One-horse town
51 Ponce de ___
52 Ferry or dinghy
53 Back then
54 Nieuwpoort's river
56 On the ___ vive
57 Form 1040 org.

by John Underwood

128

ACROSS

1 Catch on a ranch
6 Root beer brand
10 In
13 W.W. II conference site
14 Counterpart of lyrics
15 Ending with pay or plug
16 #1 hit
18 Brooch
19 Country's McEntire
20 Summer coolers
21 Comforting words
23 Magazine and newspaper revenue source
25 Larger-than-life
26 Some 1960s–'70s attire
31 Potpourri holder
35 Directional suffix
36 WWW page creation tool
37 English horn relatives
38 It can precede the starts of 16-, 26-, 43- and 58-Across and 10- and 33-Down
39 Muslim pilgrim's goal
40 Alan of "Betsy's Wedding"
41 Sunday offering: Abbr.
42 Faulty shot, as in tennis
43 Watch
46 Carter of "Gimme a Break!"
47 Spa treatment
52 Madrid museum
54 Not orig.
56 Middle name at Menlo Park
57 ___ shot (joke follow-up)
58 However

61 Rocks in a glass
62 Skyrockets
63 Prince's "Raspberry ___"
64 Deletes, with "out"
65 "That wasn't good!"
66 Dropped a line

DOWN

1 Stretchy synthetic
2 Sounded content
3 Hearty slices
4 Feedbag part
5 Feedbag morsel
6 Pull a fast one on
7 Egyptian slitherers
8 Casino cube
9 Actor's reading
10 Playground game
11 Mixed bag
12 Fail miserably
14 Strut on the runway
17 "Be silent," in scores
22 Worshipers' payments
24 Lincoln and Vigoda
25 Seeming eternity
27 '60s guru Timothy
28 Shiverer's sound
29 Start of the 22nd century
30 Strip under the mattress
31 Enjoy a tub
32 Up to the task
33 Manhattan Project and Operation Overlord
34 Piled up
38 Competition of sorts
39 Give a darn
41 NBC hit starting in '75
42 Yap, so to speak
44 Mourning of the N.B.A.

45 Sends out
48 Farm bundler
49 Bygone Olds
50 Cable box holder
51 Cause of sloppiness, maybe
52 ___ fixe
53 Paella need
54 Home ___
55 Staff note
59 "La-la" preceder
60 "Charlotte's Web" author's monogram

by Jim Hyres

ACROSS

1 "I'm glad that's over!"
5 "Green" sci.
9 Schindler of "Schindler's List"
14 Sound from a 57-Down
15 Writer Ephron
16 Like some Groucho Marx humor
17 Himalayan legend
18 Sketched
19 Speak histrionically
20 Revolve
23 "Honest!"
26 Put chips in a pot
27 "Don't miss the next episode . . ."
32 "Bye Bye Bye" boy band
33 Kind of sleep
34 Sleeping, say
36 Gave the thumbs-up
37 Start of many a pickup line
41 Tall tale
42 Cry
44 Luau serving
45 Set straight
47 Become a recluse, perhaps
51 Campaign fund-raising grp.
52 Rest stop features
53 Speaker of the catchphrase that starts 20-, 27- and 47-Across
58 Shade of green
59 Word with pepper or saw
60 Congregation's location
64 Signal to clear the road
65 Nat or Natalie
66 Hertz competitor
67 Courage
68 Give ___ to (approve)
69 Stun

DOWN

1 Like some humor
2 Weed whacker
3 Chow down
4 On paper
5 Evasive maneuver
6 Relative of a trumpet
7 Creme-filled snack
8 Croquet site
9 Act before the headliner
10 Indonesian island crossed by the Equator
11 The "K" in James K. Polk
12 Naysayer
13 Deli loaves
21 Robert of "Spenser: For Hire"
22 Weapon in 1940s headlines
23 Edward R. Murrow's "See ___"
24 Like a walrus
25 Talk show host Tom
28 Go around and around
29 ___ culpa
30 Do a favor
31 Pound, for example
35 Jobs for body shops
38 Geologic period
39 "___ and whose army?"
40 Arafat of the P.L.O.
43 Light muffin
46 Frog's perch
48 Inventor's goal
49 Verdi opera featuring "Ave Maria"
50 Gave birth in a stable
53 "Poppycock!"
54 Tennis's Nastase
55 Actress Sorvino
56 Org. that organizes camps
57 Big prowler
61 Longoria of "Desperate Housewives"
62 Diana Ross musical, with "The"
63 Dir. from Seattle to Las Vegas

by Mike Nothnagel

ACROSS

1 "Madness" month
6 Crime-fighter Eliot Ness, notably
10 Hug givers
14 What a sun visor prevents
15 Saab or Subaru
16 Santa's "present" for a naughty child
17 Company that clears clogged drains
19 Game with Miss Scarlet and Professor Plum
20 "Faster!"
21 Spanish squiggle
22 Uses a stool
23 Phone part
25 Rocky hill
28 "___ on your life!"
29 Following
30 With 48-Across, popular computer product
32 Second Amendment rights org.
33 Adjective follower
36 Car for a star
37 Break, briefly . . . or a hint to this puzzle's theme
39 Use a keyboard
40 Held on to
41 Suffix with expert
42 Fancy tie
43 French political divisions
45 Barn bird
47 U.S.N.A. grad
48 See 30-Across
50 The Godfather's voice, e.g.
52 Put in ___ way
53 Scenic view
57 Greek Cupid
58 Friendly tournament format
60 Baseball's Matty or Felipe
61 Ladder step
62 1940s Bikini blast, in brief
63 Subject to mildew, perhaps
64 Web destination
65 Nick of "Lorenzo's Oil"

DOWN

1 Baseball team V.I.P.'s: Abbr.
2 Gobs
3 Assign an NC-17, e.g.
4 Corn and wheat
5 Nancy Drew or Joan of Arc
6 One who knows "the way"
7 Unlikely dog for a canine registry
8 Lunched, say
9 Neither's partner
10 Mishaps
11 Silver Cloud of autodom
12 Bea Arthur sitcom
13 Winter precipitation
18 Not fooled by
21 Explosive inits.
23 Steellike
24 Way off
25 Lecture
26 "Garfield" canine
27 Classic kids' show
31 Exhortation at a pub
32 SSW's opposite
34 Atop
35 New Jersey hoopsters
37 "Lovely ___, meter maid" (Beatles lyric)
38 Entry-level position: Abbr.
42 Ross Perot, in 1992 and 1996
44 Tummy muscles
45 Like pumpkins and traffic cones
46 Harry Potter prop
48 In front
49 Nurse Espinosa on "Scrubs"
51 Prefix with -plasm
53 Football kick
54 Cain's brother
55 Aerosol spray
56 Poker stake
58 Monopoly quartet: Abbr.
59 Pro vote in a French referendum

by Steve Kahn

ACROSS

1 Bird in the "Arabian Nights"
4 Traffic tie-up
9 Morning hour
14 Actor Gulager
15 Playful sprite
16 Throat dangler
17 Alphabetic trio
18 38-Across, in a sense
20 Decides one will
22 Afternoon social
23 Request to a switchboard oper.
24 Secular
25 Composer of the "Brandenburg Concertos," in brief
28 38-Across, in a sense
31 Throw out
35 Verdi aria
36 Squanders
38 1964 #1 hit by the Shangri-Las . . . or this puzzle's theme
42 Excite
43 Italian flowers
44 Mural site
45 38-Across, in a sense
49 Personify
52 Five-star
53 Letters before a pseudonym
56 U.R.L. ending
57 "Uncle" of old TV
59 38-Across, in a sense
63 Former Vladimir Putin org.
64 Zhou ___
65 Being of service
66 Funnyman Philips
67 Seat that may have a swivel top
68 All-night trucker's aid
69 Tibetan beast

DOWN

1 Soft drink since 1905
2 Friend since high school, say
3 Place for chalk
4 Petty quarrel
5 One-named singer for the 1960s Velvet Underground
6 Firefighter's tool
7 Resort city that shares its name with a Duran Duran hit
8 Did not disturb
9 Rapper Shakur
10 "Little" '60s singer
11 Hosiery shade
12 Third baseman Rodriguez
13 Schooner part
19 Pirate's domain
21 Plan
25 Mil. plane's boosted launch
26 Discarded: Var.
27 Setting for TV's "House"
29 War god on Olympus
30 Muddy area
32 Actress Hagen
33 Jiffy
34 "Naughty!"
36 Often-misused pronoun
37 Prefix with space
38 Murphy's is well known
39 Period to remember
40 Gmail alternative
41 Microscopic
45 Area connected to a kennel
46 Computer user's shortcut
47 Conundrum
48 Adidas competitor
50 It merged with Exxon
51 "What's shakin', ___?"
53 Skunk River city
54 Categorical imperative philosopher
55 Guthrie who sang about Alice
57 Opposite of bueno
58 "Mockingbird" singer Foxx, 1963
60 Southeast Asian language
61 Oklahoma native
62 Prefix with afternoon

by Barry C. Silk

132

by Richard Silvestri

ACROSS

1 Slightly
5 Got rid of a chaw
9 Perfume from petals
14 Formal fabric
15 Corrida creature
16 Pleasant Island, today
17 Kelly Clarkson or Taylor Hicks
18 Broadway's __ Jay Lerner
19 Like unfortunate bullfighters
20 Stealing some computer memory?
23 Roll-call vote
24 Go off course
25 "Too bad!"
27 Squeegees' kin
30 Homework assignments
33 Stash away
34 Jackknife, for one
35 Tale of the gods
37 Stateside Ltd.
38 Narrow pieces
41 Kung fu star
42 Most of I-76 across Pennsylvania
44 Word of agreement
45 Lincoln Center offering
47 Beermat, e.g.
49 Drank slowly
50 Sig Chi, e.g.
51 Where Fermi went to university
52 Queasy
54 Always use the term "coloring agent"?
60 Sent out beams
62 Graph line
63 Tiger club
64 Where the action is
65 Bean town?
66 Maritime: Abbr.
67 Twangy
68 School in Berkshire, England
69 Sandwich from a sidewalk stand

DOWN

1 Found a perch
2 Vocal fanfare
3 Running __
4 Come through
5 Puts on
6 Arctic
7 Djellaba wearer
8 "West Side Story" role
9 San __, Tex.
10 Chinese cosmic order
11 Ways to make lefts and rights?
12 Realtor's calculation
13 Basketball's Tomjanovich
21 "Revenge of the __"
22 Get to the point?
26 Outfielder's asset
27 Senate figure
28 Ancient Greek dialect
29 Assorted hydroxides?
30 Don or Lena
31 Square
32 Cordwood measure
34 Makeshift screwdriver
36 John, at sea
39 Coffeehouse order
40 "El Capitan" composer
43 Audio receiver
46 Saying grace
48 Huarache
49 Toyota rival
51 First-rate
52 Where Farsi is spoken
53 1965 Julie Christie role
55 Lowland
56 Take off
57 Sledge
58 Part of B.Y.O.B.
59 Inner, in combinations
61 Faline's mother, in "Bambi"

ACROSS

1 Footlong sandwiches
5 Lost traction
9 Post office purchase
14 Fairy tale meanie
15 Hatcher of "Lois & Clark"
16 Himalayan kingdom
17 Short on dough
19 Play a role none too subtly
20 Kind of paper for gift-wrapping
21 Short on dough
23 ___ to stern
25 Dedicatory verse
26 Sports org. for scholars
29 Finger food at a Spanish restaurant
32 Over-the-top review
36 The "A" in A/V
38 Howard Stern's medium
40 Tiny criticism to "pick"
41 Short on dough
44 Part of an iceberg that's visible
45 Sarge's superior
46 Aquafina competitor
47 Aardvark's fare
49 Attack en masse, as a castle
51 Architect Saarinen
52 ___ Beta Kappa
54 Individually
56 Short on dough
61 Bits of wisdom?
65 One washing down a driveway, e.g.
66 Short on dough
68 Eye-teasing paintings
69 Saskatchewan Indian
70 Teeny bit
71 See 22-Down
72 "Thundering" group
73 Agts. looking for tax cheats

DOWN

1 Downy
2 Wrinkly fruit
3 Garments that usually clasp in the back
4 Takes off on a cruise
5 Avenue
6 Fierce type, astrologically
7 Annoys
8 Jenny Craig regimen
9 Three-time P.G.A. champ
10 Word repeated after someone starts to show anger
11 Individually
12 Chess ending
13 Begged
18 ". . . and nothing ___"
22 With 71-Across, "White Men Can't Jump" co-star
24 Ballet's Fonteyn
26 Can./U.S./Mex. treaty
27 Give hints to
28 Good (at)
30 Barbecue area
31 Stick (to)
33 "___ Get Your Gun"
34 Church official
35 Prefix with -centric
37 Something good to strike
39 Unclose, poetically
42 Polite refusal
43 "Enough already!"
48 Globe
50 In an atlas, e.g.
53 #1 to Avis's #2
55 So-so grade
56 Restaurant acronym
57 "Uh-uh"
58 Nicholas I or II
59 Do art on glass, say
60 Partner of truth
62 "A ___ of One's Own"
63 Instrument that's plucked
64 Baseball's ___ the Man
67 Individually

by Harriet Clifton

ACROSS

1 Former U.N. chief Javier ___ de Cuéllar
6 Colorist
10 Black Power symbol
14 Site of Crockett's demise
15 Gutter site
16 Creep (along)
17 Spoonerism, usually
20 Something that may be brought back from the beach
21 Abbr. in a help wanted ad
22 Instruments played with bows
23 Sight along the Thames
28 Most acute
30 Bran material
31 Draft org.
32 Get on one's nerves
33 Indiana ___
35 Actress Roseanne
36 Word that can follow the starts of 17-, 23-, 51- and 59-Across
38 Clickable image
42 Baby screecher
44 Observe Yom Kippur
45 Deadly viper
48 "The Star-Spangled Banner" contraction
49 Like some dental floss
51 Hoedown folks
54 Author Vonnegut and others
55 General on a Chinese menu
56 Lilliputian
59 San Francisco tourist attraction
64 Modern ice cream flavor
65 Little explorer on Nickelodeon
66 Raise
67 Pete Rose's team
68 Small bit
69 Actress Moorehead

DOWN

1 Previous
2 Singer Fitzgerald
3 Slickers and the like
4 Akihito's title: Abbr.
5 Madhouse
6 Abhor
7 Popular e-mail provider
8 Grandmother of Enoch
9 Abbr. after some generals' names
10 That's all
11 Metal bars
12 Crews' craft
13 Postdocs often publish them
18 Gangsters' foes
19 Elliptical
24 Emcee's delivery
25 Word between two last names
26 Etymological basis
27 Axes
28 Putin's former org.
29 Pitcher's stat
33 Small bit
34 Instrument often accompanied by a pair of small drums
36 Swiss painter Paul
37 "Happy Days" put-down
39 Crew's leader
40 Atomic number of hydrogen
41 Flanders of "The Simpsons"
43 "It's ___ than that!"
44 Great reverence
45 Request
46 Future knight
47 Puckered
49 Open, in a way
50 Cpls. and others
52 One of the Three Musketeers
53 Centipede maker
57 Gaelic language
58 Newts
60 Tpkes.
61 Back-to-school time: Abbr.
62 "Huh?"
63 Big bike

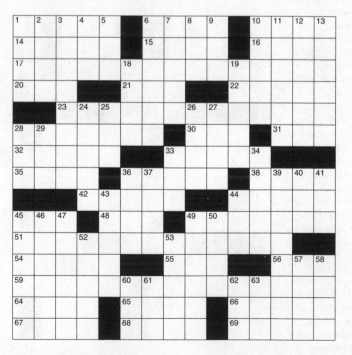

by Jonathan Gersch

ACROSS

1 Classic muscle cars
5 Stellar bear
9 Not be able to take
14 Juillet's follower
15 Gad about
16 Valuable find
17 Scrap the original strategy
19 Party spreads
20 Bikini, for one
21 Part of a suit
23 Rap's Dr. __
24 Big spread
26 Mrs., in Madrid
27 __ Mae (Whoopi's "Ghost" role)
28 Broke ground
30 Loop looper
33 Restrained
35 Chapel fixture
36 Three-time 60-homer man
37 Personal quirk
39 Anthem starter
43 Bandleader Eubanks, familiarly
46 Metropolis figure
49 Muscle shirt, e.g.
53 Rock's __ Lonely Boys
54 Pewter component
55 Glass of "This American Life"
56 Lock
58 Common Market inits.
59 Cyclist Armstrong
61 "Cool!"
64 Unaided
66 What the ends of 17-, 30- and 49-Across spell
68 Comic Amsterdam
69 Pandora's boxful
70 Cry after the sound of a bell
71 Dag Hammarskjöld, for one

72 Cry after the sound of a bell
73 PC suite components

DOWN

1 Totally smitten
2 Attention-getting sound
3 On empty
4 Took off with
5 Location to bookmark: Abbr.
6 Driver's license prerequisite
7 All there
8 Plot feature in many a western
9 Calm
10 Support, of a sort
11 Ballpark buy
12 Take too far
13 Use again, as a Ziploc bag

18 Catcher's place
22 Blood's rival
25 __ Na Na
28 When added to 29-Down, tres
29 See 28-Down
31 Big copper exporter
32 Wanted G.I.
34 One of 10,000 in Minnesota
38 "Who's on first?" asker
40 Spicy bowlful
41 2008, por ejemplo
42 What a nod may mean
44 Curse, of sorts
45 Designer Wang
47 Neighbor of Leb.
48 Gregg pro
49 Cooks, in a way
50 Stay out of sight

51 Call for more
52 "The Blues Brothers" director John
57 Mattress giant
60 Knick rival
62 Fill-in
63 Bauxite and others
65 Prof. Brainard of "The Absent-Minded Professor"
67 AOL, e.g.

by Curtis Yee

136

ACROSS

1 #1 number two who became the #2 number one
6 Actors who mug
10 Talking equine of '60s TV
14 Roll over, as a subscription
15 Neighbor of Yemen
16 Toy on a string
17 Food from heaven
18 Lot in life
19 ___-again (like some Christians)
20 She offered Excalibur to the future King Arthur
23 Garment accompanying a girdle
24 Last letter, in London
25 Gordon of "Oklahoma!"
29 Went out, as a fire
31 Club discussed in clubhouses: Abbr.
34 Guiding philosophy
35 Couch
36 Standard
37 Popular canned tuna
40 Word of invitation
41 Broadway award
42 Alleviates
43 Nile stinger
44 Hockey legend Gordie
45 Handles the food for the party
46 Big bird of the outback
47 Quilt locale
48 Columbia, in an old patriotic song
55 Witty Ephron
56 Lamb: ewe :: ___ : mare
57 Ram, astrologically

59 Voting no
60 Warren of the Supreme Court
61 Do, as a puzzle
62 Something to slip on?
63 Whirling current
64 County ENE of London

DOWN

1 Elbow's place
2 "Are we agreed?"
3 Late celebrity ___ Nicole Smith
4 Repair
5 Sag on a nag
6 Labor leader Jimmy who mysteriously disappeared
7 Amo, amas, ___ . . .
8 Trig or geometry
9 Take lightly

10 "Oops! I made a mistake"
11 Castle, in chess
12 "Jane ___"
13 "___ we now our gay apparel"
21 Valuable rock
22 ___ Zeppelin
25 Holy city of Islam
26 One of the Three Musketeers
27 Cheeta, in "Tarzan" films
28 Serving with chop suey
29 "Lorna ___"
30 Questionable
31 Rapper's entourage
32 Garson of "Mrs. Miniver"
33 Accumulate
35 The white in a whiteout

36 Tidy
38 Crayfish dish
39 One who could use a shrink
44 Medical care grp.
45 Corporate V.I.P.
46 EarthLink transmission
47 Stomach
48 Disappeared
49 Old Harper's Bazaar artist
50 Wart causer, in legend
51 Rocklike
52 Greek love god
53 Needs medicine
54 Campbell of "Scream"
55 40 winks
58 Topic for Dr. Ruth

by Randall J. Hartman

ACROSS

1 The gamut
5 Places to kick habits
11 Merino mother
14 Comic Chappelle
15 Like a paradise
16 Gen __
17 Cool treats
18 Wildlife manager
20 Home of Smith College
22 Like some heirs
23 Flop or lop follower
26 100 square meters
29 Home of the U.S. Military Academy
33 Run out
35 Like a greenhorn
36 Start the kitty
37 Suffix with psych-
38 Leopold Bloom's creator
40 Maryland collegian
41 Unicorn in a 1998 movie
42 Words of commitment
43 Correo __ (words on an envelope)
44 Home of Notre Dame
48 In position
49 "Blame It __" (Michael Caine film)
50 Most-cooked parts of roasts
52 Home of Michigan State
59 Sites for stargazers
61 With 64-Across, 2005 Charlize Theron title role
62 Author Rand
63 Way past ripe
64 See 61-Across
65 "Absolutely!"
66 Ball
67 Puts into play

DOWN

1 Score after deuce
2 Food in a shell
3 [see other side]
4 Citrus peels
5 Wine and dine
6 Mingo player on "Daniel Boone"
7 Source of hashish
8 Work without __
9 Steven __, real-life subject of the 1987 film "Cry Freedom"
10 Act starter
11 Former lovers, e.g.
12 Minuscule
13 Mess up
19 Flow out
21 "The Battle Hymn of the Republic" writer
24 It may come with more than one side
25 Colorist's vessel
26 "The Tempest" king
27 Mete out
28 Devotees of fine dining
30 Test for fit
31 __-Man
32 Have a tab
34 Nova __
38 Triangular sail
39 Lyric poem
43 "The King __"
45 Boorish sorts, in Canada
46 Naysayer
47 Ready for the rubber room
51 Major mess
53 Sporty auto roof
54 Plasterer's strip
55 Johnson of "Laugh-In"
56 Salon goos
57 Pouting look
58 "Need You Tonight" band
59 Compensation
60 Caustic alkali

by John Underwood

138

ACROSS

1 With 1-Down, 1982 Richard Pryor/Jackie Gleason film
4 Half court game?
7 Part of an auto accident
13 Crude structure?
15 Tourist's aid
16 "Understood!"
17 Like a band of Amazons
18 Iran-Contra grp.
19 Draftsman's tool (and a hint to this puzzle's theme)
20 Satchel in the Hall of Fame
23 Little squirt
24 Poli ___
25 Aunt of Prince Harry
26 Dogma
28 Conclusion, in Germany
31 Levy on a 33-Across
33 Place to build
35 63-Across, in Málaga
36 Like vinegar
37 Cookout sites
39 Foundation exec.
40 Frank McCourt memoir
42 A few
43 Suffix with exist
45 Means of fortunetelling
47 ___ account (never)
48 "___ got it!"
50 King in a celebrated 1970s U.S. tour
51 Clampett player
52 Attend to the final detail
54 Crimson foe
55 Commits to, as an interest rate

56 Ferris in film
60 Intent, as a listener
61 Field of unknowns?
62 Hand-color, in a way
63 Rotation period
64 Muesli morsel

DOWN

1 See 1-Across
2 Shake a leg
3 Old N.Y.C. lines
4 Title guy in a 1980 Carly Simon hit
5 A Waugh
6 Any part of Polynésie
7 Where Mosul is
8 Waiter's armload
9 Guard's workplace
10 Iroquois and others

11 Grammar concern
12 Plays a campus prank on, informally
14 Gridiron formation
15 Dutch beer brand
19 Big load
20 1974 Medicine Nobelist George ___
21 Bayer alternative
22 Influential group
23 Singing Ritter
26 Implied
27 Go ___ (deteriorate)
29 Quints' name
30 Hardly strict with
32 Relative of a chickadee
34 Fashion a doily
38 Big name in cellular service
41 "___ Cheerleaders" (1977 film)

42 "I'm kidding!"
44 Brought forth
46 Endless 9-to-5 job, e.g.
49 Op-ed, typically
51 Poem of lament
52 E. ___
53 What to call a king
54 Faulkner's ___ Varner
55 Iron pumper's muscle
56 No longer edible
57 Wall St. action
58 Diamond stat
59 Disloyal sort

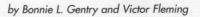

by Bonnie L. Gentry and Victor Fleming

ACROSS

1 "Get out of here!"
5 Scott who draws "Dilbert"
10 Heart problem
14 Tortoise's race opponent
15 Argue against
16 Attempt at a basket
17 Fe, chemically
18 Actress Verdugo
19 Loving strokes
20 Course option
23 Hold the wheel
24 "___ So Fine," #1 Chiffons hit
25 Double curve
28 Old photo shade
32 Space cut by a scythe
34 ___ Khan
37 Response option
40 Ballet skirt
42 Dweller along the Volga
43 Signal hello or goodbye
44 Electric light option
47 Hedge plant
48 Person under 21
49 Group singing "Hallelujah!"
51 Sault ___ Marie
52 Stout drink
55 Parts to play
59 Quiz option
64 Advertising award
66 "Praise be to ___"
67 Lhasa ___
68 Easter servings
69 String bean's opposite
70 Person under 20
71 Optometrists' concerns
72 Department of ___
73 Ocean eagle

DOWN

1 Freighters, e.g.
2 Diamond weight
3 Came up
4 Tightens, with "up"
5 Space
6 Place to get an egg salad sandwich
7 Eve's second son
8 Chew (on)
9 Old hat
10 Nile nippers
11 Shoo off
12 Mouth-burning
13 Travelers from another galaxy, for short
21 Glenn of the Eagles
22 Professional grp.
26 Comedian Martin
27 "The Taming of the ___"
29 Consumers of Purina and Iams food
30 Vidi in "Veni, vidi, vici"
31 Playful trick
33 Opposite ENE
34 They're smashed in a smasher
35 "Go fast!," to a driver
36 Back then
38 Courtroom affirmation
39 Western U.S. gas giant
41 Carrier of 13-Down
45 Berlin Mrs.
46 Take on, as employees
50 Spin
53 Pages (through)
54 Key of Mozart's Symphony No. 39
56 Outcast
57 Ruhr Valley city
58 Gem
60 One of TV's "Friends"
61 ___Vista (search engine)
62 Final
63 Mule or clog
64 Revolutionary Guevara
65 Make, as a wager

by Kurt Mengel and Jan-Michele Gianette

140

ACROSS
1 Director Kazan
5 Singer Lane of old TV
9 Challenge in a western
13 Artist Chagall
14 Developer's land
16 A pop
17 Computer introduced by Steve Jobs
18 ___ dish (lab item)
19 Full of pep
20 First showing at an all-day film festival? (1988)
23 Genetic material
24 Prankster's bit
25 Second showing (1970)
34 First sign, astrologically
35 Crystal-lined rock
36 Rocky peak
37 Highland headgear
38 Paycheck booster
39 Packed away
40 Greek H
41 Von Richthofen's title
42 Disloyal
44 Third showing (1975)
47 Taking after
48 Motorists' org.
49 Final showing (2004)
57 Graph line
58 Wipe clean
59 The Hawkeyes of college sports
60 Beanery handout
61 Hearing-related
62 "Beg pardon . . ."
63 Mideast's Gulf of ___

64 Avian sources of red meat
65 Ticked off

DOWN
1 Send out
2 Poor, as excuses go
3 It includes Mesopotamia
4 Damn
5 Having fun
6 La ___ Tar Pits
7 Upside-down sleepers
8 Neutral shade
9 Create fashions
10 Speaks ill of
11 Plot unit
12 Tot's repeated query
15 Self-important sorts

21 Printers' supplies
22 Red in the middle
25 Assigned stars to
26 Muse with a lyre
27 Joltin' Joe
28 Ancient marketplace
29 A little before the hour
30 Climb onto
31 Novelist Calvino
32 "That's a lie!"
33 Eco-friendly
38 San Francisco and environs
41 Place for a hayfork
42 Herr's mate
43 Biblical liar
45 Nissan, once
46 Atelier sights
49 Pink-slipped
50 Speeder's risk
51 Loyal

52 Damage
53 Biblical twin
54 Gallery-filled part of the Big Apple
55 Basin accompanier
56 Unlikely to bite
57 Physicians' grp.

by Ray Fontenot

ACROSS

1 Great Trek participant of the 1830s
5 Courtroom fig.
11 Bake sale grp.
14 Bowed, in music
15 "Yippee!"
16 Alley __
17 Newts and such
19 "The Addams Family" cousin
20 Nocturnal beetle
21 Sugar suffix
22 __ equal footing
23 Senior Saarinen
24 Take apart
26 Setting for a chaise longue
28 In groups
29 Deflating sound
30 When repeated, part of a Beatles refrain
33 Services' partner
34 Go-between, and a clue to 17-, 24-, 49- and 57-Across
37 Prized violin, briefly
40 Canned fare since 1937
41 Univ. staffers
44 School papers
46 Downsize, maybe
49 Salon job
52 __ Potti
53 Totally confused
54 In the style of
55 Hit close to home?
56 Kick __ storm
57 Locale of Uhuru Peak
59 Israeli airport city
60 Lover of Cesario, in "Twelfth Night"
61 Neighbor of Wash.
62 City grid: Abbr.
63 Take stock of
64 Features of greenhouses

DOWN

1 Stout-legged hounds
2 Sources of wisdom
3 Bakery treats
4 Lion, for one
5 Ill-fated captain
6 Trinity member
7 "Me too"
8 Long lock
9 Risktaker's challenge
10 "I see" sounds
11 Indicate, in a way
12 Came to
13 Suitability
18 Actress Powers of "Cyrano de Bergerac"
22 Something to cry over?
24 Knight's list
25 Bit of plankton
27 Dancer Charisse
31 Eiger, for one
32 Soul mate?
34 "__ mia!"
35 It pops into the head
36 Tussaud's title: Abbr.
37 Wren's cathedral
38 X marks it
39 Double-checks
41 Rarer than rare
42 Took in, perhaps
43 Old salts
45 Garden pests
47 Worked like Rumpelstiltskin
48 Swindler's work
50 __ Island (museum site)
51 Dewy-eyed
55 Lambs' laments
57 R.V. hookup provider
58 Wrong start?

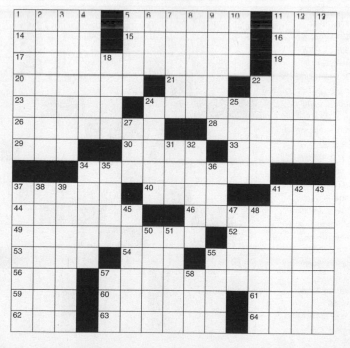

by Barbara Olson

ACROSS

1 Gem units
7 Revolutionary Guevara
10 Sea creature that moves sideways
14 Common recipe amount
15 Actor Holbrook
16 Turner of Hollywood
17 Masonry work that may be smoothed with a trowel
19 Grace finisher
20 Deadly snake
21 Shoving away, football-style
23 Director Bob who won a Tony, Oscar and Emmy all in the same year
24 Evicts
25 Quester for the Golden Fleece
28 Hen's place
30 "It's a sin to tell ___"
31 Goes 80, say
34 Fellow
37 More rain and less light, e.g., to a pilot
40 Sault ___ Marie
41 Ill-___ gains
42 Hitchhiker's need
43 Tabbies
44 Person whose name appears on a museum plaque, e.g.
45 Zorro's weapon
48 Colorado resort
51 Some memorization in arithmetic class
54 Airport overseer: Abbr.
57 Director Kazan
58 Earlier . . . or a hint to the words circled in 17-, 21-, 37- and 51-Across

60 Book after John
61 Coach Parseghian
62 White fur
63 Two tablets every six hours, e.g.
64 Thieve
65 Target and J. C. Penney

DOWN

1 ___ Nostra
2 Six-legged intruders
3 Sign on, as for another tour of duty
4 N.C. State's group
5 University of Arizona's home
6 Leopard markings
7 Rub raw
8 .5
9 Singer Fitzgerald
10 Zip one's lip
11 Harold who directed "Groundhog Day"
12 Concerning
13 Hair over the forehead
18 State known for its cheese: Abbr.
22 Hen's place
23 Enemies
25 1975 thriller that took a big bite at the box office
26 Very much
27 Father
28 Give
29 Chief Norse god
31 Many a person whose name starts Mac
32 Flower holders
33 Suffix with differ
34 Enter

35 Ruin
36 Belgian river to the North Sea
38 "Zounds!"
39 Laundry implement that might make a 43-Down
43 See 39-Down
44 Gobi or Mojave
45 Lieu
46 Radio word after "Roger"
47 Skips
48 Popular BBC import, for short
49 ___-mo replay
50 Israel's Shimon
52 Skier's transport
53 Prefix with -nautic
54 Light-skinned
55 Actress Heche
56 Citrus coolers
59 M.D.'s group

by Peter A. Collins

ACROSS

1 It's a no-no
6 Up for it
10 Hook attachment
14 Shia's deity
15 Letter-shaped beam
16 Long ago
17 Colorful food fish
18 Kid around
19 Mix up
20 Deeply hurt
23 Benevolent fellow
25 Poem of exaltation
26 Quitter's cry
27 Abs strengtheners
29 Big bash
32 Partner of poivre
33 Ark complement
34 Checks for errors
36 Ramadan observance
41 Be testy with
42 Pride member
44 Little terror
47 Genesis garden
48 Attached, in a way
50 Racial equality org.
52 Whale group
53 Suffix with butyl
54 Gulliver's creator
59 Mineralogists' samples
60 Met solo
61 Game played on a wall
64 Scot's attire
65 Took a turn
66 Like leprechauns
67 To be, to Brutus
68 Scots' turndowns
69 Conical dwelling

DOWN

1 "___ Te Ching"
2 Yodeler's setting
3 Semiformal
4 Pearl Harbor site
5 "Come on, that's enough!"
6 Doll for boys
7 Help in wrongdoing
8 Kind of note
9 Art Deco notable
10 Petty officer
11 Class clown's doings
12 Yule tree hanging
13 Pulitzer winner Studs
21 N.F.L. six-pointers
22 Drink heartily
23 "I know what you're thinking" ability
24 Fish story teller
28 WWW addresses
29 Wordless "Ouch!"
30 Summer month, in Paris
31 Rock's ___ Lobos
34 Sherlock Holmes prop
35 Red tag event
37 Klutzy
38 ___ about (rove)
39 Excursion diversion
40 Cel character
43 S.F.-to-Spokane direction
44 Bit of humor most people can't get
45 Native New Zealanders
46 Discussion groups
48 Wrecker's job
49 "Finally finished!"
51 Social stratum
52 Jr.-year exams
55 Goldie of "Laugh-In"
56 General vicinity
57 Punch-in time for many
58 MetroCard cost
62 "The Waste Land" monogram
63 ___-crab soup

by Norma Johnson

144

When this puzzle has been completed, shade in the letters of 35-Across everywhere they appear in the grid, revealing three letters and three lines.

ACROSS

1 Karate blow
5 Winkler role, with "the"
9 Cartoon pics
13 Wertmüller who directed "Seven Beauties"
14 "___ Gold"
16 Sky lights?
17 Brewery fixture
18 Knocking sound
20 Solid alcohol
22 All you need, in a Beatles song
23 Have a TV dinner, say
24 Fire sign?
26 Late singer Rawls
29 Classic Mercedes-Benz roadsters
30 Homes that may have circular drives
32 Long, long time
33 Soviet labor camp
34 Automaker Ferrari
35 July 4th message to America
40 Theological schools: Abbr.
41 Buys for brew lovers
42 Grand ___ Opry
43 How many teens go to movies
46 Not many
49 160, once
50 Mentholated cigarettes
51 Gawk (at)
53 Brief moments
54 Regains one's senses, with "up"
55 Memorable title film role of 1971
60 Some nest eggs, for short
61 Risk-taking Knievel
62 Prod

63 ___-Rooter
64 Old comics boy
65 Those, to Carlos
66 Official with a list

DOWN

1 Shutters
2 Having a gap
3 Initiations
4 "Gloria ___" (hymn start)
5 Roll up
6 Suffix with pay
7 Web
8 Fanatic
9 Adorable
10 Pond denizen
11 Mauna ___
12 Sound barrier breaker: Abbr.
15 Tend the hearth
19 Greetings of long ago

21 Early Ping-Pong score
24 Puncture
25 Enchanting
26 Horne who sang "Stormy Weather"
27 Like mud
28 3 − 2, en español
31 Cunning
33 Some docs
34 Masthead names, for short
35 "War is ___"
36 Green card?
37 "Phooey!"
38 Lao-___
39 "___ Fine" (1963 Chiffons hit)
40 Assn.
43 ___-doke
44 Opposite of día
45 Medicinal amount

46 Denmark's ___ Islands
47 Mistakes
48 Big name in oil
52 Snazzy Ford debut of 1955
53 Capital of Manche
54 Dict. offerings
55 Opium ___
56 Correct ending?
57 Part of a sleep cycle
58 Some football linemen: Abbr.
59 Down Under hopper

by Patrick Blindauer

145

ACROSS

1 Warm-blooded animal
7 Polite concurrence
14 Neighbor of Sudan
16 Behind on payments, after "in"
17 Five-pointed ocean denizen
18 Short sleeps
19 Charged particles
20 1950s Wimbledon champ Lew
21 Singer Morissette
24 Justice div. that conducts raids
25 And so on: Abbr.
28 Pepsi and RC
29 Viewer-supported TV network
30 Sag
32 E. __ (health menace)
33 Help
34 Sportscaster Howard
35 Opposite WSW
36 Creature suggested by this puzzle's circled letters
38 __ v. Wade
39 Criticize in a petty way
41 Cleaning tool in a bucket
42 Turner who sang "Proud Mary"
43 __ firma
44 __ Bartlet, president on "The West Wing"
45 Trigonometric ratios
46 Michigan's __ Canals
47 Sn, in chemistry
48 Unpaired
49 Threadbare
51 "What were __ thinking?"
52 Driver's levy

55 Drinkers may run them up
59 Kansas expanse
60 Back: Fr.
61 Coarse-haired burrowers
62 2001 Sean Penn film

DOWN

1 Enero or febrero
2 "You __ here"
3 "Mamma __!"
4 Where Moses got the Ten Commandments
5 Stella __ (Belgian beer)
6 Tilts
7 Regatta boats
8 __ Good Feelings
9 Spanish Mlle.
10 Darners
11 Tiny battery type
12 Dadaist Jean
13 Editor's work: Abbr.
15 __ poetica
21 One of two in "résumé"
22 Cuckoos
23 Fast, in music
24 Body's midsection
26 Jewelry for a sandal wearer
27 Rank below brigadier general
29 Cherry seed
30 Uno y uno
31 "The magic word"
33 1 or 11, in blackjack
34 Saucer's go-with
36 Suffix with pay
37 Pea's home
40 Fade
42 "Tip-Toe Thru' the Tulips" singer

44 They cause bad luck
45 __ Mist (7 Up competitor)
47 Characteristic
48 Puppeteer Lewis
50 Other, south of the border
51 Abbr. in TV listings
52 Tach measure, for short
53 ". . . man __ mouse?"
54 River to the Rhine
56 D.D.E. defeated him
57 Playtex item
58 Half a year of coll.

by Peter A. Collins

146

ACROSS

1 Completely wreck
6 Pipe shape
9 Twin Falls's home
14 High home
15 Finder's reward
16 Generous soul
17 Loan to a company before it goes public, say
20 Computer command after cut
21 Gill opening
22 D.C. insider
24 N.F.L. position: Abbr.
26 Lake that is a source of the Mississippi
30 Spilling out
34 Director Browning
35 Russian country house
36 Slangy turndown
37 History chapters
38 Periods of unrest
42 Life stories
43 Unedited
44 South Beach plan and others
46 Seating info
47 Remover of impurities
50 "___ Song" (John Denver tune)
52 ___ one-eighty
53 Mormons, initially
54 Crash-probing agcy.
56 Place to shop in Tokyo
59 The starts to 17-, 30-, 38- and 47-Across, collectively
65 Arboreal Aussie
66 Be short
67 Pour out from
68 On the tail of
69 Ernie of golf
70 Social level

DOWN

1 Treater's pickup
2 "___ the land of the free . . ."
3 Racing feat
4 Broadway musical with the song "The Gods Love Nubia"
5 Crab morsels
6 Lacking vigor
7 Handout at a tiki bar
8 Shutterbug's purchase
9 Set off
10 Formal rulings
11 Bird: Prefix
12 Old biddy
13 .com alternative
18 Impress clearly
19 Land (on)
22 Part of a commercial name after "i"
23 It may be standing
25 Extended, as a membership
27 Lights on posts, perhaps
28 Didn't work that hard
29 They may pop up nowadays
31 Greek R's
32 Greek T
33 Nascar ___
37 Expressionist Nolde
39 Harsh and metallic
40 Long. crosser
41 ___ Amin
42 It has a supporting role
45 Grads-to-be: Abbr.
47 Home mixologist's spot
48 ___ gallery
49 Go bankrupt
51 Fireplace
55 Fraternal org.
57 Tiny fraction of a min.
58 Coors brand
59 Calypso cousin
60 Punch-in-the-gut response
61 Rebellious Turner
62 Saddler's tool
63 Baseball's Master Melvin
64 Carrie of "Creepshow"

by Pete Muller

ACROSS

1 SeaWorld attractions
6 50 Cent piece
9 Constantly change lanes
14 "Peachy!"
15 Voters liked him twice
16 Stan's partner in old films
17 Poke, in a way
18 Mature before being picked
20 Sport played on the first word of its name
22 Ax user, e.g.
23 Page turner
28 Eerie
29 Tot's wheels
32 Say "uncle"
33 Popular clog-buster
34 California's state bird
35 Sport played in the first word of its name
39 Gucci competitor
40 Scrabble draw
41 Prefix with -gon
42 The lion in "The Lion, the Witch and the Wardrobe"
43 Go out, as embers
46 Organized crime
48 "You can come out now"
51 Sport played on the first word of its name
54 It may get stuck in a movie theater
58 Home of Brigham Young University
59 Fictional Scarlett
60 Lead-in to many a chef's name
61 Fan's opposite

62 "Shucks!"
63 Horse color
64 Alley pickup

DOWN

1 Boxing combo
2 Installed anew, as flooring
3 Took a taxi, with "it"
4 Ringlike island
5 Scattered over the earth
6 They run rapids
7 Related
8 William for whom a colony was named
9 Not as good
10 Inventor Whitney
11 European peak
12 Compete
13 Poetic darkness

19 Limerick's home
21 Neon ___ (fish)
24 Contents of una fontana
25 Use a rotary phone
26 Dr. ___ of "Austin Powers" films
27 Divinity sch. subject
30 How sardines are often packed
31 Pitcher who says "Oh, yeaahh!"
33 Crime lab evidence
34 Some hikers' targets, for short
35 St. Louis attraction
36 Appraise
37 Noted cheese town
38 Tither's amount
39 Poker payoff
42 Irish Rose's beau

43 Some Plains Indians
44 "Should that come to pass"
45 Pooh's mopey pal
47 Words after court or rule
49 Frosh, next year
50 Consign to the junkyard
52 "Yikes!"
53 Corker
54 Conk
55 Dull responses
56 Cry from Scrooge
57 Strapped wear

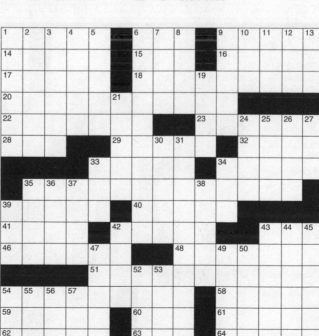

by Patrick Merrell

148

ACROSS

1 Cutlass or 88, in the auto world
5 Result of a serious head injury
9 Refrigerates
14 Hilarious happening
15 Not new
16 Big foil maker
17 *It rolls across the Plains
19 Poverty-stricken
20 Church music maker
21 Bean from which sauce is made
23 18, e.g., as a minimum for voting
24 When repeated, a Hawaiian fish
27 Kevin of "Field of Dreams"
29 Psychiatrists' appointments
33 Western Indians
34 First responder, say: Abbr.
35 ESE's reverse
36 Spoke roughly
39 Former coin in the Trevi Fountain
41 Barely chewable
43 "It is so"
44 California city on a bay, slangily
46 Shooters' org.
47 Coach Parseghian
48 Edith who sang "La Vie en Rose"
49 Responsible for, as something bad
52 Wife of Marc Antony
55 Vivacity
56 "The Tell-Tale Heart" teller
57 1967 Montreal attraction
59 Saint ___, Caribbean nation
63 Range maker
65 *Beehive contents

68 Put back to 0000, say
69 Preppy shirt label
70 Jai ___
71 Birch and larch
72 Politicos with a donkey symbol
73 Barber's call

DOWN

1 Roughly
2 False witness
3 Rapper Snoop ___
4 Really ticks off
5 Snarling dog
6 The Buckeyes, for short
7 Result of a ransacking
8 Like some committees
9 Card game with melding
10 Bullfight cry
11 *Juice drink brand
12 Where Moose meet
13 Follower of nay or sooth
18 ___ B'rith
22 See 25-Down
25 With 22-Down, what the ends of the answers to the four starred clues are examples of
26 ___ way, shape or form
28 Try out
29 ___-help
30 Mideast leader
31 *Alluring dance
32 Moved like a pendulum

37 Coin across the Atlantic
38 Unhearing
40 Land east of the Urals
42 Eats
45 Cautions
50 Easter bloom
51 Big-billed bird
52 Bedazzling museum works
53 Person who shows promise
54 Green garden bug
58 Seep
60 ___ slaw
61 Large-screen cinema format
62 Not much
64 Maiden name preceder
66 ___ de plume
67 Mag. staffers

by Elizabeth A. Long

ACROSS

1 Rocker Ocasek
4 "American Pie" beauty
9 Window area
13 Sufficient, old-style
15 Walt Whitman's "___ the Body Electric"
16 Far from harbor
17 *1942 film with the line "What makes saloonkeepers so snobbish?"
19 Look inside?
20 Prefix with mural
21 Long-distance letters
23 Commercials
24 *Bench sharer
28 One with fingers crossed
30 Lead-in to while
31 "Illmatic" rapper
32 Like a clock that has hands
34 Ensembles of eight
37 You might crack one while playing
38 Word before pool or park
41 *Japanese grill
43 "Get it?"
44 "Me, Myself & ___," 2000 Jim Carrey film
46 Peter of "Goodbye, Mr. Chips"
48 When Alexander Hamilton and Aaron Burr dueled
50 Goof
51 Letters
55 Actor Milo
56 *Underwater creature whose males give birth
58 "Finger-lickin' good" restaurant
59 Fort ___, N.J.

61 Had dinner at home
62 Not at home
64 How the answer to each of the nine starred clues repeats
68 Barely cooked
69 Bor-r-ring voice
70 Alternative to truth in a party game
71 Uno + uno + uno
72 The "S" in WASP
73 "Help!"

DOWN

1 Say, as a pledge
2 More ludicrous
3 Sportscaster Bob
4 Nothing
5 Blind ___ bat
6 Clamor
7 Old llama herder
8 Christie who created Hercule Poirot
9 Instrument that wails
10 *They live on acres of Acre's
11 *Rick Blaine in 17-Across, e.g.
12 Sets (down)
14 Start liking
18 "Kapow!"
22 Throat part
25 "Nay" sayer
26 Popular aerobic program
27 *Many-acred homes
29 Bobby's wife on "Dallas"
33 "Well, that beats all!"
35 Bawled (out)
36 It might need to be settled
38 Secretive org.

39 *Classic Chinese military treatise, with "The"
40 *Fearful 1917–20 period
42 Bar mitzvah dance
45 Slangy denial
47 Hammed it up
49 River nymphs, in Greek myth
52 Basketball venues
53 San ___, Argentina
54 Camera eyes
57 Derisive laugh
58 Mario ___, Nintendo racing game
60 More, in commercialese
63 Verbal nod
65 Be a pugilist
66 Plastic ___ Band
67 Evening hour

by Natan Last

150

ACROSS

1 Example of 41-Across
7 Example of 41-Across
15 Like "Survivor" groups
16 "That's fine"
17 ___ Quimby of children's books
18 Most finicky
19 Not fighting
21 Squeezed (out)
22 Ballerina's digit
23 Suffix with racket or rocket
25 Weakens, as support
29 Line up
32 Push (for)
36 Needle part
37 Mauna ___
39 Example of 41-Across
41 Theme of this puzzle
45 Example of 41-Across
46 90° pipe joint
47 Result of getting worked up
48 Call the whole thing off
50 On the wagon
54 Eton students, e.g.
56 Symbol of sturdiness
58 City map abbr.
59 Tacks on
63 Works of Swift and Wilde
66 They're over the hill
70 Dancing locale
71 "Be delighted"
72 Low tie
73 Example of 41-Across
74 Example of 41-Across

DOWN

1 Rock bands?
2 Keynote speaker, e.g.
3 Less firm
4 Instrument with a conical bore
5 Sha follower
6 French ice cream
7 Bush league?: Abbr.
8 Merle Haggard, self-descriptively
9 Sail a zigzag course
10 Little one
11 Put up with
12 Bread for a Reuben
13 Speakers' no-nos
14 Amount left after all is said and done
20 Unagi, at a sushi restaurant
24 Actress Dawson of "Rent"
26 Polar denizen
27 Polar explorer
28 Salty septet
30 Therapeutic plant
31 "___ got mail"
33 Humanities degs.
34 Memory unit
35 Cries from the woods
38 "I love him like ___"
40 Defendant's plea, informally
41 Not work out
42 Kirlian photography image
43 Four-footed TV star
44 Jar part
49 Thank-yous along the Thames
51 Black Russians may go on it
52 ___ Brothers
53 Fix, as a shoe
55 Buffalo hockey player
57 Barbecue offering
60 Bug juice?
61 Like Radio City Music Hall, informally
62 Hitch
64 Pint-size
65 "Mm-hmm"
66 Chart topper
67 "Do ___ do"
68 It may be tidy
69 ___-Cat

by Tibor Derencsenyi

ACROSS

1 Toast to one's health
6 Whooping ___
11 Belle of the ball
14 Humiliate
15 Ship from the Mideast
16 Commercial cousin of crazy eights
17 Traps off the coast of Maine
19 Get-up-and-go
20 Horn sound
21 Urns
22 Nozzle site
23 Southerner in the Civil War
25 "___ you asked . . ."
26 Part of a TV catchphrase from Howie Mandel
28 Ball catcher behind a catcher
31 Thesis defenses
32 Identical to
33 Twisted, as humor
34 Source of disruption to satellites
36 "My man!"
39 Disobeys
40 Letter-shaped skyscraper support
42 Sleeveless shirts
45 Strained relations?
46 Bakery fixtures
47 Goad
48 Moist, as morning grass
49 Los Angeles's San ___ Bay
52 Mayberry lad
55 Santa ___ winds
56 Gotham tabloid
58 Yank
59 Kennel club classification

60 Guy
61 Wide shoe spec
62 Put a hex on
63 Fish basket

DOWN

1 Pepper's partner
2 "Peek-___"
3 Jerry Lewis telethon time
4 Andrew Carnegie corp.
5 Investigator: Abbr.
6 Reef material
7 Steals, with "off"
8 Skin cream ingredient
9 New Jersey hoopsters
10 Places to see M.D.'s in a hurry
11 Company behind nylon and Teflon
12 Georges who composed "Romanian Rhapsodies"
13 "Little" shepherdess of children's verse
18 Daredevil Knievel
22 Serpentine sound
24 Droopy-eared hounds
25 Rink activity
26 This instant
27 Bobby ___, the only N.H.L.'er to win the Hart, Norris, Ross and Smythe trophies in the same year
28 Points on a diamond?
29 Roadies' loads
30 Corporate V.I.P.
32 Salon sound
35 Roswell sighting

36 Tall, skinny guy
37 Like vegetables in salads
38 Mantra syllables
39 Designer letters
41 Knee-slapping goof
42 Thus far
43 Street
44 Music genre for Enya
45 Aviation pioneer Sikorsky
47 Wash away, as soil
49 Andean land
50 Pitcher
51 Turns red, perhaps
53 "Survivor" setting, sometimes
54 And others, briefly
56 Peacock network
57 Col. Sanders's chain

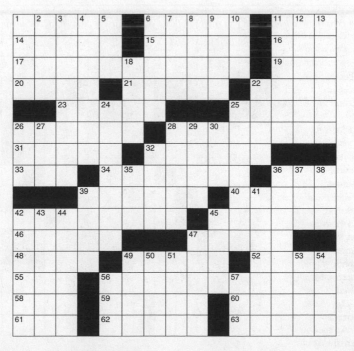

by Randall J. Hartman

ACROSS

1 Language in which plurals are formed by adding -oj
10 Wrist timer
15 Christian Dior, e.g.
16 Drop a line from a pier, say
17 Angry rabbits in August?
19 Windsor's prov.
20 Prefix with identification
21 Hard-to-miss hoops shots
22 Handheld computer, briefly
24 Give a card hand
25 Hens at the greatest altitude?
32 Battery part
33 Houston skaters
34 Horse at the track
36 Villain's reception
37 Green card holder
38 Whence Goya's duchess
39 Memphis-to-Chicago dir.
40 Tourneys for all
41 Have ___ (revel)
42 Cat lady's mission?
45 Channel
46 Finder's ___
47 Shortly, after "in"
50 Have a bug
52 Tussaud's title: Abbr.
55 What a Chicago ballpark bench holds?
59 Apply, as coat of paint
60 Beach cookouts
61 Mensa-eligible
62 Private chat

DOWN

1 Greek nymph who pined away for Narcissus
2 "Any day now"
3 Any miniature golf shot
4 And more: Abbr.
5 Play about robots
6 Scents
7 Not yet final, in law
8 Trueheart of "Dick Tracy"
9 Poet's planet
10 Classifieds
11 Tree rings
12 Happy hour cry
13 Staff symbol
14 Dame Myra
18 Given experimentally
22 Many profs.
23 Actor Billy ___ Williams
24 Most calamitous
25 1944 Chemistry Nobelist Otto
26 Permanently written
27 "Take a look!"
28 Scouts seek it
29 Life form
30 China's Zhou ___
31 Luxurious fur
35 Guys' pals
37 Zeniths
38 French cleric
40 Luxuriant
41 Face on a fiver
43 Masthead title
44 On fire
47 Pointy tools
48 Impact sound
49 Informal "Welcome!"
50 Auto shaft
51 "___ first . . ."
52 Karaoke need
53 Track event
54 In ___ (existing)
56 Columbus Day mo.
57 Hoops org.
58 Rebellious Turner

by Bruce Adams

ACROSS

1 "Vissi d'arte" opera
6 Rx, for short
11 Fed. holiday, often
14 Not just question
15 Evidence of pain
16 So-so grade
17 Part 1 of a snarky quote by 54-Across
19 D.C. clock setting
20 Admiral Bobby who directed the N.S.A. under Jimmy Carter
21 Unwordy
23 Prime status
24 Photo ___
27 Sibling of 54-Across
28 With 53-Across, noted comedy group, in brief
29 Geisel's pen name
32 ___-chef (kitchen #2)
33 "It's nobody ___ business"
35 Picks off, as a pass
37 Proposal fig.
38 Middle of the quote
41 Take steps
44 Showed fright
45 ___ Ark
49 "Cheers" character
51 Baseball exec Bud
53 See 28-Across
54 Speaker of the quote
56 General on Chinese menus
57 Celeb fired in 2007
58 Pale yellow Danish cheese
61 Ribbed, like corduroy
63 Japanese waist material?
64 End of the quote

68 Narrow inlet
69 Some are Dutch
70 Web mag
71 N.L. insignia
72 Iran-Contra name
73 Prepare to fire again

DOWN

1 ___ Friday's
2 1st or 2nd, e.g.
3 Parties to a contract
4 Punch lines, e.g.
5 Menlo Park middle name
6 Farm enclosure
7 Golden parachute receiver, maybe: Abbr.
8 Actor Julia
9 Rombauer of cookery
10 Coll. course
11 Tennis star-turned-analyst
12 Antigone's father
13 What you pay
18 Slaughter in baseball
22 Western treaty grp.
23 Cockney's abode
25 Apothecary tool
26 Snowbirds' destination
30 Some OPEC officials
31 ___ Snorkel of the funnies
34 National Chicken Mo.
36 Thing to confess
39 Some batteries
40 Put into action
41 Firmly ties (to)
42 Share digs
43 Worth bubkes

46 Yerevan's land
47 Master escapologist
48 Radiator sound
50 Longtime Elton John label
52 Cap's partner
55 Bean on-screen
59 Record for later viewing
60 Anatomical canal
62 Golden ___ (senior)
65 "We know drama" channel
66 Sort of: Suffix
67 Pro ___ (for now)

by Ed Early

154

ACROSS
1 Old ___ tale
6 Fiction's opposite
10 Two-wheeler
14 Novelist Zola
15 "Are you ___ out?"
16 Luau instruments, informally
17 Wee
18 Cost of an old phone call
19 Check for a landlord
20 Game equipment for an old sitcom star?
23 Son of Seth
24 Organic salt
25 Greek T
28 ___ Kippur
29 Chem. or biol.
30 Captains of industry
32 Sudden outpouring
34 Mark in "piñata"
35 Game location for an actress?
38 Major mix-up
40 Deflect, as comments
41 IBM/Apple product starting in the early '90s
44 Pull tab site
45 Pinup's leg
48 Product pitches
49 Carved, as an image
51 Florence's river
52 Game site for a popular singer?
54 Plastic building block
57 Mélange
58 When repeated, classic song with the lyric "Me gotta go"
59 Rainbow goddess
60 Pasta sauce first sold in 1937
61 Ponders
62 Like some Steve Martin humor
63 "___ It Romantic?"
64 "Give it ___!" ("Quit harping!")

DOWN
1 Actor Snipes of "Blade"
2 Prefix with suppressive
3 Owner of MTV and BET
4 New York Harbor's ___ Island
5 Order in a bear market
6 Faithfulness
7 Licoricelike flavor
8 Hand-to-hand fighting
9 8-Down ender
10 Singer Ives
11 "I Like ___" (old campaign slogan)
12 Barbie's doll partner
13 Inexact fig.
21 Train that makes all stops
22 Speaker's spot
25 Spilled the beans
26 &
27 "It's no ___!" (cry of despair)
29 Go all out
31 Like a mechanic's hands
32 Ump's call with outstretched arms
33 Paranormal ability
35 Tools with teeth
36 Wasn't turned inward
37 Tehran native
38 Place for a mud bath
39 Doze (off)
42 A ___ (kind of reasoning)
43 Maria of the Met
45 Bellyache
46 "___ Song" (John Denver #1 hit)
47 Not given to self-promotion
50 Winston Churchill flashed it
51 Love of one's life
52 Inquisitive
53 ___ mater
54 Gossipy Smith
55 Pitcher's stat.
56 Beefeater product

by Elizabeth A. Long

ACROSS

1 Chews the fat
5 Cleveland cagers, briefly
9 1986 Indy winner Bobby
14 ___ breve
15 Writer Waugh
16 Maine college town
17 Paper quantity
18 Zig or zag
19 Pooh's creator
20 *Line formatting option
23 Go off course
24 Blockbuster aisle
25 Prerequisite for sainthood
27 Nixon's 1968 running mate
30 Big top noise
31 Coke competitor
34 Not of the cloth
36 Pawn
39 In the style of
40 *Hipster
43 Cyndi Lauper's "___ Bop"
44 Accompanying
46 Explorer Zebulon
47 Book before Joel
49 Lacking slack
51 Get going
53 Kind of pool or medal
56 Common TV dinner
60 Part of Ascap: Abbr.
61 *Education overseers
64 Ring-tailed mammal
66 Jason's craft
67 Wharton degs.
68 Sought answers
69 Old female country teacher
70 Der ___ (Konrad Adenauer)
71 Model/volleyballer Gabrielle
72 Commoner
73 Coward of the stage

DOWN

1 Singer Brooks
2 Last Oldsmobile to be made
3 Britain's P.M. until 2007
4 Tennis star Pete
5 Grotto
6 Pub servings
7 27-Across, e.g., informally
8 "Get out!"
9 Cesar who played the Joker
10 "Exodus" hero
11 *College in Worcester, Mass.
12 One-year record
13 Lerner's musical partner
21 Sound reasoning
22 About, in dates
26 Satisfied sigh
28 "The Time Machine" race
29 Word following the last parts of the answers to the five starred clues
31 Pussy foot?
32 QB Manning
33 *Kids' game
35 "Ricochet" co-star
37 Rebel Guevara
38 Mauna ___
41 Fiber-___ cable
42 Pulsate
45 Prosciutto
48 Living room piece
50 Positive aspect
52 Self-assurance
53 Musician/wit Levant
54 Not tied down
55 Titleholder
57 Artist Picasso
58 Really steamed
59 Collectible Ford product
62 Voiced
63 Fairy-tale fiend
65 Private eye, slangily

by Allan E. Parrish

156

ACROSS

1 Latin 101 word
5 Flip
9 Early third-century year
14 "Norma Rae" director
15 Sport with jabs
16 They make lawns green
17 1966 Lincoln Center role for 21- and 28-Across
19 Grind down
20 Pong maker
21 With 28-Across, a late, great entertainer
23 Insignificant
26 Silas Marner's adopted daughter
27 "As I Lay Dying" father
28 See 21-Across
30 Mark permanently
33 Scatterbrained
35 Retort to "Not so!"
36 ___-10 Conference
39 See 29-Down
42 Quick to pick up things
43 Balkan native
45 Numbered clubs
47 Mexican accord?
48 1970 Covent Garden title role for 21- and 28-Across
50 Increase
54 The Dixie Chicks and others
56 Common cleanser
58 Childhood nickname of 21- and 28-Across
60 "Dynasty" actress
61 Stretches out?
62 1955 "Die Fledermaus" debut role for 21- and 28-Across
65 Really big
66 Giant-screen movie format
67 Tony-winning Carter
68 Ruhr Valley city
69 Strike out
70 Coll. seniors' tests

DOWN

1 Mysteries
2 "Paradise Lost" author
3 Starting lineups
4 Celebrated in the past
5 Earl Grey, e.g.
6 Elect, with "for"
7 Balkan native
8 Conger, e.g.
9 Unlikely candidate for Mr. Right
10 Running back's stat
11 "La Traviata" role for 21- and 28-Across
12 May race, familiarly
13 Expert finish?
18 ___ money
22 They may report to C.E.O.'s
24 In connection with
25 Slip of the tongue, maybe
29 With 39-Across, 21- and 28-Across, for one
31 Flatfoot
32 Much sought after
34 Believer: Suffix
35 It's charged
36 Mac alternatives
37 D-backs, on a scoreboard
38 Stage wear for 21- and 28-Across
40 "Sempre libera" e.g.
41 Linguist Chomsky
44 Flying home?
46 Nudging, and then some
48 Internet chuckle
49 Requirement to buy on eBay
51 More ludicrous
52 Cause to burn
53 Canvas sites
55 "The Wild Duck" playwright
57 Radio executive Karmazin
58 Short dos
59 A few
61 Cedar Rapids college
63 ___ soda (textile bleacher)
64 Chopper

by David J. Kahn

ACROSS

1 Do very well (at)
6 Alabama march city
11 U.K. channel
14 Pope before Paul V, whose papacy lasted less than four weeks
15 Loud, as a stadium crowd
16 Yahoo! competitor
17 Result of hitting the pause button on a movie
19 Dundee denial
20 Have concern
21 Authoritative order
23 Vegetarian's protein source
26 Volcanic emission
28 The "B" in L.B.J.
29 Hall-of-Fame QB Johnny
31 Enzyme suffix
33 Low-lying area
34 Uncovers
35 Chief Pontiac's tribe
37 Coast Guard rank: Abbr.
38 Extra
40 Nightwear, briefly
43 Buses and trains
45 "Honest to goodness!"
47 Sit for a picture
49 __ compos mentis
50 Try hard
51 Book size
53 NNE's opposite
55 Part of a list
56 Chatty birds
58 "The Censor" of ancient Rome
60 Tire pressure meas.
61 Old-time songwriters' locale
66 "Horrors!"
67 Online birthday greeting, e.g.

68 Go out
69 Go blonde, say
70 Seized vehicles, for short
71 Channel with cameras in the Capitol

DOWN

1 North Pole toymaker
2 Generation __ (thirtysomething)
3 Cedar Rapids college
4 Carry out, as an assignment
5 Multitalented Minnelli
6 Bank fixtures
7 Goof up
8 Rich soil
9 "Goldilocks" character

10 Football bowl site
11 Dairy Queen offering
12 Overnight accommodations by the shore
13 John who starred in "A Fish Called Wanda"
18 Times on a timeline
22 Temperamental performer
23 TV, slangily, with "the"
24 __ empty stomach
25 Attack before being attacked
27 Millinery accessories
30 "The Thin Man" canine
32 "Immediately," in the O.R.
35 __ buco

36 Departed
39 Having been warned
41 Hepcat's talk
42 Appear to be
44 Derrière
46 Baltimore nine
47 Like some balloons, questions and corn
48 Playwright Sean
50 Ugly duckling, eventually
52 Person in a polling booth
54 A whole slew
57 Jacket fastener
59 After-bath powder
62 Con's opposite
63 Nascar unit
64 Longoria of "Desperate Housewives"
63 Desire

by Allan E. Parrish

158

ACROSS

1 Liquor holder in a coat pocket
6 Wonderment
9 Taxi sounds
14 Milk: Prefix
15 First word of every Robert Ludlum title but one
16 Extreme
17 Ward off
18 Texas tea
19 Sectors
20 "Just like that!"
22 Electronic toll-collecting system in the Northeast
23 Walk in water
24 In the past
25 "Not on your life!"
30 Torment
31 ___ in Show (Westminster prize)
32 Temporary drop
34 Subj. in drawing class
35 Cargo area
36 Rick's "Casablanca" love
37 Holiday ___
38 Planning detail
40 Gold standards
42 "Yeah, wanna start somethin'?"
45 War ender
46 Create, as a phrase
47 No-goodnik
50 "The Sopranos" clip? . . . or where you might hear 20-, 25- and 42-Across
54 Continent separator
55 Embargo
56 One of the Carpenters
57 Make joyous
58 Israeli-invented gun
59 Goaded, with "on"

60 Like notepaper or subjects of a king
61 Fed. monitor of stock fraud
62 Midterms and finals

DOWN

1 "Spare tire"
2 Content of some cones
3 Nailed
4 Farmer's headwear
5 Toiletries holders
6 Made amends (for)
7 Henry Clay, politically
8 Conger or moray
9 Army barber's specialty
10 Ran off to the marrying judge
11 Italian source of 2-Down
12 White House occupant: Abbr.
13 Snippiness
21 Midmonth time
22 Grandson of Adam
24 Love, honor and ___
25 Rear end
26 Heavens: Prefix
27 Taken ___ (surprised)
28 Religion with the Five Pillars
29 Small bite
30 "Bali ___"
33 Good time, slangily
35 Frequent target of engine wear
36 Circus animal enclosure
38 Tarnished
39 Walk to and fro

40 Old TV feature
41 Start of an Ella Fitzgerald standard
43 Timely news bulletin
44 Like some sacred art
47 Afrikaner
48 Legal rights org.
49 Successful conclusion of a negotiation
50 Labyrinth
51 Pieces of work?
52 Nair competitor
53 Conclusions
55 Vehicle with a route

by Daniel Kantor

ACROSS

1 Toyota Camry model
7 Dietary needs
11 Balaam's beast
14 1980 John Carpenter chiller
15 Sarcastic reply
16 Rap's Dr. ___
17 Channel swimmer Gertrude
18 Novelist Jaffe
19 Crude, e.g.
20 Back-to-the-slammer order?
23 Readies, briefly
24 "___ a traveler from an antique land": "Ozymandias"
25 Son of Judah
27 Opposite of ecto-
28 Hard-rock connector
29 Cheerful
30 Reason the kids were left alone?
34 Eiger, e.g.
37 A/C meas.
38 ___ Na Na
39 Get stuck with, as the cost
40 Reward for a Ringling invention?
44 In progress
45 La-la lead-in
46 Devil Ray or Blue Jay, for short
50 Prefix with cab or cure
51 Baba ___, Gilda Radner "S.N.L." character
53 Coward's lack
54 Scuff marks on the prairie?
57 Bespectacled dwarf
58 "Young Frankenstein" hunchback
59 TV's Howser

60 "Norma ___"
61 Poetic times
62 Museum guide
63 Since Jan. 1
64 Be in a stew
65 Alley pickups

DOWN

1 Grassy expanse
2 "Shoot!"
3 Looked like a wolf
4 Music from across the Atlantic
5 Diner basketful
6 Posthumous Pulitzer winner
7 Dalmatian's master, sometimes
8 Superior to
9 Group doctrine
10 Marquee topper
11 "Oklahoma!" gal
12 Ceylon, now

13 Condiment for pommes frites
21 Revolt
22 Go bad
26 Duma denial
28 Graphic ___
29 1970s tennis great Smith
31 Border on
32 Woman's shoe style
33 1969 and 2000 World Series venue
34 Put ___ on (limit)
35 1944 Hitchcock classic
36 Cranked out
41 Do
42 Least favorably
43 Starchy dessert
47 Hang around
48 Object of a tuneup
49 Turns to 0, say

51 It might be placed at a window
52 Without equal
53 Hawk's descent
55 Feudal estate
56 Throws in
57 Prohibitionist

by Donna S. Levin

160

ACROSS

1 Town known for witch trials
6 __-friendly
10 Jane Austen heroine
14 Politician who wrote "The Audacity of Hope"
15 Senate errand runner
16 Authentic
17 Fortune-seeking trio
19 Formerly
20 Hrs. in a Yankee schedule
21 Mimicked
22 Feels sorry for
24 Hits the roof
26 Brought to ruin
27 Barely make, with "out"
28 Peru-Bolivia border lake
31 Mosey along
34 Walnut or willow
35 Oozy roofing material
36 Grass-eating trio
40 One of the Manning quarterbacks
41 Giant birds of lore
42 Brain sections
43 Pedestrian's intersection warning
46 Soccer Hall of Famer Hamm
47 Exclamations of annoyance
48 Took a load off one's feet
52 Respectful tribute
54 War on drugs fighter
55 China's Chairman __
56 Enthusiastic

57 Gift-giver's trio
60 Frilly material
61 Pint, inch or second
62 Bird on the Great Seal of the United States
63 Ran away from
64 Turner of "Peyton Place," 1957
65 Sticks around

DOWN

1 They're always underfoot
2 Put up with
3 Coffee concoction
4 Aid provider to the critically injured, briefly
5 "Nonsense!"
6 Increased
7 Uttered

8 Omelet ingredient
9 Peaceful interludes
10 Titillating
11 Trio at sea
12 Riot-control spray
13 Draft picks in pubs
18 Fencing sword
23 Amin of Africa
25 Peddle
26 Food regimens
28 Racecourse
29 Casual eatery
30 Obedience school sounds
31 In the sack
32 Venus de __
33 Trio on the run
34 Hammers and hoes

37 Appreciative
38 Minor hang-ups
39 Highway or byway
44 Sent to another team
45 Jokester
46 Painter Chagall
48 December list keeper
49 Alpha's opposite
50 In a weak manner
51 Sniffers
52 50%
53 Football-shaped
54 Dresden denial
58 Cell's protein producer
59 Item with a brim or crown

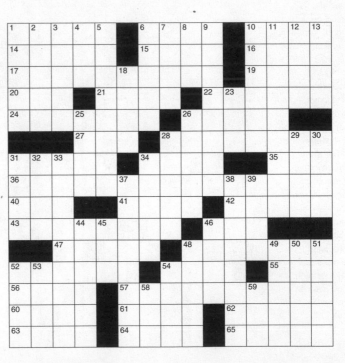

by Lynn Lempel

ACROSS

1 Private stash
6 Eighty-six
10 Very smart
14 Earthy pigment
15 Double-reed woodwind
16 Ruffian
17 Police ploys
20 Old Russian ruler
21 Lid trouble
22 Omar of TV's "House"
23 ___ of Man
25 Farm milk producers
27 Type
30 End-of-day spousal salutation
35 Clear, as a winter windshield
37 Crossed out
38 Sign of things to come
39 When said three times, a W.W. II movie
40 Give the giggles
42 Gallery showing works by Turner, Reynolds and Constable
43 Calendario units
44 Debussy's "La ___"
45 Lead down the aisle
46 "Call when you get the chance"
50 Flutter
51 Pocket particles
52 Sandbox item
54 Univ. lecturer
56 Way to go
58 Duchess of ___, Goya subject
62 Bogart/Hepburn film
65 Work in the garden
66 Use of a company car or private washroom, say
67 Took a shot at
68 Birds whose heads can rotate 135° left or right
69 "Got it"
70 Full of lip

DOWN

1 How much to pay
2 Play parts
3 Quickly growing "pet"
4 Painter Matisse
5 Wee bit of work
6 Best-seller list
7 Toe the line
8 What a welcome sight relieves
9 Neptune's realm
10 Lofted approaches to the green
11 Earring shape
12 Charged particles
13 They may be burned and boxed
18 1993 Israeli/Palestinian accords site
19 Swarm
24 "___ Drives Me Crazy," #1 hit by the Fine Young Cannibals
26 Like some smiles and loads
27 Holder of a dog's name and owner info
28 Téa of "Spanglish"
29 Russian ballet company
31 Outlying community
32 D-Day beach
33 Apportioned
34 First month in Madrid
36 Social workers' work
40 "You got that right!"
41 Pastries in "Sweeney Todd"
45 Action film firearm
47 Tick off
48 Mental grasp
49 Newswoman Paula
53 First lady after Hillary
54 "What a relief!"
55 Rod's partner
57 Decent plot
59 Island garlands
60 Theme of this puzzle
61 Pop artist Warhol
62 First and last digit in a Manhattan area code
63 Sch. in Troy, N.Y.
64 Parts of gals.

by Tom Heilman

ACROSS

1 Lovers' scrap
5 Nanki-Poo's father
11 Cabinet dept.
14 Samovars
15 Artillery unit member
16 Some eggs
17 McGarrett's TV catchphrase
19 Unit of RAM
20 Father figure?
21 By way of
22 600-homer club member
23 Alights
24 Question for a hitchhiker
26 Giant in Cooperstown
27 Eggs, in labs
29 Biblical landing spot
30 Putting a toe in the water, say
32 Hockey position
35 Paris Métro station next to a music center
36 Shout from the phone
39 Resident of Medina
42 ___' Pea
43 Type size
47 Cause of odd weather
49 Wrap up
51 ___ de plume
52 Chevy truck slogan, once
55 John of London
57 Ward (off)
58 Sellout sign
59 World Cup chant
60 Italian diminutive suffix
61 Singles bar repertoire (and a hint to 17-, 24-, 36- and 52-Across)

63 Make darts, say
64 Cry after "Psst!"
65 For fear that
66 Farm brooder
67 Casually add
68 Pseudocultured

DOWN

1 Side story
2 Apportion, as costs
3 Rubs oil on
4 Clicked one's tongue
5 Ones minding the store: Abbr.
6 Birth control option, briefly
7 Scalawag
8 ___ Hall, Diane Keaton role
9 "Gracias" response

10 Cortés's prize
11 Tall wardrobe
12 Succeeds in a big way
13 Yachting event
18 "Happy Motoring" brand
22 Top-notch, to a Brit
24 Innocents
25 Suffix with buck
28 Bugs on a highway
31 Straightened (up)
33 "___ what?"
34 Rosetta stone language
37 Yothers of "Family Ties"
38 Kobe cash
39 Me-first
40 Property recipient, in law

41 Hardly a celebrity
44 Chanter
45 Least ruffled
46 General pardon
48 "Twelfth Night" lover
50 Secluded valley
53 Violists' places: Abbr.
54 Burger go-withs
56 Hyams of 1920s–'30s films
59 Shop window sign
61 Word with boss or bull
62 New England state sch.

by Patrick Blindauer

ACROSS

1 It's rounded up in a roundup
5 Propel a bicycle
10 Pinnacle
14 Hawaii's "Valley Isle"
15 "___ Get Your Gun"
16 Linen fiber
17 Operation for a new liver or kidney
20 Home (in on)
21 Mao ___-tung
22 That woman
23 "The Sweetheart of Sigma ___"
26 Refuses to
28 Encourages
30 Jane who wrote "Sense and Sensibility"
32 Take home a trophy
34 Beer component
35 Swains
36 Cry after a bad swing
37 Decorates, as a cake
38 Beneficial substance in fruits, vegetables and tea
41 Feature of many a wedding dress
43 Picking ___ with
44 Alto or soprano
47 Letter-shaped building support
48 Small number
49 Yuletide songs
50 Mortarboard addition
52 Face-to-face test
54 Puppy's bite
55 Inventor Whitney
56 Grain in Cheerios
58 Great-great-great-great-great grandfather of Noah

60 Literary genre popular with women
66 Shortly
67 Message from a BlackBerry, maybe
68 Tiny critters found twice each in 17-, 38- and 60-Across
69 Impose, as a tax
70 Car dings
71 Yuletide

DOWN

1 Insurance grp.
2 Where a phone is held
3 Oriental ___
4 Actress Cameron
5 Sponsor
6 Company with a spectacular 2001 bankruptcy
7 Reproductive material
8 "___ it the truth!"
9 Made smaller
10 C.I.O.'s partner
11 Kind of suit
12 Street opening for a utility worker
13 Spreads
18 Most recent
19 Place to hang one's hat
23 Taxi
24 Shade
25 "I, Robot" author
27 Four
29 Key of Saint-Saëns's "Danse macabre"
31 Radio receiver parts
33 Eye part
36 ___ gras

39 Puffed up
40 King Arthur's burial place
41 Without metaphor
42 Mother-of-pearl source
45 151, in old Rome
46 Telepathy, e.g.
49 "Streets" of Venice
51 Period in history
53 Size again
57 It heals all wounds, in a saying
59 ___ Lee of Marvel Comics
61 One or more
62 Soup container
63 Year, in Spain
64 Sault ___ Marie
65 Fashion inits.

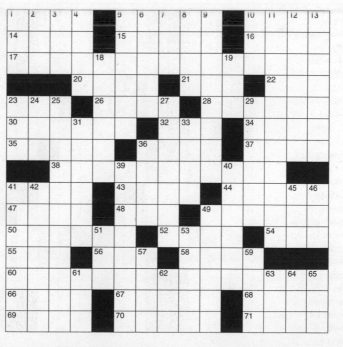

by Steven Ginzburg

ACROSS

1 Russian space station
4 "The Song of ___," old French epic
10 Spill the beans
14 Half of dos
15 Blackboard appurtenance
16 Like hands after eating potato chips
17 It's worth listening to
19 Info in a used car ad
20 Toll
21 Conduct a survey
23 Republic from which Montenegro gained its independence
25 ___-jongg
26 Sherlock Holmes portrayer
33 Nabokov heroine
35 "Don't ___ on me" (slogan of the American Revolution)
36 Where San Diego is: Abbr.
37 Art ___
39 Expensive coat
41 Cravings
42 Not silently
44 Laughing
46 Drivers' org.
47 Perfect shape
50 Building wing
51 Sale markdown indicator
54 Variety of rose
60 Decorative sofa fabric
61 River of Switzerland
62 Where the first words of 17-, 26- and 47-Across may be found
64 It may be in the doghouse

65 Its alphabet starts with alif
66 Bard's "before"
67 Hightail it
68 Tennessee team
69 "Help!"

DOWN

1 Scents used for perfume
2 Senseless
3 English philosopher called "Doctor Mirabilis"
4 One who sees it like it is
5 Fort ___, former Army post on Monterey Bay
6 Source of basalt
7 Purchase stipulation
8 Place for a crick
9 Imagined
10 Cry of glee
11 Stead
12 Chester Arthur's middle name
13 Polar explorer Richard
18 Isle of exile
22 Sis-boom-bahs
24 Snobs put them on
27 Memorize, as lines
28 Raging mad
29 He lost to Dwight
30 They're controlled by the moon
31 "Peter Pan" dog
32 Actress Lanchester, who married Charles Laughton
33 "Madam, I'm ___"
34 Place to get a Reuben
38 Catcher of sound waves
40 ___'acte
43 Mid seventh-century date
45 Haberdashery items: Var.
48 Dated
49 Smell
52 Old Oldsmobile
53 They may be dominant
54 Knife handle
55 Where Bill and Hillary met
56 La ___ Tar Pits
57 Hatcher or Garr
58 Part of Q.E.D.
59 "I Do, I Do, I Do, I Do, I Do" group
63 Winning cry in a card game

by Linda Schechet Tucker

ACROSS

1 Steering wheel option
5 Superior to
10 Pacific island nation
14 Gas leak evidence
15 20 Mule Team compound
16 Canadian dollar bird
17 Nativity trio
18 Ain't grammatical?
19 Wilson of "Zoolander"
20 Expresses scorn
22 Means' partner
23 Swiss artist Paul
24 Early TV comic Louis
26 Blowhard's speech
29 1966 Rolling Stones hit
34 Give a keynote
35 Eco-friendly
36 Author Fleming
37 Hose woes
38 Nymph of Greek myth
39 ___ breve
40 Upper-left key
41 Prison-related
42 Prefix with task
43 Scan
45 Start a new hand
46 Part of H.R.H.
47 Tubular pasta
48 Place to dock
51 Human hand characteristic
57 In good shape
58 Rhone feeder
59 Back muscles, for short
60 Loafing
61 Word before tube or self
62 Neutral shade

63 Face, slangily
64 They may be the pits
65 Percolate

DOWN

1 Barnum midget
2 Actress Lupino and others
3 Business card graphic
4 Tchotchkes
5 Brought down
6 Held up
7 Creme-filled snack
8 U-Haul rentals
9 Like some warranties
10 Lapel insert
11 Corn Belt state
12 "Friends" spinoff
13 Roadside stops

21 Gen. Robert ___
25 Nikkei average currency
26 It may stick out
27 Pie part
28 Dressing choice
29 Dickens's ___ Heep
30 Boortz of talk radio
31 ___ Lacs, Minn.
32 Big Three meeting place
33 Kind of sketch
35 What a prisoner's tattoo may signify
38 Anxiety may be a symptom of it
39 Quarterbacks' play changes
41 Rue Morgue's creator
42 Prefix with physics

44 Rappers' skill
45 Stair parts
47 Stopped listening, with "out"
48 Swab name
49 Pakistani tongue
50 Has a fever, say
52 Plexiglas unit
53 Corn bread
54 Queen Anne's ___
55 To be, in France
56 Encouraging sign

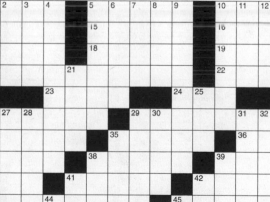

(1) THUMB (2) THUMB (3) THUMB (4) THUMB

by Jayne and Alex Boisvert

166

ACROSS

1 Exercises sometimes done cross-legged
5 Basement's opposite
10 Place for a ship to come in
14 Rightmost bridge position
15 Grand Canyon transport
16 Western native
17 Base for turkey stuffing, often
19 Wagering parlors, for short
20 Madison Square Garden is one
21 On ___ (when challenged)
22 J. R. of "Dallas"
25 Leave furtively
28 Taoism founder
30 New Balance competitor
31 Opposed to
32 They're seen at marble tournaments
35 What the easiest path offers
41 Waiting to be mailed
42 "O.G. Original Gangster" rapper
43 Items in a "bank"
46 Off-course
48 Long-lasting housetop
51 Thrill
52 Appointed
53 Native of Tehran
55 "___ cost you!"
56 Sob stories
61 Orange throwaway
62 Miserable weather
63 Cash drawer
64 This, to Tomás
65 Pal
66 Cherry throwaway

DOWN

1 "Sure thing!"
2 Morsel for Dobbin
3 Overseer of govt. office bldgs.
4 Legendary sunken island
5 French cleric
6 Blinkers signal them
7 "My ___" (dinner host's offer)
8 Levin who wrote "Rosemary's Baby"
9 Fish-and-chips fish
10 Thingamajig
11 Canada's capital
12 Snake charmers' snakes
13 "One Flew Over the Cuckoo's Nest" author Ken
18 Work units
21 Preferred invitees
22 Carrier to Tel Aviv
23 Decrease gradually
24 Greek "I"
26 Have a home-cooked meal, say
27 "___ Fideles"
29 Salary recipient
33 Painting surface
34 Enzyme ending
36 Like a good-sounding piano
37 Emergency military transports
38 Annual hoops championship organizer, for short
39 Penny
40 Suffix with marion
43 Stack in a kitchen cabinet
44 "To be or not to be" speaker
45 Verdi opera
47 City near Lake Tahoe
48 Relative of the sandpiper
49 Lubricated
50 Emancipated
54 Regarding
56 "Naughty, naughty!"
57 "Float like a butterfly, sting like a bee" boxer
58 ___ and wisdom
59 Bullring shout
60 Shade tree

by Sarah Keller

ACROSS
1 Missing Jimmy
6 Hit the slopes
9 General feeling
14 Paula of "American Idol"
15 Chum
16 Take forcibly
17 Big spender's woe?
19 "Mule Train" singer, 1949
20 Bête ___
21 Gum arabic-yielding tree
22 Where to find the headings Books, Dolls & Bears, and Collectibles
25 Revolver toter?
27 The Ewings' soap
29 ___ Tin Tin
30 Letter-shaped support
31 Huge expanses
33 Clinic name
37 MasterCard-carrying ecclesiastic?
40 New York home of Rensselaer Polytechnic Institute
41 Give the boot to
42 Green of "Bonanza"
43 Mark, as a ballot square
44 "Blah, blah, blah . . ."
45 Peter?
51 Deck wood
52 Country singer Milsap
53 Quick Pick game
55 Worse than bad
56 Where this puzzle's theme pairs would like to meet
60 Chain unit
61 Reproductive cells
62 Condor's nest
63 Tender spots
64 Prickly husk
65 Pasta sauce brand

DOWN
1 Witchy woman
2 Sapporo sash
3 Rx watchdog
4 1975 Barbra Streisand sequel
5 Chorus voice
6 Richard's first vice president
7 Superman's birth name
8 Under the weather
9 Spock, on his father's side
10 Asimov of sci-fi
11 LaCrosse carmaker
12 Bert's Muppet pal
13 Pickle portion
18 Some ballpoints
21 Imitative in a silly way
22 Papal bull, e.g.
23 Kiddie lit elephant
24 Olds discontinued in 2004
26 Developer's plot
28 "___ Blue?"
31 Spa feature
32 Overhead trains
33 Reggie Jackson nickname
34 Think alike
35 Buttinsky
36 Vacuum maker
38 Library no-no
39 Supermodel Carol
43 "Trust No One" TV series, with "The"
44 Sermon ending?
45 Lacking couth
46 Self-help category
47 Due to get, as punishment
48 Toughen
49 Romantic message, in shorthand
50 Without face value
54 Pipe section
56 Cry out loud
57 Seam material
58 Rug, of a sort
59 Zodiac beast

by Larry Shearer

168

ACROSS
1 Trots
5 Seaweed product
9 Visual movement popularized in the 1960s
14 Twist-apart treat
15 God, for George Burn or Morgan Freeman
16 U.P.S. supply
17 One . . .
20 Artist's mishap
21 79, for gold: Abbr.
22 Brenner Pass locale
23 Many a TV clip
25 "i" completer
27 Helpless?
30 Headed out
32 Averse
36 Noted polonaise composer
38 Kind of vaccine
40 Horse course
41 Two . . .
44 Prefix with con
45 W.W. I German admiral
46 Rafael's wrap
47 On edge
49 Big atlas section
51 Fateful March date
52 Mother's hermana
54 Cable for money?
56 Iolani Palace locale
59 Simmer (down)
61 "I wanna!"
65 Three . . .
68 End of a fight
69 Langston Hughes poem
70 Largest volcano in Europe
71 Athenian lawgiver who introduced trial by jury
72 Big do
73 "Durn it!"

DOWN
1 Writes quickly
2 City near Provo
3 Subject of modern "mapping"
4 Fizzy drinks at a five-and-ten
5 J.F.K. posting: Abbr.
6 Start limping
7 One, two and three . . . or this puzzle's title
8 Guide strap
9 Baby docs, briefly
10 It has eyes that can't see
11 1½ rotation leap
12 Bring in the sheaves
13 Tut's kin?
18 Goof
19 O.K. sign
24 Confess (to)
26 Half an old comedy duo
27 Bloodhound's trail
28 "Golly"
29 Access the Web
31 "Don't give up!"
33 In first place
34 Brownish gray
35 Ballyhoos
37 Immigrant from Japan
39 Analyze, as ore
42 Grant-giving org.
43 High school course, for short
48 Wall plaster
50 "Yes, you are!" retort
53 Crackerjack
55 Mom's skill, briefly
56 Makes up one's mind (to)
57 Sleek, in auto talk
58 Burglar's booty
60 "You wish!"
62 Prefix with physical
63 Thomas who wrote "The Magic Mountain"
64 Slate, e.g., for short
66 Rooster's mate
67 It goes for a buck

by Manny Nosowsky

ACROSS

1 It may be held together by twine
5 Bit of broccoli
10 Tussle
15 ___ Turing, the Father of Computer Science
16 Usher's domain
17 Incinerator deposit
18 Do a post office job
19 Prenatal
20 It leaves the left ventricle
21 Start of an idle question
24 Long look
25 Canasta plays
26 Kon-Tiki Museum site
30 Mid-sixth-century year
31 ___-cow
34 Robbie Knievel's father
38 Blow a mean horn
40 Ruby's victim
42 Middle of the question
45 Book before Jeremiah
46 Drink with tempura
47 Antelope's playmate
48 Inc., in St. Ives
49 Insolence
51 Rover's pal
53 Low-fat breakfast dish
55 Cambria, today
60 End of the question
66 Tenth of a decathlon
67 Manhattan Project result
68 Contact at a hospital, say
69 Pad paper?

70 Bottom line
71 Tropical spot
72 Went white
73 In need of middle management?
74 "Bang Bang" singer, 1966

DOWN

1 Groundwork
2 In the air
3 Pre-chrysalis stage
4 Record
5 Call at first
6 Painter Mondrian
7 Is, to Isabella
8 Chili rating unit?
9 Depended
10 Miles from Plymouth
11 Boxing punch
12 Few and far between

13 Hammett pooch
14 Excellent, slangily
22 Prefix with thermal
23 Licit
27 Language from which "safari" comes
28 Part of a science course
29 Museum display
31 Final check
32 Ye follower
33 Gas leak giveaway
34 Satanic
35 Endow with authority
36 "Zounds!"
37 Luau favor
39 Fall faller
41 Chewing gum mouthful
43 Masterful
44 Runner with a turned-up nose

50 Victim of ring rot
52 Have title to
53 Parson's place
54 Big shot
56 Molded jelly
57 Collar attachment
58 Top scout
59 Have the tiller
60 Fab Four film
61 Part of the eye
62 Square thing
63 Learning method
64 "___ corny . . ."
65 Up to snuff

by Richard Silvestri

ACROSS
1 Nightfall
5 Sonnet and sestina
10 The Beatles' "Back in the ___"
14 Korea's continent
15 Kind of ink
16 Artsy N.Y.C. locale
17 Many a Westminster show exhibitor
19 Aliens' craft, for short
20 Parrot
21 Makes a cartoon of
23 Robin or swallow
25 Swiss peak
26 Shepherd's domain
29 Mathematician John von ___
33 Play part
36 ___ Remus
38 Predestination
39 Cabbage salad
40 Features found in 17- and 64-Across and 11- and 28-Down
43 Hydrochloric ___
44 ___ noire
45 Sir or madam
46 The "r" in Aristotle
47 It is golden, it's said
49 Superlative ending
50 Louse-to-be
52 Ayatollah's predecessor
54 Walked unsteadily
59 "Lose Yourself" rapper
63 Sailor's greeting
64 Longtime Wal-Mart symbol
66 Grain grinder
67 Tarzan's transports
68 Fox TV's "American ___"

69 Gallup sampling
70 Shareholder's substitute
71 Beach composition

DOWN
1 Miami-___ County, Fla.
2 Quadrennial games org.
3 Sound of relief
4 Skewered lamb, e.g.
5 South Dakota's capital
6 Word before "ignition . . . liftoff!"
7 Icelandic epic
8 Demeanor
9 Wrap for Indira Gandhi
10 Everyday

11 Rear of the roof of the mouth
12 Home for an "old woman" in a nursery rhyme
13 Seamstress Betsy
18 Queens of France
22 Homo sapiens
24 Camper's bag
26 Kind of eclipse
27 Cain's eldest son
28 G.I. Joe, for one
30 Dull photo finish
31 Parthenon's home
32 Born: Fr.
34 Charges on a telephone bill
35 Little bird's sound
37 Ushered
39 Biol. or chem.

41 Geisha's sash
42 Like a sauna room
47 Jeanne d'Arc, e.g.: Abbr.
48 Shabby
51 Pastoral composition
53 Old 45 players
54 Wettish
55 Birthplace of seven U.S. presidents
56 Answer, as an invitation
57 Mideast potentate
58 T. Rex, e.g.
60 Zippo
61 Supply-and-demand subj.
62 Blend
65 Superman enemy ___ Luthor

by Edward M. Sessa

ACROSS

1 The whole ball of wax
5 Court cry
9 Last budget category, usually: Abbr.
13 Loafer, for one
14 Fabricate
15 Mediterranean island country
16 Golf club used in a bunker
18 Bird-related
19 USAir rival
20 Like Methuselah
21 Invent
22 Butcher's device
25 Examine
29 Pizazz
30 At full speed
31 Xerox machine output
36 Architect Ludwig Mies van der
37 Krispy __ Doughnuts
38 Nabisco cookie
39 Tourist shop purchases
41 Avoid, as work
42 N.Y.C. cultural institution
43 Taste bud locale
44 U.S.S. Nautilus, for one
49 Show to be false
50 Computer file name extension
51 Haw's partner
54 Sierra __
55 Spider-Man or the Green Lantern
58 Religion of the Koran
59 Like the Sahara
60 Singer Fitzgerald
61 Cop's path
62 "Toodles," in Milan
63 Marvel Comics mutants

DOWN

1 Secretary: Abbr.
2 Microwave option
3 Mrs. Chaplin
4 1-Across's end, in England
5 Frittata, e.g.
6 When said three times, et cetera
7 Heart chart, for short
8 New York's Tappan __ Bridge
9 Expert
10 Troy story?
11 Union member
12 Chair person?
15 Name after Dan or San
17 "Pretty __" (Richard Gere/Julia Roberts movie)
21 Shipping container
23 Iran's capital
24 __ on to (grabs)
25 Swedish version of Lawrence
26 Melville novel
27 Waikiki Beach locale
28 Ukraine's capital
31 __ ballerina
32 Big band saxophonist Al
33 Not a reproduction: Abbr.
34 The Pan-American Highway runs through it
35 Oxen holder
37 Séance sound
40 Rapper Marshall Mathers, familiarly
41 On the wagon
43 Some supper club attire
44 Improvise
45 Reagan cabinet member
46 Deadly virus
47 Charge
48 Brownish photo tint
51 Captain's position
52 Writer __ Stanley Gardner
53 Séance sound
55 Pouch
56 "Psychic" Geller
57 Voodoo doctor's doing

by Christina Houlihan Kelly

ACROSS

1 Mountain goat's spot
5 Letter-shaped fastener
10 Shake up
14 Hold sway
15 "Socrate" composer
16 Co. bigwig
17 "You said it!"
18 Dress design
19 "Jaywalking" personality
20 Smash
23 Pipe type
24 Once-common skyline sights
28 Head of state?
29 Athlete seated at a table, maybe
33 "Shrek" princess
34 "It's Impossible" crooner
35 Advice to a Harley passenger
39 Cracked a bit
41 County near Tyrone
42 Fits perfectly
46 Jiffy
49 Soccer forward
50 Put on
52 Sprint to the tape . . . and a hint to this puzzle's theme
56 Pacific retreat
59 Like any of seven Nolan Ryan games
60 Similar
61 Tom Joad, for one
62 With 57-Down, 1950s campaign slogan
63 Hawaii's state bird
64 Does a dog trick
65 Break off
66 Windsor, for one

DOWN

1 Tarzan portrayer
2 They spread fast
3 Joan's "Dynasty" role
4 Salami variety
5 B-1 letters
6 Hope/Crosby "Road" destination
7 Ear-related
8 Going from A to B, say
9 [Giggle]
10 Suffered from an allergy, maybe
11 Send packing
12 Meditative sect
13 "Foucault's Pendulum" author
21 Hardly robust
22 Employer of many auditors: Abbr.
25 Plenty
26 Apollo vehicle, for short
27 Good sign for an angel
30 Retinal cell
31 Phone trigram
32 Fish in a John Cleese film
33 Enriches with vitamins
35 "Aquarius" musical
36 Asian holiday
37 High dudgeon
38 Destined for the record books
39 Onager
40 Stick out
43 Do moguls, say
44 Court action
45 A.L. East player
46 Not tacit
47 Cause of weird weather
48 Young swan
51 Short-sheeting, e.g.
53 Weapon in a rumble
54 Scout outing
55 Poll closing?
56 Watch attachment
57 See 62-Across
58 Energetic dance

by Alan Arbesfeld

ACROSS

1 With 68-Across, bell ringer
5 Doing nothing
9 Speechify
14 Fashion designer Rabanne
15 Vehicle on tracks
16 Pugilist
17 No. on a bank statement
18 Grotto
19 Material for Elvis's blue shoes
20 Bell ringer
23 "California, ___ Come"
24 Spouse's meek agreement
28 See 52-Across
29 Cy Young Award winner Blue
33 Home that may have a live-in butler
34 Less certain
36 Archaeological site
37 Bell ringer
41 Go backpacking
42 Inside info for an investor, maybe
43 Sheep's cries
46 Unskilled laborer
47 Ordinal suffix
50 Kids' game involving an unwanted card
52 With 28-Across, winner of golf's 1997 U.S. Open
54 Bell ringer
58 Org.
61 Club that's not a wood
62 Al or Tipper
63 Book after Jonah
64 Emperor who reputedly fiddled while Rome burned
65 God of love

66 "Lord, ___?" (biblical query)
67 Pop music's Bee ___
68 See 1-Across

DOWN

1 Geronimo's tribe
2 Poet Lindsay
3 Happens
4 ___ Dame
5 Poison ivy symptom
6 Sketch
7 ___ lamp (1960s novelty)
8 Manicurist's item
9 Dwell (on)
10 Point A to point B and back
11 Firefighter's tool
12 Slugger Williams
13 "Able was I ___ I saw Elba"
21 Honda model
22 Joey with the Starliters
25 Waters, informally
26 Going ___ (fighting)
27 Stimpy's cartoon pal
30 Post-op spot, for short
31 One running away with a spoon, in a children's rhyme
32 Greek fabulist
34 Heartthrob
35 Baptism or bar mitzvah
37 Bit of medicine
38 Squeezed (out)
39 Palindromic tribe name

40 Forty-___ (gold rush participant)
41 "Curb Your Enthusiasm" airer
44 Chinese martial art
45 "___ 'em!"
47 "Bewitched" witch
48 Steering system component
49 Religious dissent
51 Faulkner's "As I Lay ___"
53 Star in Orion
55 Native Canadian
56 Stories passed down through generations
57 1961 space chimp
58 Pal in Paris
59 ___ boom bah
60 Lab field: Abbr.

by Sarah Keller

174

ACROSS

1 Inane
5 ___ scan (biometric authentication method)
9 Districted
14 Cynic's comment
15 Payload delivery org.
16 Beam
17 Helpful person's line
20 Spiral in space
21 Most comfy
22 Jazz dance
23 Vice squad arrestees, perhaps
25 Perturbation
27 Autumn bloomer
32 With 42-Across, helpful person's line
37 Mesa tribe
38 Philosophy of bare existence?
39 Log-in info
41 Writer Waugh
42 See 32-Across
46 Like good pianos and engines
48 Levitated
49 Versatile fabric
51 Lives on
56 Spode ensembles
60 Coterie
61 Helpful person's line
64 Popular place for 18-Down
65 Tied up
66 Reel in
67 With cunning
68 St. Andrew's Day observer
69 Virtual mart

DOWN

1 Small jobs for a body shop
2 Kriegsmarine vessel
3 ___ Park (noted lab site)
4 Substitute players
5 Annual racing classic
6 Squealer
7 Prefix with tonic
8 "Hello, Dolly!" jazzman
9 One of the Gabors
10 Bygone Dodge
11 Giant in footwear
12 Graceful shaders
13 It's repellent
18 Sojourners abroad, for short
19 Darlin'
23 Elbow
24 Prospecting find
26 1989's ___ Prieta earthquake
28 Flushing stadium
29 Having a hard time deciding
30 Like "Paradise Lost"
31 Ferris wheel or bumper cars
32 Swarm member
33 "To Sir With Love" singer, 1967
34 Mideast harbor city
35 Cubes at Harrah's
36 Bother
40 ___ Artois beer
43 Agrees
44 Sellout letters
45 Lithium-___ battery
47 Stylish
50 Dough producer, briefly
52 Airplane seating request
53 Fowl entree
54 ___ deaf ear to
55 Not yet gentrified
56 Much of a waitress's income
57 And others, for short
58 Cockeyed
59 Clipper's sheet
60 ¢
62 Piping compound, briefly
63 Fierce type, astrologically

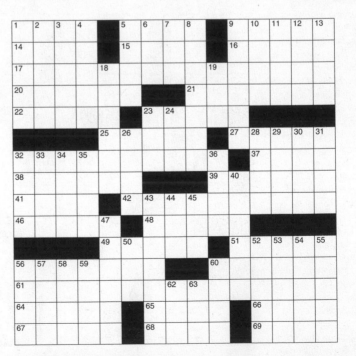

by Chuck Deodene

ACROSS

1 "That stinks!," quaintly
4 Ladder danger
8 It makes Frisky frisky
14 Evangelical sch. with a 4,000+ enrollment
15 On the deep
16 Top gun
17 Alternative to Gleem
18 "Pretty Woman" and "Waiting to Exhale"
20 Shul's shepherd
22 On its way
23 Stew (over)
24 Shepherds' locales
26 Like harp seals
28 Actor who got his start on TV's "Gimme a Break!"
32 Roadie's load
33 "Master"
34 "I Love Lucy" costar
38 Wing, e.g.
40 Archie Bunker, famously
42 Belgrade resident
43 Dummy Mortimer
45 Hit Sega title character
47 Gene material
48 Shooter of westerns
51 What virgin drinks lack
54 1847 novel subtitled "A Narrative of Adventures in the South Seas"
55 Gladly
56 Oscar-winning role for Helen Mirren, in brief
59 Part of a metropolitan area
62 They're exercised when cycling
65 ___ Canals
66 Rival of Old El Paso
67 Opera's ___ Te Kanawa
68 Useful insect secretion
69 Not just hypothesize
70 It's hard to believe
71 Singer Sumac

DOWN

1 Animal hunted in one of Hercules' 12 labors
2 ___ da capo
3 It's embarrassing to eat
4 Spa offerings
5 Tree of life, in Norse myth
6 Kauai keepsakes
7 Some needlework
8 Beach cover-up
9 Be indisposed
10 Those who don't behave seriously
11 Mother-of-pearl
12 Clinton adviser Harold
13 Termites and such
19 Patella
21 Old Turkish title
25 Fashion designer Elie
27 Pioneer in 33⅓ r.p.m. records
28 Photocopier woes
29 Land on the end of a peninsula
30 Sounds from a teakettle
31 Ordeal's quality
35 With shaking hands, perhaps
36 "Rule, Britannia" composer
37 Letter-shaped beam
39 Automatic-drip machine maker
41 Busy viewer's convenience
44 "What an idiot I am!"
46 Arrives
49 Plumlike Chinese fruit
50 Fish eaten cold
51 Foil-making giant
52 Specialists in storytelling?
53 Druids, e.g.
57 Totally gross
58 Pelvic bones
60 Go far and wide
61 Part of Florida's Gold Coast, informally
63 Restaurant V.I.P.: Abbr.
64 Misreckon

by Stella Daily and Bruce Venzke

ACROSS

1 Put out, as a fire
6 Furry TV extraterrestrial
9 Arouse, as interest
14 "In my opinion . . ."
15 Place for sheep to graze
16 Mrs. Bush
17 Utensil used with flour
18 Perry Mason's field
19 Out of kilter
20 Old "Tonight Show" intro
23 Fork over
24 Word after show or know
25 Bygone Rambler mfr.
27 Classic arcade game
31 Set free
36 Pungent-smelling
37 Expensive tooth filling material
38 Sport with beefy grapplers
39 Admonition to a showboating athlete
42 Notes after do
43 Doll's cry
44 Almost any doo-wop tune
45 What a driver's license shows proof of
47 Makes tough
48 Understood
49 By way of
50 "Cheers" bartender
53 Kid's book with a hidden character
60 Atlantic or Pacific
62 Buddhist sect
63 Squirrel away
64 Suspect's story
65 Stephen of "The Crying Game"

66 Out of favor, informally
67 Derby prize
68 The whole shebang
69 Activities in 57-Down

DOWN

1 Satellite TV receiver
2 Garfield's pal, in the funnies
3 ___-friendly (simple to operate)
4 Put money in the bank
5 Poker player's headgear
6 Give the O.K.
7 Wife of Jacob
8 Young Bambi
9 Benchwarmer's plea
10 The Beatles' "___ the Walrus"

11 Wit's remark
12 Celestial bear
13 "Piece of cake!"
21 Rock's Bon Jovi
22 Nita of silent films
26 Windsor, notably
27 Father: Prefix
28 Felt sore
29 Oreo's filling
30 Sinking in mud
31 Hardly cramped
32 Director Kazan
33 Napped leather
34 Cybermessages
35 Stadium toppers
37 Pesky swarmer
40 Most common U.S. surname
41 Zero

46 Local noncollegian, to a collegian
47 Bro's sibling
49 Open to bribery
50 Suds maker
51 Rights org.
52 Golda of Israel
54 Poet Pound
55 Walk drunkenly
56 Top-rated
57 Features of science classes
58 "Dang!"
59 5:2, e.g., at a racetrack
61 Muscles to crunch

by Fred Piscop

ACROSS

1 ___ Bartlet, president on "The West Wing"
4 John of "Full House"
10 Voodoo charm
14 Org. that publishes health studies
15 Butt in
16 One who may be caught off base?
17 Food transportation . . . that Harry Belafonte sang about
19 Place for a footballer's pad
20 Indiana and Ohio State are in it
21 Play ice hockey
23 Charles Lamb, pseudonymously
24 . . . that's an ambulance, in slang
28 It ends in the fall: Abbr.
29 Shade of green
31 Helpful
32 Symbol of love
36 "Sometimes you feel like ___"
37 . . . that a rube might fall off
39 Al Jazeera viewer, typically
41 He danced in "Silk Stockings"
42 Put on the payroll
44 Stimpy's cartoon pal
45 Org. for drivers?
48 . . . that may be upset
52 Place to load and unload
53 R & B singer Mary J. ___
54 Sen. Feinstein
56 Pork chop?
59 . . . that's a source of easy money

61 Declare
62 Cliff hangers?
63 Some like it hot
64 Word with telephoto or zoom
65 San Fernando Valley district
66 Doofus

DOWN

1 Poked
2 Communicates with online
3 "Phooey!"
4 Trig function
5 Tax cheat chaser, informally
6 Alert for a fleeing prisoner, in brief
7 Bullwinkle, e.g.
8 Japanese city whose name means "large hill"

9 Go after
10 Stick out one's tongue, maybe
11 Hold title to
12 Coffee, slangily
13 Corrida cheer
18 One ___ time
22 Afternoon hour
24 Home run hero of '61
25 Icky stuff
26 Home of the Cowboys: Abbr.
27 New Jersey cager
29 Part of r.p.m.
30 Novelist Ferber
32 Mingle (with)
33 Make a choice
34 Crank up
35 Keystone State port
37 Rain delay roll-out

38 Caterer's coffee holder
39 "So it's you!"
40 Boot Hill letters
43 Actor Benicio ___ Toro
45 Party animal?
46 Wish offerers
47 Soccer venues
49 Prop for Groucho Marx
50 See eye to eye
51 Plays parent to
52 72, at Augusta
54 Turned blue, maybe
55 "___ deal!"
56 Kilmer who once played Batman
57 She raised Cain
58 Bridge capacity unit
60 Compete

by Randall J. Hartman

Note: The answers to the 13 starred clues have something in common.

ACROSS

1 *Stone in Hollywood
7 *Home for Will Rogers and Garth Brooks
15 1950s All-Star outfielder Minnie
16 *What some unscrupulous e-businesses do?
17 Arthurian paradise
18 Bejeweled pendant
19 *Torn
20 Regatta crew leaders
21 Govt. code-breaking group
22 Wish to take back
23 Song syllable
25 U.S. mil. medal
27 Whence the line "A soft answer turneth away wrath"
31 *Extremely narrow winning margin
35 *Kind of club
37 Mother of Queen Elizabeth I
38 Lingerie shade
41 *A Perón
42 Mercury model
43 TV Dr. of note
44 *Student of Dr. Pangloss
46 *Lover of Radames
47 Like some nursery care
50 Cape Town's country: Abbr.
53 Oz. and kg.
54 Washington ballplayer, briefly
56 Study
59 Class __
62 *Renown
63 Nullify
65 Air __
67 *Site of much horsing around?

68 Architectural decoration
69 *Perform ostentatiously
70 *Destiny

DOWN

1 Astrologer Sydney
2 Meet, as expectations, with "to"
3 Goofier
4 Battery unit
5 That, in Tijuana
6 Friend of Harry and Hermione
7 Capital near the 60th parallel
8 2001 film set in a mental institution
9 Washed
10 Collect

11 Anthropomorphic cinema computer
12 Lena of "Chocolat"
13 Place to which Bart Simpson makes prank calls
14 Gillette brand
20 Dodge on the road
23 New Deal program, for short
24 Renaissance instrument
26 Home in the Alps
28 Eyepiece
29 Curer of feta cheese
30 Lay
32 Even one
33 Wayfarer's stop
34 King's title
36 Sully
38 Clean Air Act org.
39 The Bears, on scoreboards

40 Completely free
45 Some "Law & Order" figs.
48 Ancient garland
49 Kind of class
51 Cancel
52 __ Viejo (California city near Laguna Beach)
55 Creed element
56 Medics
57 Cole Porter's "Well, Did You __?"
58 "Quo Vadis" role
60 Old music halls
61 Result of a whipping
62 End-of-wk. times
64 Big fight
65 1991 film directed by 1-Across
66 "Either he goes __ go!"

by Lee Glickstein and Craig Kasper

ACROSS
1 Wager
4 Gush
10 Willie of the 1950s-'60s Giants
14 Israeli submachine gun
15 Last words of the Pledge of Allegiance
16 ___ vera
17 Atomic energy org.
18 *Popular Sunshine State vacation destination
20 Prepare to shoot
22 Docs
23 Stop for the night, as soldiers
25 Daughter's counterpart
26 Dartboard, for one
28 The "I" of I.M.F.: Abbr.
30 Austrian affirmatives
33 "The Thin Man" pooch
34 Rim
36 Put (down), as money
38 Theater focal point
40 Select, with "for"
41 Language akin to Urdu
42 Serious drinker
43 Arnaz of "I Love Lucy"
45 Depression-era migrant
46 "But I heard him exclaim, ___ he drove . . ."
47 Take too much of, briefly
49 Objected to
51 Brouhaha
52 Keep just below a boil
54 Not deceitful
58 Deck covering to keep out moisture

61 *Like players below the B team
63 "This means ___!"
64 Sets of points, in math
65 "Relax, soldier!"
66 U.K. record label
67 Newspaper essay
68 Mascara goes on them
69 King, in old Rome

DOWN
1 Part of a suicide squeeze
2 Poet Pound
3 *Material for an old-fashioned parade
4 Wipe off
5 Decorate with leaves
6 Erich who wrote "The Art of Loving"
7 Bygone Mideast inits.

8 Slender
9 Firstborn
10 "___ Whoopee!" (1920s hit)
11 One of the Baldwin brothers
12 Toy that might go "around the world"
13 Period in Cong.
19 Coach Rupp of college basketball
21 Take on
24 *Sties
26 One of the five senses
27 Fur trader John Jacob ___
29 Basketball rim attachments
30 Location for the ends of the answers to the four starred clues
31 Actress MacDowell
32 Schussed, e.g.

35 Dumbbell
37 Hampton of jazz fame
39 Wore away
44 Really, really big
48 ___ fin
50 Representations
51 Pungent-smelling
53 N.B.A. coach Thomas
54 Normandy town
55 Breakfast restaurant letters
56 "Good shot!"
57 Kett of old comics
59 Designate
60 Cereal whose ads feature a "silly rabbit"
62 ___ ipsa loquitur

by Allan E. Parrish

180

ACROSS

1 "Do you like green eggs and ham?" speaker
7 In the style of
10 Lao-tzu's way
13 Meeting handout
14 Broke from the band, maybe
17 Cosmopolitan staple
19 Date
20 Uncertainties
21 It can be silly
22 Spot en el mar
24 W.W. I German admiral
26 N.F.L. star
32 Slip
33 Conquistador's quest
34 Actress Turner
36 Opposite of WSW
37 Period of human benightedness
41 Stroke
42 Overall feel
44 Coquettish
45 Relative of a mole
47 Colorful bed cover
51 Corrida cheers
52 Pageant adornment
53 Highest peak of Crete
56 Egg: Prefix
57 Wide shoe spec
60 "Behave!" . . . and a hint to this puzzle's theme
65 Representative
66 Tie, as a score
67 Cry between "ready" and "go!"
68 "Kid-tested" breakfast cereal
69 Keep

DOWN

1 Fools
2 Author James
3 Slight
4 Special connections
5 Bustle
6 Port seized by Adm. Dewey, 1898
7 Poking tools
8 Luau offering
9 Queen of the hill?
10 Ballyhoo
11 Dismounted
12 Like mud
15 Easygoing
16 Sound at a greased pig contest
18 In the distance
22 Figs. clustered around 100
23 Like a malfeasant, often
24 Fluids in bags
25 Bull Moose party: Abbr.
26 Appeal
27 Incurred, as charges
28 "La Traviata," e.g.
29 Site of the first Asian Olympics
30 Kind of pants
31 Prepare to propose
35 1, for hydrogen: Abbr.
38 What a massage may ease
39 Theater seating
40 Titles for attys.
43 In disagreement
46 "Say what?"
48 Pottery materials
49 Reply, briefly
50 Onetime German leader
53 Mlles. after marriage
54 Red-bordered magazine
55 The "W" in Geo. W. Bush, e.g.
56 Straight-horned African animal
57 Author Ferber
58 Prefix with distant
59 "SportsCenter" channel
61 Yellow ribbon holder, in song
62 Geller with a psychic act
63 St. crosser
64 Bring home

by Oliver Hill

ACROSS

1 A diehard enemy might want yours
6 Gather
11 QB's goals
14 Amor vincit ___
15 Milk: Prefix
16 In
17 Call in roulette
19 Suffix with fish
20 For smaller government, presumably
21 One who supplies the means
23 Knocks off
25 Gun dealer's stock
26 Norway's patron saint
30 Call in blackjack
34 Robot maid on "The Jetsons"
36 Buttresses
37 Call in many a betting game
44 Impart
45 Broadcast portion
46 Call in draw poker
52 John P. Marquand detective
53 Signify
54 Prefix with carpal
56 Sounds of walking in moccasins
60 Deicing tool
65 Detroit-to-Philadelphia dir.
66 Call in craps
68 Family room
69 Challenge to ___
70 Family girl
71 Inexact fig.
72 Request to meet in person
73 Photographer Adams

DOWN

1 It has arms, legs and a back
2 "Let's go!"
3 "Sometimes you feel like ___ . . ."
4 Italian river valley in W.W. II fighting
5 Page of music
6 Cosmonaut Leonov, the first human to walk in space
7 "Holy moly!"
8 Fair-sized plot
9 Old British gun
10 Fountain offering
11 1991 Geena Davis title role
12 "The Sound of Music" hit
13 "Sophie's Choice" author
18 Per
22 Catch
24 Celebrity
26 Fort ___ on Monterey Bay
27 W.C.
28 Tempe sch.
29 Tiny tale
31 Part of r.p.m.: Abbr.
32 Pre-1868 Tokyo
33 Dog in 1930s films
35 Fitzgerald who sang "A-Tisket, A-Tasket"
38 Comics cry
39 Start of long-distance dialing
40 Make music on a comb
41 Answer before exchanging rings
42 Have a ___ to pick
43 Sentimental drivel
46 Hinder
47 Some auto deals
48 Present but not active
49 Contents of some shells
50 Be cozy
51 Write permanently
55 Rock concert setting
57 Pitchers' stats
58 Depended (on)
59 Pivot
61 Score after deuce
62 Bakery display
63 "___ homo"
64 Line holder
67 NASA vehicle

by Robert Dillman

182

ACROSS
1 Witty sorts
5 Make sense
10 Choice word
14 Think tank nugget
15 On the lam
16 Gerund, e.g.
17 Bond villain
19 Saw red?
20 Ph.D. thesis: Abbr.
21 Gets corroded
22 Bemoan
25 "Beats me" gesture
28 Rub out
29 Certain trout
33 Basis of a suit
34 Endless, poetically
35 Fraternity P
36 "Survivor" shelter
37 Some red wines
38 Obey the coxswain
39 Cheroot residue
40 Wings it
41 Place for a hoedown
42 Classic blues musician
44 Intuit
45 The "35" in John 11:35
46 Prodded
47 Woods or Irons
50 Flair
51 Laugh heartily
52 Patriarchal gorilla
58 Pond organism
59 Primp
60 Natural soother
61 Lounge in the sun
62 Feel nostalgia, e.g.
63 Crips or Bloods

DOWN
1 Faux 'fro?
2 Brouhaha
3 Goo in a do
4 Most mournful
5 Most-wanted group for a party
6 Puts on
7 Follow everywhere
8 Put to work
9 Part of r.p.m.
10 "Stop!"
11 Wall Street minimums
12 Fatty treat for birds
13 Pulls the plug on
18 Ticket cost?
21 Game sheet
22 Deadly
23 Work up
24 First first lady
25 Germ-free
26 As a result of this
27 Patronizes U-Haul, e.g.
29 Plays for time
30 Gofer's job
31 When repeated, cry by Shakespeare's Richard III
32 Consumed heartily
34 Octogenarian, for one
37 Pole tossed by Scots
41 Nontraditional chair style
43 Czech composer Antonín
44 Go up, up, up
46 Filmdom's Close
47 Omani, e.g.
48 Fast-food drink
49 Makes "it"
50 ". . . ___ after"
52 U-2 pilot, e.g.
53 Ill temper
54 Grazing ground
55 Carte start
56 Bamboozle
57 Fraternity party setup

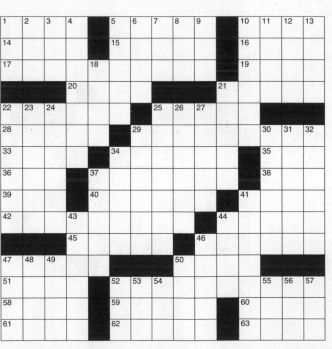

by Steve Kahn

ACROSS

1 Speaks, informally
4 Speak
9 Smokey Robinson's music genre, for short
14 ___ de France
15 End of a hangman's rope
16 Love to bits
17 BORE
20 Have ___ in one's head
21 ___ and outs
22 The "I" in T.G.I.F.
23 BOAR
28 Nap
29 "Golden" song
32 Ad-lib, musically
35 Sign before Virgo
36 Person performing an exorcism
37 Gives a stage cue
40 Honeybunch or cutie pie
41 Glowing remnants of a fire
42 Abbr. after many a general's name
43 Meyerbeer's "___ Huguenots"
44 Painting surface
45 Publisher of Cosmopolitan and Good Housekeeping
48 BOER
53 Before, in poetry
55 Baseballer Mel
56 "Maria ___," Jimmy Dorsey #1 hit
57 BOHR
62 Actress Garbo
63 "Er . . . um . . ."
64 Old tennis racket string material
65 Stand for a portrait
66 Taboos
67 Cry before "Get your hands off!"

DOWN

1 Have a chair by, as a table
2 ___ Yale, for whom Yale University is named
3 Six in 1,000,000
4 Out of sight
5 Also
6 ___ Sawyer
7 Reverse of WNW
8 Fix the electrical connections of
9 Didn't have enough supplies
10 Problem in focusing, for short
11 "Don't worry about it"
12 "Phooey!"
13 Panhandles
18 Club with a lodge
19 Bankbook abbr.
24 Knuckleheads
25 Tribulations
26 ___ dye
27 Lena or Ken of film
30 "This ___ . . . Then" (Jennifer Lopez album)
31 French summers
32 Computer image file format
33 French weapon
34 Sights at after-Christmas sales
36 Lab's ___ dish
38 Mini-plateau
39 "Will you marry me?," e.g.
40 Brandy fruit
42 Hoops official
45 Sticker through a lady's headgear
46 Coils of yarn
47 Soft powder
49 Biblical suffix
50 Stable sound
51 Come afterward
52 Wretched
53 Scoring advantage
54 ___ avis
58 Suffix with Israel
59 Dr. provider
60 Japanese moolah
61 ___ Paulo, Brazil

by Timothy Powell

184

ACROSS

1 C-shaped gadget
6 Breastplate, e.g.
11 "Kinda" suffix
14 Spokes, essentially
15 Break from service
16 E-file preparer, briefly
17 Good-looking, briefly
19 Part of a confession
20 Oscar winner Tomei
21 Like a woodland
23 Inventor Rubik
24 Bounty letters
26 Thumbscrew ridges
27 Final Four org.
29 Dom or earl
30 Low man
33 Taylor Hicks, e.g.
35 Sharp as a tack
38 Cable network owned by NBC Universal
39 Oh-so-cute carnival prizes, briefly
42 Pirouette pivot
43 Adoption agcy.
45 Projector unit
46 "Jerusalem Delivered" poet
48 Of yore
50 Fall setting
52 Dry rot, e.g.
54 Bustle
55 "Don't forget . . ."
59 Prayer wheel inscriptions
61 "Oops!" list
63 Phoenix-to-Albuquerque dir.
64 Risky person to do business with, briefly
66 Holy ones: Abbr.
67 Made public
68 Possessive pronoun in an old hymn
69 It may be cocked
70 Some are proper
71 Church assembly

DOWN

1 ___ fraîche
2 Agent Swifty
3 Deck out
4 Flunkies
5 Places to refuel
6 Toby filler
7 Marine hazards
8 Deli supply
9 It's too much
10 Take umbrage at
11 Winter hazards, briefly
12 Hawker's line
13 Deck crew
18 "That's a laugh!"
22 Be a sourpuss
25 Fair one?
28 "Le ___ d'Or"
29 Rang out
30 H.O.V. lane user
31 Shakespeare's "poor venomous fool"
32 Student writing competition, briefly
34 Buck's mate
36 Aurora, to the Greeks
37 Opposite of paleo-
40 Fortress of old
41 Sault ___ Marie Canals
44 Kelp, for one
47 Possible result of a natural disaster
49 Victim of Macbeth
51 Active sort
52 Crayola color changed to "peach"
53 ___ Mountains, home of King's Peak
54 Ghostly pale
56 Like most South Americans
57 Note taker
58 Propelled a shell
60 Hose shade
62 Mafiosi who "flip"
65 Online revenue sources

by Robert Zimmerman

ACROSS

1 Indifferent to pleasure or pain
6 Close
10 Jacket
14 Toyota rival
15 Impulse
16 ___ of office
17 Taking back one's words in humiliation
19 "Oh, that's what you mean"
20 Excitement
21 ___-de-sac
22 Receiver of a legal transfer
24 Actress Zellweger
26 Anger
27 Negotiating in a no-nonsense way
32 Baby kangaroos
34 Joel who directed "Raising Arizona"
35 "These ___ the times that . . ."
36 One-named Art Deco designer
37 Vehicles in airplane aisles
39 "Love ___ the air"
40 Big elephant feature
41 Theater award
42 Prayers' ends
43 Pretending to be dead
47 The "et" of et cetera
48 Lock of hair
49 Rip off
53 Moo goo ___ pan
54 Ewe's call
57 Supervising
58 Raising a false alarm
61 Roman statesman ___ the Elder
62 Daylight saving, e.g.

63 ___ Rae (Sally Field title role)
64 Didn't just guess
65 Locales of mineral waters
66 Say with one's hand on the Bible

DOWN

1 New York stadium
2 Relative of a frog
3 Seeing through the deception of
4 Dictator Amin
5 Calls off
6 Cell centers
7 Misplay, e.g.
8 Slack-jawed
9 Edits
10 Neologist
11 Kiln

12 Suit to ___
13 Biblical pronoun
18 Sticky matter
23 Give ___ for one's money
24 Comedic actress Martha
25 Put into cipher
27 Four: Prefix
28 "___ Milk?"
29 Casey with a radio countdown
30 Land o' blarney
31 Achings
32 Army transport
33 Spoken
37 Leads, as an orchestra
38 "Hulk" director Lee

39 Don with a big mouth
41 One of the Sinatras
42 Hands out, as duties
44 Peter of Peter, Paul & Mary
45 Unrestrained revelries
46 Actor Penn
49 Marina fixture
50 "___ Almighty," 2007 film
51 Honor with a roast, say
52 What icicles do
54 Drill
55 ___ mater
56 Many miles away
59 Singer Sumac
60 "Man alive!"

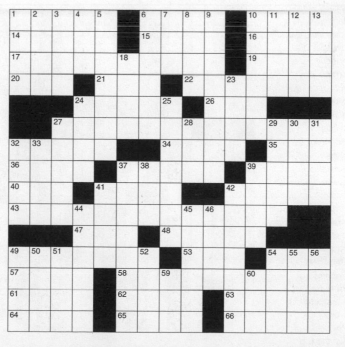

by Andrea Carla Michaels

186

ACROSS

1 Show anger
5 Round before the final
9 Washroom tub
14 Ph.D. awarder
15 Gave the boot
16 Blessing-inducing sound
17 Flank
18 Gimlet garnish
19 Crockpot concoctions
20 Relax during a drill
23 Temp's work unit
24 Polite affirmation
25 Brazilian dance
27 Big Apple awards
30 Like hair, usually, after combing
33 Post-O.R. stop
36 Craps natural
38 Impoverished
39 Sgt. Friday's org.
41 Calendar units hidden in 20- and 61-Across and 11-and 35-Down
43 Worker's pay
44 Like a brainiac
46 Fire remnants
48 The "R" in Roy G. Biv
49 Trojan War hero
51 Popular snack chip
53 Surveyor Jeremiah, for whom a famous line is partly named
55 Beatle, endearingly
59 Meadow sound
61 Sunshine State school
64 Minute Maid Park player
66 Baylor's city
67 Sp. girl
68 Rodeo animal
69 From the top
70 Ticks off
71 TV shout-out from the team bench
72 It's sold in skeins
73 "Great" kid-lit detective

DOWN

1 Hard to please
2 Bring together
3 Greedy monarch
4 "Nevertheless . . ."
5 On the payroll
6 Lighted sign in a theater
7 Hand-waver's cry
8 They may be bright
9 One in the infield
10 Follow direction?
11 Show sadness
12 Political caucus state
13 Like a yenta
21 "That's mine!"
22 Deplete, as energy
26 Cold one
28 FEMA recommendation, briefly
29 Play by a different ___ rules
31 Upper hand
32 Like batik fabrics
33 Ingrid's role in "Casablanca"
34 Showed up
35 "Time to rise, sleepyhead!"
37 Within earshot
40 Zwei follower
42 Lose the spare tire
45 Schedule B or C, e.g.
47 Ancient Greek colonnade
50 La preceder
52 Chooses to participate
54 "Impossible!"
56 ___ firma
57 Largish combo
58 Terrible twos, e.g.
59 Bad-mouth
60 Sparkling wine city
62 ___ deficit (lost money)
63 Pastry prettifier
65 Vintage auto

by Michael Kaplan

ACROSS
1 The Velvet Fog
6 Casino pair
10 Cabaret, e.g.
14 Smuggler's stock
15 Giant-screen film format
16 Summer wine selection
17 All the rockets in existence?
20 Ask for
21 Some emergency cases, for short
22 Place for shots
23 Noughts-and-crosses win
25 Brand of shaving products
26 "Dry-clean only," e.g.?
33 Empty (of)
34 Small, as a Beanie Baby
35 First course option
36 Does as told
38 ___ Andreas fault
39 Like déjà vu
40 Turner who sang "The Best"
41 Marzipan ingredient
43 Piggy
44 Cooking utensil from central Spain?
47 Like a starless sky
48 Alt. spelling
49 Iran-___
52 Debtor's letters
54 ___ buco
58 HAL 9000, in "2001: A Space Odyssey"?
61 First-year J.D. candidate
62 Restaurant chain acronym
63 Thus far
64 A sergeant might ask a soldier to pick it up
65 I.R.S. ID's
66 Recipe parts

DOWN
1 Tabbies' mates
2 Mayberry boy
3 Angry reaction
4 Animal with a shaggy coat
5 U.K. record label
6 Fizzled out
7 Radio's "___ in the Morning"
8 Poky
9 Mutual fund redemption charge
10 Deep fissure
11 Oral history
12 "Evil empire" of the '80s
13 "It's ___ real!"
18 Sarge's superior
19 Brewery units
24 Baseball's Ed and Mel
25 Relative key of C major
26 Second-longest human bone
27 Utopias
28 Stahl of "60 Minutes"
29 As a friend, to the French
30 Outlet of the left ventricle
31 Astronaut ___ Bluford, the first African-American in space
32 Sport with lunges
33 Mil. option
37 First N.F.L. QB with consecutive 30-touchdown passing seasons
39 Novelist Ferber
41 Acid neutralizers
42 "___ Organum" (1620 Francis Bacon work)
45 Crucifix inscription
46 Subject of the 1999 film "Le Temps Retrouvé"
49 Karate blow
50 The last Mrs. Chaplin
51 Minute part of a minute: Abbr.
52 A program usually has one
53 "Stupid me!"
55 Eyelid woe
56 Ooze
57 Table scraps
59 Geezers' replies
60 Dads

by Paula Gamache

188

ACROSS
1 Does sums
5 Pillow filler
9 Flapper hairdos
13 Scuttlebutt
14 Like a manly man
15 Escapade
16 Part of the eye that holds the iris
17 ___ and pains
18 What "thumbs up" means
19 Bandleader in the Polka Music Hall of Fame
22 Explosive initials
23 Pinocchio, famously
24 Mock
28 Dance with a wiggle
30 Lord
31 Card that's taken only by a trump
32 Mail carriers' assignments: Abbr.
34 Creamy soup
38 City where van Gogh painted sunflowers
40 Suffix with sucr- and lact-
41 Pacific republic
42 Substantial portion
45 Pile
46 Component of bronze
47 Permit
48 Washington's Capitol ___
50 Precipitates at about 32°F
52 Left hurriedly
54 New Deal program inits.
57 One who lost what's hidden in 19-, 34- and 42-Across
60 Hawaiian isle
63 More than perturbed
64 "Unfortunately . . ."
65 Give a hard time
66 Nobodies
67 Small field size
68 Branch of Islam
69 Plow pullers
70 Jean who wrote "Wide Sargasso Sea"

DOWN
1 No longer a minor
2 Couch
3 Made a stand and would go no further
4 Polaris, e.g.
5 Bangladesh's capital, old-style
6 Color of fall leaves
7 "Thank goodness!"
8 Rhinoplasty
9 Chap
10 Tree loved by squirrels
11 Maidenform product
12 Cloud's site
14 Psycho
20 90° turn
21 Ushered
25 "Fantastic Voyage" actress
26 Honda division
27 Get ready to drive, in golf
29 ___-friendly
30 Agents under J. Edgar Hoover, informally
32 Balsa transports
33 Path
35 Booty
36 Tempe sch.
37 Comedian Mort
39 1972 U.S./U.S.S.R. missile pact
43 Latin American with mixed ancestry
44 Oedipus' realm
49 Wedding vow
51 Doolittle of "My Fair Lady"
52 Distress signal shot into the air
53 Divulge
55 Explorer who proved that Greenland is an island
56 Basilica recesses
58 Fearsome dino
59 Jack of early late-night TV
60 ___ Butterworth's
61 What a doctor might ask you to say
62 Israeli gun

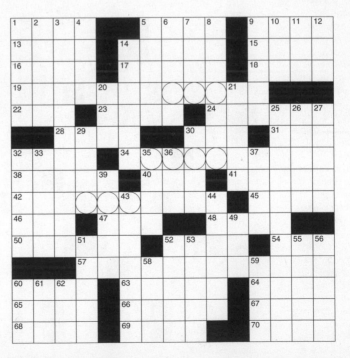

by Lynn Lempel

ACROSS

1 Play place
6 Ballroom dance
11 Chart-topper
14 Sign of spring
15 Mountaineer's tool
16 ET's ride
17 Play follower, usually
19 Unruly do
20 Amateurish
21 "___ economy is always beauty": Henry James
23 Buggy rider
26 Loofah, e.g.
30 108-card game
31 Start the pot
32 Pest control brand
33 Spoil
35 Bibliophile's suffix
36 Tipplers
37 Circulatory system flow
41 Singer ___ P. Morgan
43 Early 11th-century year
44 Back at sea?
47 Actress Chase of "Now, Voyager"
48 For dieters
51 Smidgen
52 Shoot-'em-up figure
54 Harmony, briefly
55 Clobber, biblically
56 Computer that uses OS X
58 Director Lee
59 What the starts of 17-, 26-, 37- and 52-Across are
66 Crib cry
67 Burger topper, maybe
68 Site of Ali's Rumble in the Jungle
69 Salon job
70 Cuts and pastes
71 TV awards

DOWN

1 Amniotic ___
2 Play about Capote
3 Put on TV
4 Manage, barely
5 Jacob's twin
6 G.I.'s helmet, slangily
7 Duke's sports org.
8 "Read Across America" grp.
9 Guy's partner
10 Primrose family member
11 Saroyan novel, with "The"
12 "It slipped my mind!"
13 Letterman lists
18 ID on a dust jacket
22 Acknowledges nonverbally
23 PC glitch
24 "Wheel of Fortune" buy
25 Hoops coach with the most NCAA Division I wins
27 Playful mockery
28 Rural event on horseback
29 Work out in the ring
31 Commotion
34 Red Sox div.
38 Old Dodge
39 Singer of the 1962 hit "The Wanderer"
40 Guinness Book suffix
41 Tools for making twisty cuts
42 Barnard grads
45 Bled, like dyes
46 "Deal or No Deal" network
49 Fakes, as an injury
50 Weaponry
53 Leave alone
54 "Beat it!"
57 Wood-shaping tool
60 Suffered from
61 Here, in Paris
62 "I'm kidding!"
63 Deadeye's asset
64 Dryly amusing
65 Nintendo's Super ___

by Alan Arbesfeld

ACROSS

1 7-Up flavor
5 Easter serving
9 Funny ones
14 "Just ___!"
15 Succulent plant
16 Clinker
17 Locker room supply
18 *Solid ground
20 *You should have the body
22 Online currency
23 Catches in the act
24 Pro at balancing
27 Big pet food brand
30 Pageant wear
32 Erica who wrote "Any Woman's Blues"
35 Bottom of a lily
38 Bank rights
39 Schoenberg's "Moses und ___"
40 *From the beginning
42 Gray-brown goose
43 "The Taming of the Shrew" setting
45 Sport whose name means "gentle way"
46 Formerly, once
47 Kind of number
49 7'1" N.B.A. star, informally
51 Pince-___
52 Shout to a team, maybe
55 Fall colors
59 *The die is cast
62 *Always the same
65 "Warm"
66 They're rather pointless
67 "Camelot" actor Franco
68 Other, in the barrio

69 Charges
70 Innovative 1982 Disney film
71 Like a busybody

DOWN

1 Wood-turning tool
2 Stern that bows
3 Nellie of opera
4 *Behold the proof
5 Back muscles, for short
6 "The Black Stallion" boy
7 Idiot
8 He said "Slump? I ain't in no slump. I just ain't hitting"
9 Turndown
10 Van Gogh floral subject
11 Bobby of Boston
12 Male cat
13 Title in S. Amer.
19 Getaway alerts, for short
21 Cry before "It's you!"
24 All alternative
25 ___ Grove, N.J.
26 Money in the bank, e.g.
28 Part of a C.E.O.'s résumé
29 Topic: Abbr.
31 *Without which not
32 Black lacquer
33 Filibuster, in a way
34 Alertness aid
36 Bud's comedy sidekick

37 Briefs, briefly
41 "Isn't that beautiful?!"
44 Lacking purpose
48 Round dance official
50 Gallery display
53 Canonized figure
54 One who's not "it"
56 Look after
57 Some Peters
58 Homeless animal
59 Mimicked
60 Pertaining to flying
61 "Follow me!"
62 Leave in stitches?
63 Air quality org.
64 Debussy's "La ___"

by Patrick Blindauer

ACROSS

1 Started a cigarette
6 Sail supporter
10 Rooters
14 Left one's seat
15 Gumbo vegetable
16 Track shape
17 Allotment of heredity units?
19 Parks who pioneered in civil rights
20 Our language: Abbr.
21 Took the blue ribbon
22 Room to maneuver
24 Nuclear power apparatus
27 Top 10 tunes
28 Hole-punching tool
29 Slender cigar
33 Prefix with -hedron
36 Is false to the world
37 Get from ___ (progress slightly)
38 Battle of the ___ (men vs. women)
39 Stadium section
40 Studied primarily, at college
42 Holder of 88 keys
43 Caveman's era
44 Vintage automotive inits.
45 Tennis great Arthur
46 Mediums' meetings
50 Stewed to the gills
53 King Kong, e.g.
54 Lacto-___-vegetarian
55 Sitarist Shankar
56 Preacher's sky-high feeling?
60 Twistable cookie
61 Turn at roulette
62 Decaf brand
63 Give an alert
64 Direction of sunup
65 Sticky problem

DOWN

1 Hearty brew
2 Jim Carrey comedy "Me, Myself & ___"
3 Kingdom east of Fiji
4 Milk for all its worth
5 Pay-___-view
6 Travel by car
7 Closely related (to)
8 Sign at a sellout
9 Bikini wearers' markings
10 TV channel for golfers?
11 State frankly
12 Shuttle-launching org.
13 Murder
18 Delinquent G.I.
23 Greek H's
25 Pasta-and-potato-loving country?
26 Former rival of Pan Am
27 Safe place
29 Mischievous sprite
30 Director Kazan
31 Claim on property
32 Prefix with dynamic
33 Scots' caps
34 Coup d'___
35 Japanese P.M. during W.W. II
36 Mantel
38 Equine-looking fish
41 Take a siesta
42 Split ___ soup
44 Fishing line winder
46 Paid out
47 Nickels and dimes
48 Call to mind
49 Sunken ship finder
50 Furrowed part of the head
51 Dr. Zhivago's love
52 1964 Dave Clark Five song "Glad All ___"
53 Hertz rival
57 Mileage rating org.
58 Cleopatra's biter
59 Eastern "way"

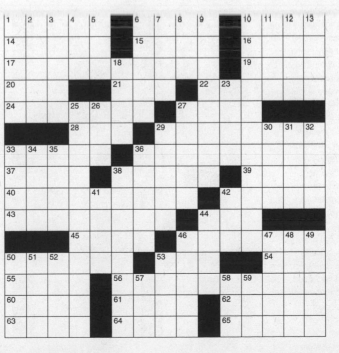

by Fred Piscop

ACROSS

1 Peak
5 Chattered incessantly
10 TV horse introduced in 1955 . . . or a Plymouth model introduced in 1956
14 Partiality
15 Seeing red
16 Prime draft status
17 Drug-yielding plant
18 Opposite of serenity
19 Cartoonist Al
20 Scary sound from the ocean?
23 Park, e.g., in N.Y.C.
25 "Sting like a bee" athlete
26 Having seniority
28 Scary sound from a war zone?
33 Juillet's season
34 Kodiak native
35 Physics unit
36 Theory's start
37 Scary sound from a cornfield?
41 Splinter group
44 Motel-discount grp.
45 Sales slips: Abbr.
49 Galley implement
50 Scary sound from a steeple?
53 Tedious
55 Boot part
56 "Whew!"
57 Misspells, say, as a ghost might at 20-, 28-, 37- and 50-Across?
62 Abominate
63 African antelope
64 Hot rod's rod
67 ___ Lackawanna Railroad
68 Countryish
69 Boot part
70 Card game for three
71 Walk leisurely
72 Stealth bomber org.

DOWN

1 Charles Gibson's network
2 A.F.L.-___
3 Cane cutter
4 Biblical son who sold his birthright
5 Wavelet
6 Language whose alphabet starts alif, ba, ta, tha . . .
7 Child's caretaker
8 Suffix with hypn-
9 Part of a bottle or a guitar
10 Kind of point
11 Helpless?
12 Filled to the gills
13 Big fat mouth
21 Country just south of Sicily
22 Moo goo gai pan pan
23 Lawyers' org.
24 Kilmer of "The Doors"
27 ___ Irvin, classic artist for The New Yorker
29 Cowlick, e.g.
30 Fit for a king
31 Blunder
32 "Long ___ and far away . . ."
36 Creep (along)
38 Name that's an anagram of 27-Down
39 ___ de mer
40 Egyptian dry measure equal to about five-and-a-half bushels
41 Soak (up)
42 Tag for a particular purpose
43 Neighbor of Slovenia
46 Co. addresses, often
47 A duo
48 Crafty
50 Tournament pass
51 Like some music
52 Musically improvise
54 Sport utilizing a clay disk
58 Hospital shipments
59 Styptic agent
60 Part of a fishhook
61 Island with Waimea Bay
62 Gentlemen
65 Meadow
66 Shoemaker's helper, in a fairy tale

by Gary Steinmehl

ACROSS

1 Big stingers
6 Johnny Fever's workplace, in 1970s–'80s TV
10 Amt. at a car dealership
14 Ancient marketplace
15 Mixed bag
16 Siouan tribe
17 Some horizontal lines
18 Carries
19 Birthstone of someone born on Halloween
20 Professional secrets
23 Muslim holy man
26 Amanda of "The Whole Nine Yards"
27 Off-site meetings, maybe
28 Promoted, as a pawn
30 look to court
32 Went bad
33 Formal discourse
34 "Choosy moms choose ___"
37 Ham it up
38 ___ pop
39 Ride the ___ (sit out a baseball game)
40 Heros
41 Red in the middle
42 Large, at Starbucks
43 Elec. Day, e.g.
44 Hockey feat
45 Some urban legends
46 Aussie's neighbor
47 Like some old stores
48 Early seventh-century year
50 Wander
52 Whirlpool
53 U.N. ambassador under Reagan
56 Shows

57 Entr'___
58 Certain flower girl
62 Focal point
63 Honolulu's home
64 Reese of "Touched by an Angel"
65 Plea
66 Swill
67 Balance sheet listing

DOWN

1 Candle material
2 Turkish title
3 Red ___
4 Stain looseners on washday
5 Lip
6 Gobbled up, with "down"
7 Movie for which Jane Fonda won an Oscar
8 Starboard

9 You might strike one
10 Docked
11 Mid-March honoree
12 Map lines
13 New York Cosmos star
21 Like some columns
22 Fig or fir
23 Hurdle for Mensa membership
24 Hawaiian dress
25 Organism needing oxygen
29 Born
31 Can. neighbor
33 Something said while holding a bag
34 Having bad luck, say
35 Mean
36 Spunky
38 Like The Onion
39 War enders

41 Uncooked
42 Designer Diane ___ Furstenberg
44 Honey site
45 Rope material
46 "Sexual Behavior in the Human Male" author
47 Begin, as a hobby
48 Two-sport Sanders
49 Entertainment from a magician
51 Brand name in lawn care
53 Chimpanzee researcher Goodall
54 "Get Smart" org.
55 ". . . ___ bottle of rum"
59 Choices for Chicago commuters
60 Cavs, on a scoreboard
61 Nag (at)

by Ken Stern

194

ACROSS

1 "Lady Marmalade" singer ___ LaBelle
6 Musical phrase
10 On the briny
14 Birdlike
15 Poet ___ Khayyám
16 Butter slices
17 T. S. Eliot title character who measures out his life with coffee spoons
20 Not just recent
21 Muck
22 "The Simpsons" bartender
23 Light throw
26 Studio sign
29 Actress MacDowell of "Groundhog Day"
32 Really impressed
34 Geller with a spoon-bending act
35 Light golden lager
38 ___ Bator, Mongolia
39 Editor out to smear Spider-Man
42 Parti-colored
43 Dance class outfit
44 Quantity: Abbr.
45 Sheep cries
46 Rapids transits
50 A goose egg
52 Phobia
55 Unfortunate sound when you bend over
56 Hay storage locale
58 Saw-toothed
61 Vice president who once famously mashed "potato"
65 Come to shore
66 Baby bassoon?
67 War horse
68 Lyric poems
69 Puppy bites
70 Sexy nightwear

DOWN

1 ___ party (sleepover)
2 Frankie of "Beach Blanket Bingo"
3 Cultivated the soil
4 President who later served as chief justice
5 Initials on a cross
6 Where you might hear "Ride 'em, cowboy!"
7 Little devil
8 Distant
9 Lively '60s dance
10 Kitchen spill catcher
11 Brazil's largest city
12 And so on: Abbr.
13 "___ and ye shall receive"
18 CPR pro
19 Grocery offering
24 California city in a 1968 Dionne Warwick hit
25 Accumulation on the brow
27 Persia, today
28 ___ Tin Tin
30 Its first ad touted "1,000 songs in your pocket"
31 German article
33 Humorist Bombeck
36 Singsong syllables
37 Grain bundle
38 Beef quality graders: Abbr.
39 Guitarist Hendrix
40 747, e.g.
41 Be mistaken
42 La ___, Bolivia
45 Hit, as on the noggin
47 Worn at the edges
48 Like the Marquis de Sade or the Duke of Earl
49 Rapid
51 Unilever skin cream brand
53 Fireplace remnants
54 Necessary: Abbr.
57 Roger Rabbit or Donald Duck
59 Corrosion sign
60 Appraise
61 Female singer's 2001 album that debuted at #1
62 "Dear old" guy
63 Slugger's stat
64 Blouse or shirt

by Jeremy Horwitz

ACROSS

1 Home in an old warehouse district
5 Virus named for a river
10 Trans-Siberian Railroad stop
14 Peculiar: Prefix
15 U.S./Canada early warning syst.
16 City bond, for short
17 Eisenhower was one
20 Move unsteadily
21 Delon of "Purple Noon"
22 Cedar Rapids college
23 2:30, aboard ship
27 Dele undoers
29 Something new
30 Ho Chi Minh's capital
31 Boris Godunov, for one
32 Rove, with "about"
35 Full range
37 It's off the tip of Italy
40 Bad-mouth
41 ___ war syndrome
45 ___ plume
46 Chiang Kai-shek's capital
48 Mountain cats
49 Rests for a bit
52 Singleton
53 "Waiting for Lefty" playwright
54 Like Dickens's Dodger
57 Shortly after quitting time, for many
62 Forearm bone
63 Shul V.I.P.
64 Pizzeria fixture
65 Hot times in France
66 Befuddled
67 Try for a role

DOWN

1 Brit's elevator
2 Garfield's foil
3 Nickel
4 Slugging it out
5 ___'acte
6 Feathery wrap
7 Bobby of the Bruins
8 Dillydally
9 Fruity quencher
10 Brunch dish
11 Wall art
12 Symbol of slowness
13 Ceramists' baking chambers
18 Welcomes, as a guest at one's home
19 Catches red-handed
23 Jack Sprat's taboo
24 Hypotheticals
25 Rome's ___ Veneto
26 Blunders
27 Outbuilding
28 Vehicle with a medallion
32 Request for a congratulatory slap
33 Pierce player
34 Gray concealers
36 End-of-workweek cry
38 At a cruise stop
39 Be worth
42 AP competitor
43 "My Name Is Asher ___"
44 "For shame!"
46 Colorful fishes
47 Helper: Abbr.
49 Brimless cap
50 At least 21
51 "The Family Circus" cartoonist Bil
54 Home to most Turks
55 Iris's place
56 Libraries do it
58 Big Band ___
59 Turn state's evidence
60 "Sesame Street" network
61 Honest ___

by John Underwood

196

ACROSS

1 Scores, as a victory, with "up"
7 Blunted blade
11 Hipster
14 Door sign
15 Fancy club trophies
16 Pale ___
17 Mongol horde, e.g.
18 Romantic goings-on
20 "Rose is a rose is a rose is a rose" writer
21 Clinton cabinet member
22 Poetic land
23 Tupperware sale event
25 Takes a turn
26 City limits sign abbr.
27 Dept. of Labor agcy.
29 N.L. Central team
32 Society column word
34 Erie Canal city
38 What 18-, 23-, 55- and 63-Across each comprises
43 Early time to rise
44 Mahmoud Abbas's grp.
45 Pro-gun org.
46 Catches Z's
49 Star pitchers
52 Chorus after a bad call
55 Catching cold?
60 Annika Sorenstam's org.
61 Fraternity letters
62 Good-looker
63 Cockpit datum
65 Whodunit plot element
66 Vane dir.

67 "You lookin' ___?"
68 Spring bloomers
69 ___ Moines
70 North Sea feeder
71 When many stores open

DOWN

1 Don't go together
2 Must
3 It means "Go with God"
4 Act as a go-between
5 Boarding site
6 Sound of a leak
7 Calculus pioneer
8 Chop-chop
9 Embassy figures
10 Suffix with Brooklyn
11 Where "Aida" premiered
12 Jude Law title role
13 Many Justin Timberlake fans
19 Smooth, musically
21 Was incoherent
24 "All the King's Men" star, 2006
28 Important airport
29 They cross aves.
30 ___-night doubleheader
31 Deli delicacy
33 Eerie ability
35 Novelist Fleming
36 N.B.A. position: Abbr.
37 "___ friend, I . . ."
39 Toto's home
40 "___ Believer"
41 Five Norse kings
42 Points that may have rays
47 Lab tubes
48 Intrigue

50 Debutante's date
51 Confined
52 Short on flavor
53 Say one's piece
54 Shrek's ilk
56 Pillow filler
57 Answer to "Who's there?"
58 David of Pink Panther movies
59 Foie gras sources
64 Pony up
65 "Mamma ___!"

by Richard Chisholm

197

ACROSS

1 Pear variety
5 Filthy place
11 Mardi ___
15 Paul who sang "Puppy Love"
16 Win over
17 Bringing up the rear
18 "Floral" film that was the Best Picture of 1989
21 Ran into
22 Some ales
23 Wilderness photographer Adams
24 Quit, with "out"
25 Glossy alternative
26 "Again!"
27 Gave utterance to
29 Customers
30 Celtic dialect
31 Regional dialect
34 "Floral" film of 2006 with Josh Hartnett and Scarlett Johansson
40 Cowboy contests
41 "Sports Center" channel
43 Feudal workers
47 Traveling group of actors
49 Motown's Franklin
50 Newspapers, TV, radio, etc.
53 Teacher's favorite
54 "Get lost!"
55 System of government
56 La ___, Bolivia
57 "Floral" film of 1986 based on an Umberto Eco novel
60 Swedish soprano Jenny
61 Like some inspections
62 ___-friendly
63 "For" votes

64 Shorthand takers
65 Fictional detective Wolfe

DOWN

1 "You'll regret that!"
2 Written up, as to a superior
3 Easily startled
4 Cleveland cager, for short
5 Group of five
6 Bar of gold
7 Entire range
8 Slug, old-style
9 ___ and turn
10 1812, 2001, etc.: Abbr.
11 Quick look
12 ___ d'être
13 State with conviction
14 Shag, beehive, updo, etc.
19 "Woe ___!"
20 From Copenhagen, e.g.
26 Kazan who directed "On the Waterfront"
28 Grade between bee and dee
29 Atlantic swimmers
31 Cushions
32 Hole-in-one
33 W.B.A. decision
35 The Creator, to Hindus
36 Name repeated in "Whatever ___ wants, ___ gets"
37 Virgo's predecessor
38 Noncommittal agreement
39 One who's making nice
42 EarthLink alternative
43 To a huge degree

44 Jughead's pal
45 One of tennis's Williams sisters
46 Bleachers
47 Gives 10 percent to the church
48 Funnywoman Martha
50 Bullwinkle, e.g.
51 Spritelike
52 "Me, too"
55 Shut (up)
58 Calendar pgs.
59 Hurry

by Harvey Estes

ACROSS

1 Prefix with sphere
5 Assigned stars to
10 Thriving time
14 Jewish ritual
15 Visibly stunned
16 Humorist Bombeck
17 Ornery sort
18 Cutoffs fabric
19 Yemeni port
20 Striptease business?
23 Drive-thru convenience, perhaps
24 Having lunch, say
25 "___ to say this, but . . ."
26 Some auto deals
28 Stereotypical sandwich board diner
31 Young 'un
32 Younger brother, say
33 Knight's attendant
35 Wrestling business?
39 Former "Dateline NBC" co-host Jane
40 Beanery sign
43 Cockpit abbr.
46 Carefully arranged
47 Portugal's place
49 The March King
51 ___-Caps (Nestlé candy)
52 Row C abbr., maybe
53 Comb business?
58 Volcano known to locals as Mongibello
59 Dweller along the Arabian Sea
60 "Darn!"
62 Goatee site
63 Mullally of "Will & Grace"
64 ZZ Top, e.g.
65 Look after
66 Dummy Mortimer
67 Thanksgiving side dish

DOWN

1 "Dancing With the Stars" airer
2 One on a board
3 Jumble
4 ___ buco
5 Figure that's squared in a common formula
6 Go-between
7 Zesty flavor
8 Cast-of-thousands film
9 Floor model
10 Place for an umbrella
11 Tough time
12 Mafia code of silence
13 Unlike drone aircraft
21 Reason to cry "Alas!"
22 Some Japanese-Americans
23 Jungfrau or Eiger
27 Metro map feature
28 A singing Jackson
29 Bacchanalian revelry
30 Polar drudge
33 TV handyman Bob
34 Kind of diagram
36 The Pineapple Island
37 Expected in
38 Sauce for some seafood
41 Cratchit boy
42 Bummed out
43 Appearance
44 Not be able to stomach
45 Submit, as homework
47 Under consideration
48 Dizzy Gillespie's genre
50 Witness's place
51 School locator?
54 Pierre, François, etc.
55 Hood fighters
56 Parakeet keeper
57 Pseudo-cultured
61 Brillo alternative

by Fred Piscop

ACROSS

1 NPR host ___ Conan
5 Prevents, in legalspeak
11 Dental device
14 Chamber music piece
15 Blubber
16 When to get to the airport to pick someone up: Abbr.
17 À la a free-for-all
19 It's definite
20 Western lily
21 Granny, for one
22 ___ Rio, Tex.
23 Become bored by
25 Really easy decision
28 Bum
30 Mimieux of "Where the Boys Are"
31 "Newhart" setting
32 World Series prize
35 Double curves
36 Slogan popularized in the 1980s . . . and a hint to 17-, 25-, 28-, 48-, 51- and 60-Across
39 Fabled "snowmen"
42 Call at home
43 Unruly do
46 Hunky sort
48 Restricted airspace
51 Pitcher's coup
53 Good horseshoe toss
54 Eastern "path"
55 BB's and shells
58 "Whoso diggeth ___ shall fall therein": Proverbs
59 Museum hanging
60 Mediocre
63 Mag. info
64 Suffragist Bloomer
65 Hatcher of film
66 Whatever amount
67 Hal David output
68 ___ race

DOWN

1 To the ___ power
2 Wind and rain cause it
3 Wing part
4 Stuck
5 Fall back
6 Overcharge
7 Of two minds
8 "The Dick Van Dyke Show" catchphrase
9 "The bill and coo of sex" per Elbert Hubbard
10 Lawn base
11 Warming, of sorts
12 Wheaties box adorner
13 Singer Ella ___ Morse
18 Shortly
22 Muralist Rivera
23 ___ Friday's
24 Holiday trees
26 "___ calling!"
27 Hi-___ monitor
29 Little foxes
33 Code-cracking org.
34 Large fishing hook
36 Self-professed ultrapatriot
37 Old Voice of America org.
38 "Gimme a C . . . !," e.g.
39 Derisive word
40 Bibliophile's concern
41 100 percent
43 Handle
44 Like Carter's presidency
45 ___ diem
47 Excessively flattering
49 Repeated word in "She Loves You"
50 1952 Brando role
52 Mideast V.I.P.
56 Saharan land
57 Ear-related
59 Things in tubes
60 Hoedown partner
61 Airline to Oslo
62 Family nickname

by Jim Page

ACROSS

1 Bit of smoke
5 "Jeepers!"
11 Burton who produced "The Nightmare Before Christmas"
14 Popular plant gel
15 Native name for Mount McKinley
16 Long-distance number starter
17 Subversive group
19 Buddy
20 Four: Prefix
21 QB Manning
22 Repulsive
23 Soap or lotion, say
27 Searched
29 Gardner of Hollywood
30 Debtor's promise
31 Wise ones
34 Suspect's excuse
38 ___ Ness monster
40 Where you may find the ends of 17-, 23-, 52- and 63-Across
42 Social slight
43 Actor Hawke
45 Sirius or XM medium
47 Three: Prefix
48 No ___, ands or buts
50 Furry burrowers
52 Notorious stigma
57 Umpteen
58 Fish eggs
59 Mullah's teaching
62 Traveler's stopover
63 Coveted film honor
66 Stocking's tip
67 Hardly hip
68 Drooling dog in "Garfield"
69 Evil spell
70 Freshman's topper
71 Spiffy

DOWN

1 Blow gently
2 Tennis champ Nastase
3 One who'll easily lend money for a hard-luck story
4 Fuel by the litre
5 U.S. health promoter: Abbr.
6 Auto last made in the 1930s
7 Shoreline opening
8 Newswoman Zahn
9 New York city where Mark Twain is buried
10 What it is "to tell a lie"
11 Subject of discussion
12 With everything counted
13 Fracas
18 Flags down, as a taxi
22 Pharmacy containers
24 Vault
25 Ventriloquist Bergen
26 Big electrical project inits.
27 Mah-jongg piece
28 Underlying cause
32 Fed. air quality monitor
33 Marsh plant
35 Period between
36 Jefferson's first vice president
37 Curve-billed wader
39 Hirsute
41 Real sidesplitter
44 Org. for Colts and Broncos
46 Eye-related
49 Calm
51 Charlton of "The Ten Commandments"
52 Suffix with black or silver
53 It gets a paddling
54 Building add-on
55 Puccini opera
56 Pretend
60 Met highlight
61 Assemble
63 Fella
64 Hawaiian dish
65 ___ du Diable

by Lynn Lempel

The New York Times

SMART PUZZLES
Presented With Style

Available at your local bookstore or online at www.nytimes.com/nytstore

St. Martin's Griffin

1

```
C R E D O   T E S S   T U F T
H O M E D   I R O N   A L O E
A G I L E   M I R E   K N O X
F U L L S P E E D A H E A D
F E E   S A W   I K O N
    T A D A   D Y N A M I C
F L E W   U R L   E B O N Y
L I M O   A P A R T   A T R A
A L I A S   M I R   C O E N
G A R B L E D   P E C K
    R U N E   T E L   C O S
  T H E G A M E I S A F O O T
W H O A   M I L D   M A T Z O
E A R S   E S M E   O T T E R
T I N T   L E S S   R E A D Y
```

2

```
A L T O   S T A R   D E C O R
D O H S   O H S O   E X L A X
Z W E I   L I A M   M E E T S
  B E R N I E M A C   C A M
O L D I E   F I N E T U N E S
L O G S O N   E A T S A T
E W E   S H A Q   R E E L S
    E S C A P E P O D
P O S S E   J U D D   D A M
T O P T E N   Q U A R T O
S H O E P H O N E   G L E E M
  L I E   L A U N C H P A D
P A L M S   T E T E   A M I E
S L E E K   E V E N   C O R Y
T A R D Y   S O R T   A N T E
```

3

```
J A L A P A   U S C G   A P E
A B A C U S   R I P A   B O X
B I Z E T S I G N A L   S O P
S T Y   T E H E E   P A O L O
    V I T O   W H A R F
A S W A N   P L A Y L I S Z T
D O I N G S   Y V E S   T O O
O O Z E   L O R E N   P E R K
P T A   S A K I   A M O E B A
T H R O W B A C H   A L L A Y
    D A I S Y   O P I E
B O O K S   B O R I S   H M S
E L F   H A Y D N G O S E E K
E G O   E L M O   G U I L T Y
P A Z   D E E R   Y I P P E E
```

4

```
C U S P   A R C S   G A F F E
A L T O   C O A T   U L C E R
S T E P   H A L E   N I C E R
T R I P L E M I L E S
S A N Y O   B A L M O R A L
  T H R E E F O R O N E
A C T   A I R   K I O W A
L O W   G Y M   P O E   S A D
O B E S E   B O W   T R Y
F R E E R E F I L L S
T A N T A L U M   P A S T A
  N O M O N E Y D O W N
R A B B I   I D O L   E N I D
A D I E U   N A S A   A N N E
T O T E M   G L E N   L Y E S
```

5

```
S N I P   A R E N A   G N A T
T O T E   L A T E R   E I N E
(E)V E R Y B I T A N A N G E(L)
M A M M A   L A P E L   H R E
    I C Y   S I N T A X
(H)A S(T)H E H O T(S)F O R
E V E   T W O T O   T R I P E
R E E D   S T A B S   A D A M
A S K U P   E R I E S   E L I
  A(B)S O L U T(E)W O R S(T)
V A S S A R   D E B
E L Y   T E R P S   D R O V E
T E(L)L S(I)T L I K(E)I T I(S)
C R U E   D E U C E   E T A T
H O M E   A S S A Y   N O L A
```

6

```
C B E R   B A B A S   P O X
H A R A   O X I D E   P O U R
E D I T   N O K I A   I O T A
E T C   S U N O N M O N D A Y
T H I G H S   S V E L T E
O R D E R   J O G   A R E E D
S O L E   D E T A I L
  W E D O N T H U R S D A Y
    L A T E N S   J E E P
A N T E D   A R T   F E R A L
S E A M E N   F E D O R A
S A T O N F R I D A Y   B L Y
I L E T   L A Z A R   B I O S
S O R E   E C O L E   A C N E
I N S   R E D I D   S S G T
```

7

```
M A P S   P R A T E   B A B A
E L O I   L O R A X   O M A N
T E L L M E M O R E   B O Y D
O C E L O T   A P T S   C O D
  M Y C H E R I E A M O U R
C R I M S O N   T R U E
L A C E   R C A   E D S E L
O V A   J A Y M O H R   T A O
D E L T A   P R O   F E S T
  A P A R   E N D I V E S
B E N J A M I N M O O R E
L E A   N A V Y   R E E D I T
I R I S   L A M M E R M O O R
T I L E   I L E N E   A R N O
Z E S T   E S T O S   N E A T
```

8

```
S M O K Y   P I L E D   C A B
L A D L E   R O A R S   I R E
O C E A N B O T T O M   N B A
P E S T   A W A I T   O D O R
      C O T   N I P P E R S
G R A H A M C R A C K E R
P A T   T A R A   G R E B E
A U T O   N O I C E   A L M A
S L A N G   S A L T   L O S
  C R Y S T A L P A L A C E
I C K Y P O O   A D A
T I D E   L O E S S   S E W S
A D O   I D O L W O R S H I P
L E G   D E L L A   B I L L Y
O R S   A R D E N   S E E D S
```

9

```
M O N E T   O K S   A N T Z
A R E N A   V I C I   L O W E
S C A D S   E L A N   I R I S
C A T A S T R O P H E   A R T
  L E A H   E A R T H L Y
B O I L   M E A S U R E
A R R   T E R P   L A T K E S
N E A T H   E A R   T E N T H
C O Q U E T   R O S A   I I E
  S W E P T U P   E T A L
M I S H E A R   T A S K
A L A   B R O K E N H E A R T
Z I N C   A L L O   I O N I A
D A T A   T E E N   P U T O N
A D A M   S E E   S T E T S
```

10

```
T E M P O   D E E R E   Z I P
A V I A N   E N T E R   U S A
C O N T R A C O S T A   L E D
I K E   E T A S   I S S U E S
T E D   C O M   B R E T
  C O M P U T E R C O D E
O G L E R S   S U E   R D A S
P O U N D   M A S   S O I R S
E I A I   R E G   S H I N T O
C O U R T E N E Y C O X
  U R D U   A I R   D A M
B I G M A C   S H O T   O U I
A V A   C O M M O N C O L D S
J E W   T A B O O   U N L I T
A S K   S T A G S   T E S T Y
```

11

```
S P C A   O S L O   C L U E S
H O Y A   I H O P   L E N T O
E N C H I L A D A   O D I S T
A I L E D   W E L T S
V E E D U B   S H E B A N G
E S S   N O S E   O R A T O R
  S N A P T O   R I S E
  S H O O T I N G M A T C H
D Y A D   T A L O N S
A N T O N Y   S E C Y   S R O
S C H M E A R   S W I P E D
  S P E W S   A N O D E
G E T A T   N I N E Y A R D S
P R E L L   T R I O   N E O S
S N A P E   S E T S   E S T A
```

12

```
O P T S   O S I E R   M E S A
H A R I   B A L S A   O P E N
M R I G G I N S A N D M I S S
S C E N E   G A U D Y   L A W
  S A R A   I N C O M E
D O O L I T T L E   E A G E R
U R U   W E E L A S S
E A T S   A R T I S   E W E R
  C A R R I O N   E S E
E N D O R   A T T E M P T T O
D I A T O M   R O E S
I C H   S E E T H   P E P S I
S O L V E A C R O S S W O R D
O L I O   R O O M Y   E T T E
N E A L   A L T E R   E S A S
```

13

R	I	L	E	S	■	W	O	O	D	S	■	J	U	T
A	R	I	E	L	■	A	T	B	A	T	■	U	N	E
C	O	O	K	I	N	G	T	I	M	E	■	S	T	A
I	N	N	■	P	I	E	■	■	I	O	T	A	S	■
E	M	I	R	■	B	R	O	K	E	N	H	O	M	E
R	A	Z	O	R	S	■	P	I	T	■	S	U	E	T
■	N	E	M	O	■	D	E	N	N	Y	■	T	D	S
■	■	■	P	O	K	E	R	G	A	M	E	■	■	■
L	A	P	■	T	U	N	A	S	■	C	U	R	E	■
O	A	R	S	■	R	I	T	■	S	A	R	O	N	G
S	M	O	K	E	D	M	E	A	T	■	O	U	Z	O
T	I	M	I	D	■	■	S	O	L	■	G	Y	N	■
A	L	I	■	I	T	S	O	K	W	I	T	H	M	E
R	N	S	■	C	R	U	D	E	■	R	U	L	E	R
T	E	E	■	T	Y	P	E	D	■	A	B	Y	S	S

14

O	M	A	N	■	P	L	U	S	■	B	R	E	W	S
D	O	L	E	■	A	D	Z	E	■	R	A	C	E	R
I	N	G	A	■	J	O	I	E	■	O	S	H	E	A
S	T	A	R	M	A	P	■	M	E	T	H	O	D	S
T	H	E	M	A	M	A	S	■	S	H	E	■	■	■
■	■	■	I	R	A	■	O	U	T	E	R	E	A	R
S	E	W	S	■	S	T	O	N	E	R	■	E	L	I
T	W	I	S	T	■	A	N	D	■	S	H	O	U	T
O	E	R	■	H	I	R	E	O	N	■	A	C	M	E
P	R	E	V	E	N	T	S	■	O	A	S	■	■	■
■	■	■	A	I	R	■	T	H	E	P	A	P	A	S
F	A	I	R	S	E	X	■	O	N	E	B	E	L	L
A	B	O	I	L	■	B	A	S	T	■	A	L	I	A
R	E	N	E	E	■	O	P	E	R	■	L	E	N	T
M	E	S	S	Y	■	X	R	A	Y	■	L	E	E	S

15

E	P	E	E	S	■	M	A	C	S	■	T	O	F	U
M	I	C	R	O	■	O	S	L	O	■	I	R	I	S
B	L	O	O	D	M	O	N	E	Y	■	N	O	N	O
L	E	N	S	■	A	R	E	A	■	M	O	T	E	S
E	D	O	■	C	H	E	R	R	Y	C	R	U	S	H
M	U	M	B	A	I	■	■	E	V	E	N	S	O	■
S	P	Y	O	N	■	I	P	S	A	■	D	E	W	■
■	■	■	R	E	D	S	T	A	R	T	S	■	■	■
H	I	C	■	■	I	M	A	X	■	H	A	Z	E	L
U	N	A	B	L	E	■	■	S	E	L	E	N	A	■
R	U	B	Y	T	U	E	S	D	A	Y	■	P	T	S
S	T	A	N	D	■	G	L	E	N	■	T	H	R	O
T	E	R	A	■	B	R	I	C	K	L	A	Y	E	R
O	R	E	M	■	M	E	T	A	■	A	C	R	E	D
N	O	T	E	■	I	T	S	Y	■	B	O	S	S	A

16

B	A	M	A	■	A	L	P	S	■	A	T	L	A	S
A	L	E	X	■	H	A	I	L	■	P	E	A	C	E
H	I	G	H	W	A	Y	T	O	H	E	A	V	E	N
A	T	S	E	A	■	S	A	T	E	■	M	A	S	T
■	■	■	A	I	M	■	■	■	E	L	S	■	■	■
R	O	A	D	T	O	P	E	R	D	I	T	I	O	N
H	A	M	■	■	M	I	R	A	■	M	E	N	S	A
O	T	A	R	U	■	N	A	B	■	B	R	A	I	N
M	E	T	E	R	■	O	T	I	S	■	N	E	C	■
B	R	I	D	G	E	T	O	N	O	W	H	E	R	E
■	■	■	D	E	M	■	■	T	W	O	■	■	■	■
G	A	T	E	■	I	D	E	S	■	I	N	U	S	E
R	O	U	N	D	T	R	I	P	T	I	C	K	E	T
I	N	N	E	R	■	O	N	U	S	■	H	E	W	N
N	E	E	D	Y	■	P	E	R	K	■	O	S	S	A

17

F	A	D	■	S	H	O	W	E	R	■	P	A	G	E
O	N	E	■	P	A	R	O	L	E	■	E	A	R	N
O	N	A	G	A	I	N	O	F	F	A	G	A	I	N
L	E	N	O	■	R	E	D	■	E	L	A	T	E	■
■	■	■	L	E	D	■	■	S	L	O	E	■	■	■
I	S	O	F	F	O	N	A	T	A	N	G	E	N	T
C	A	N	S	O	■	A	L	E	S	■	S	L	O	W
I	R	S	■	R	E	V	E	R	S	E	■	E	V	E
N	E	E	R	■	F	A	V	E	■	F	I	N	E	R
G	E	T	O	N	T	H	E	O	F	F	R	A	M	P
■	■	■	P	A	S	O	■	■	A	S	A	■	■	■
A	S	T	E	R	■	■	F	I	R	■	Q	T	I	P
S	W	I	T	C	H	P	O	S	I	T	I	O	N	S
K	I	L	O	■	A	R	L	E	N	E	■	M	C	S
S	T	E	W	■	N	O	D	E	A	L	■	E	A	T

18

M	A	R	C	■	A	C	A	R	■	D	O	V	E	S
C	L	E	O	■	S	H	O	E	■	U	P	O	N	E
D	I	D	N	O	H	A	R	M	■	M	T	I	D	A
V	E	I	G	H	T	T	B	I	R	D	■	C	O	T
I	N	G	E	A	R	■	■	N	O	U	S	E	■	■
■	■	■	R	R	A	T	E	D	B	M	O	V	I	E
M	I	L	■	E	Y	E	D	■	■	S	W	O	O	N
A	C	A	D	■	S	N	I	F	F	■	S	T	U	D
R	O	M	E	O	■	■	T	R	E	S	■	E	S	S
V	N	E	C	K	T	S	H	I	R	T	S	■	■	■
■	■	■	B	A	S	I	C	■	■	R	E	A	D	M	E
N	O	R	■	I	P	H	O	N	E	E	M	A	I	L
C	H	A	N	G	■	E	X	I	T	P	O	L	L	S
O	N	I	O	N	■	M	E	N	E	■	A	L	L	I
S	O	N	G	S	■	A	N	O	D	■	N	Y	S	E

19

```
SCRAP  ALBEE  CAT
ALAMO  BOOMS  HUE
SIMPLEASABC   IRE
HOP  LACE  RAGLAN
     DUCK  RAPIDLY
ZENITH  RECESS
ALONE  VEXED   PEA
NIPS  SELES   FLAX
EAR  ACRES  SLAVE
   OPPOSE  STAYED
ROBERTA  SOUP
ELLIOT  SELF   ROW
ADE  PIECEOFCAKE
DEM  OSCAR  EAGLE
SRO  SHOTS  DREAD
```

20

```
LIP  LASSIE   ZEDS
AKA  ELAINE   OTOE
MEW  TOWNCOUNCIL
BANDITOS   MEHTA
   TENOF  SFPD
SHIPOFFOOLS   PCS
MACON   RBI   PHAT
ARKS  GHOST  AIRE
SKEE  LOU   OILER
HST  BUSTERBROWN
   JUTE   MOVES
ASHES   SIDEDOOR
STORYTELLER   PDA
KERR  STAINS  HIP
SWAY  PEYOTE  YET
```

21

```
RARE  ASHES   SILO
EXES  STENO   INON
LITTLEONES   EDGE
OLE  CAIN   ARI
ALLAH  CALIBRATE
DALLAS  OCEANIC
   VINTAGE   ANO
EVAMARIESAINT
ALI   PULSARS
DORITOS  WOBBLE
SIGNONTHE  UNION
   IVY  DARN  MAD
JANE  DOTTEDLINE
AXIS  IRVIN  ONEA
MEAT  YESNO  LIRR
```

22

```
JAGS  RULES   VEST
IRAQ  APART   AXIS
LIEU  REPRO   VERA
LALALAND   PHASER
   ROAD  LIEV
LIVETV  LETLOOSE
ACE  SIXAM  MOBIL
SEEM  SETUP  MACE
SARAH  RERAN  MEN
OXYMORON  PAJAMA
   APEX   JADE
FITSIN  BABAWAWA
AREA  ADOBE  FLAT
MAXI  MAMBA  RENT
ESTD  EMBAR  OXEN
```

23

```
LOBBY  SANS   METZ
AWIRE  ETAT   ARIE
PENAL  NOVA   IAMB
SNOWLEOPARD   TOR
   CLEAR  LEONORA
ECU  DRIP   ANA
BALE  STA  TOCSIN
BLACK  AND  WHITE
SCROLL  DAB  OMEN
   LIE  AMAS  UMA
SPRINTS  PROWL
KOI  KILLERWHALE
USSR  TOON  HOTEL
NEED  BETE  ALOSS
KYRA  ESTD  TERSE
```

24

```
IHAD   TIED   SHAM
TOMEI  HOYA   NAPE
CROWNJEWEL   URSA
HASAGO  ADLIBBED
   ROYS   ANNO
PITSTOPS  SCORNS
CRI  SUITS  ASSOC
LICE  STEEL  EERO
ANKLE  SITAR  AMT
BALERS  NOVELLAS
   EMIT   FILA
TYPECAST  SOWETO
ASIN  CLAWHAMMER
DENT  KITE  DAMNS
ARKS  SPED   NATO
```

25

```
S T E M . U R I S . J A F A R
L A V A . P E C K . A T E I N
A L A I . T R E E . G R A D S
P E N T H O U S E S U I T E .
. . R A I N . H A S H .
O D D E S T . B E E R K E G S
F R I D A . F O L D . R O I
F I R S T C L A S S C A B I N
T E T . H A T E . A T O N E
O D Y S S E Y S . I D T A G S
. T O E S . I N R E .
. F R O N T R O W C E N T E R
S L I T S . A B O O . D E L I
C A C H E . M I N D . E X E C
I N K E D . P E T E . E T C H
```

26

```
R E A L . A D A M . K I N D A
A L T O . P A R E . A R D O R
P H O N E B I L L . B O A S T
T I M E X . S O T . O N K E Y
. . L A C . S C O W .
E A S Y M A R K . E M I L I A
B B C . S T O N E S . L A N G
E N U F . S O O T S . L Y T E
R E B A . E M B A N K . U R N
T R A S H Y . S T A N D P A T
. T E E M . S U E .
W E L B Y . I T S . T A E B O
A L O U D . S H O W E R R O D
D E C C A . E R I E . M I L E
S M O K Y . R U L E . E N D S
```

27

```
G A S . F E T U S . M A T E S
A R P . I R I S H . I C I L Y
L E I . G A M E O F C H E S S
S A D C A S E . P O K E D A T
. . E A R . R E D .
F A R R O C K A W A Y . L A G
L A N E . A N T I . L O D E
A R E S . B A S S O . O N I T
M O S S . V E E P . A G E E
E N T . S H E A S T A D I U M
. I T A . D E S .
G R A N O L A . F I D D L E S
D E C K O F C A R D S . A P E
A B O I L . T R A I T . N E W
Y A W N S . S E T G O . D E N
```

28

```
M I C E . M A I M S . R A J A
A S E A . A R D E N . E V E R
R E N T . N E E D L E W O R K
X E S . K I T E D . T A N K S
. . O P R A H . L A H R .
H U R R I C A N E L A M P .
E S S E S . E R I N . L O A
A S H Y . T O A S T . P A I L
T R I . S H U T . S A Y N O
. P O T A T O P A N C A K E
. N E I L . E D I T S .
A B I D E . A E S O P . C O E
F A C E P O W D E R . S E X Y
A L E C . T R I T E . K N E E
R I S K . B Y E A R . Y E N S
```

29

```
M E N U . U S A I R . P L O T
U S E R . R A B B I T E A R S
S T A N . T I B E T A N Y A K
T O T . O E N O . S T A .
S P H I N X . T H E T A N G O
. R E T E . A L E . C R T
G U A V A . N A Z I . S H I H
I T S A L L G R E E K T O M E
R E I N . A R A L . R A R E R
T R A . A V A . S A A R .
H O M E G A M E . B A R H O P
. I T I . T I L L . A M A
F I N A L P H A S E . B R A S
C O O P E R A T E S . I S N T
C U R E . O N S E T . C H I A
```

30

```
A K I N . A P E D . A R T O O
P A N E . L O G O . B E A N S
A B S E N C E O F M A L I C E
C O O . B O T . F U T I L E
H O L E C A R D . D E S P O T
E M E R . Y A W P . H I V E
. I S P . N A I L . P E N
. V A C U U M C L E A N E R .
B O G . I N R E . S P A .
O T I S . C T R S . T A R P
D E T A C H . S P A C E B A R
. D A Y L I T . I R E . O T O
N O T H I N G I N C O M M O N
S W E E P . I D E E . A B U T
A N D Y S . F O R D . E S T O
```

31

```
J E F F █ S P A T █ P A W A T
O P I E █ H U G O █ A S I D E
G E N T L E B E N █ R I N D S
S E N I O R █ R E D C R O S S
█ █ D E P P █ W E E █ █
O P T █ W A R M W E L C O M E
C R O W S █ F A I L █ A N O N
T I K I █ L I S Z T █ L E N D
E D E N █ U R S A █ B L U T O
T E N D E R M E R C Y █ P E W
█ █ C R I █ D A N K █ █
L O C H N E S S █ N O I D E A
E L L I E █ K I N D W O R D S
G L O M S █ I D O L █ S E N T
S A G E T █ M E R E █ K W A I
```

32

```
R U B I K █ S N U B █ J P E G
O T E R I █ K A T O █ U R G E
W I E S T █ A R A L █ B A R R
S L R █ K I T C H E N I T E M
█ B L A M E S █ R E L E T S
S I E S T A █ M O R E █ █
C O I T █ G A P E █ D E P T H
A W L █ B E L O N G S █ O U I
M A Y B E █ E T U I █ E K E S
█ █ R I A S █ N L W E S T
L E G E N D █ E A S I E R █
I L L E G A L D R U G █ T O M
B R O Z █ G I S T █ H E A V E
R O B E █ E R E I █ T Y K E S
A Y E S █ S A L E █ S E E R S
```

33

```
B I L █ A T E M P O █ P A A R
E M U █ S A L A A M █ R A M A
A C C O W L I N G S █ E M I L
C L I N I C █ O K S █ I L L
H O N O R █ L C D █ A D L A I
E N D █ L E I L A █ Y E N T E
D E A F █ A L A █ I N N E E D
█ █ O J S I M P S O N █ █
C A P L E T █ P I E █ Y A P S
O L D I E █ D O T E D █ R O T
M A J O R █ A N Y █ E A G L E
P B A █ S I P █ S A V O I R
T A M A █ D H L A W R E N C E
O M E N █ O N E B I T █ N E O
N A S T █ L E G A T O █ E D S
```

34

```
B A A █ T E R M █ W R E S T S
E L L █ A L E E █ E A R T H A
R E G █ L A V E N D E R O I L
G R A P E N U T S █ A N N E
S T E R N █ E S C █ N N E
█ █ I T S █ H O T T U B
S P A S █ N I S S A N █ O N A
P L U M T U C K E R E D O U T
C O I █ O B E Y E D █ E L M S
A D O P T S █ Y E P █ █
█ P O E █ A W E █ M O R O N
S T A T █ L I L A C T I M E
P U R P L E P R O S E █ P E I
U N T I E S █ E P E E █ E G G
R E S E T S █ D E A D █ N A H
```

35

```
H I F I █ C A N D O █ E T N A
A R A N █ S H I E R █ T H E N
H O D S C I E N C E █ T A R T
A N S E L █ M O O G █ A T O Z
█ █ T A B █ O O P S █ █
T S P █ N A T I O N A L G O D
W O R M █ A R C S █ T A R R Y
A R I A █ L A I R S █ C O A L
N E C K S █ I N I T █ E S T A
G R E E T I N G C O D █ S E N
█ G M A N █ W E S █ █
A H O Y █ A L E E █ L I M I T
L O U D █ B O D C O L L E G E
T O G A █ I D I O M █ A M O S
O K E Y █ T E E N S █ S O R T
```

36

```
P I U S █ B O R N █ S H O T S
E G G O █ E L I A █ T O U C H
C O L D S N A P S █ O U T E R
K R I S T I █ A P O S T L E
█ █ A C E S █ A G E O L D
C O N C R E T E █ R E V █ █
U S E A S █ T R U E █ O L G A
P H A T █ C A L L S █ T E E N
S A L T █ A S I N █ C E D E D
█ █ L O P █ N A G A S A K I
F L E E C E █ G E A R █ █
R E A P E R S █ L O W K E Y
I N T R A █ L O C A L H E R O
E Y E O N █ I B E X █ A M I D
S A N D S █ T I N Y █ M O N A
```

37

```
B L I G H   A R C H   S T I R
A I M E E   M I C A   T A D A
M E E T M E I N S T L O U I S
B O A S   A D S   P O P T O P
A N N O Y S   E M I R S
      R E E D   I N D U T C H
S L E E P L E S S   S P R A Y
K A T   S C O U T   O L D
I D T A G   I N S E A T T L E
S E E S R E D   E S A I
      A I M E D   T R E M O R
D E A R M E   U K E   D O R A
A U T U M N I N N E W Y O R K
U R A L   D R N O   E E R I E
B O D E   S K E W   E D E N S
```

38

```
H B O M B   G U A R D   T H E
M O T E L   E N L A I   R A T
M A C A U   S P A N G L I S H
      D E S T E   R E N T A
S O W   S T A G F L A T I O N
C H O R T L E   R I M
A G R E E   S E Z   S H O O
P O R T M A N T E A U W O R D
E D Y S   B O Y   N A N A S
      F I T   T A N G E L O
G U E S S T I M A T E   S S N
U N L I T   E R M A S
C A M C O R D E R   T H A W S
C P O   P A U S E   L I G E R
I T S   S P E E D   Y P R E S
```

39

```
G A Z A   R E P E L   M O J O
A W E S   E R O D E   A B U T
P A R T   D I G I T   N E M O
  Y O U R E N O T M Y T Y P E
      D E E   E A R
I N E E D M O R E S P A C E
T A R N S   V I N E S   O P T
C O N T   M E L E E   P I S A
H M S   S O R E R   G A L O P
  I T S N O T Y O U I T S M E
      P A D   G P S
W E V E G R O W N A P A R T
E L S E   I H E A R   J I N X
A M I D   N I G H T   A G U Y
R O X Y   G O O S E   K A T Z
```

40

```
E A S E   B O O N S   T H A T
B L O C   R A D I O   H O P S
B A D H A I R D A Y   A R I E
      O N E   C A B I N E T
I N P E N   T R I   A L E C S
L A O S   S A N D R A D E E
L I L   D I A L   I B N
  L I V E F R E E O R D I E
  O A S   I L S A   D A B
P L A Y D O U G H   T O R O
A U R A E   P H I   J O L L Y
T R I G R A M   C O W
R I S E   P O S T A G E D U E
I N T R   E S T E S   R O S A
A G A S   S T Y L E   S T A R
```

41

```
A C S   D E I O N   I N A W E
R U E   A R T O O   C U T I N
R O W I N G I M P L E M E N T
O M E N S   P R E   B E G S
W O R D O F C H O I C E
      N I L   B A R R E L
D I S C   J O B   A T B A T
O P P O S I T E O F N E A T H
Z O R R O   T A O   N Y S E
  D Y N A S T   K I D
  B R U I N S L E G E N D
A F A R   N E O   C O L O R
M I N E R S D I S C O V E R Y
O C T A L   U S H E R   C A L
R A I D S   P E E L S   T H Y
```

42

```
T A T S   E B A Y   C H U M P
W H I M   L O M E   Y E N T A
I O T A   L O A M   B L A N D
X M A R K S T H E T O P S
T E N T O   N O R   H U E
  S H O O T I N G R A T S
M A G   L U L U   S E M I S
A L O E   R E R I G   D E L E
S O B E R   O D E S   D E N
T H E L A S T W A R T S
S A T   F I E   A U R A E
  W A T C H Y O U R P E T S
A D E L E   R O L L   P L O T
S N E E R   A R E A   L A N E
P A N E S   N E O N   E Y E S
```

43

```
A V E C   S T R A W   S Y N C
H I L O   P R A D A   H E A L
A V E R   R E P E L   R O S A
B A C K B A Y     L E E W A Y
      T O N S   S P E W
A D D I N G   B I L L D A N A
W I E L D   O N U S   S E M
A X L E   S L A N G   S C A B
S I T   I N O R   P E A R L
H E A D C O L D   E L A P S E
      H O W L   A X E L
V A C A N T   S I D E B E T
I G O R   I M A C S   V O T E
S E A M   R O B O T   E R O S
A S T A   E T A T S   L E N T
```

44

```
A L K A   S L A V   F L O R A
L A N G   H A L O   L E M O N
I T E R   E X C I T A T I O N
C E L E B   A L O T   T K O
E X T E R M I N A T O R
      T E A R   S U B W A Y
E X P O R T E R S   T I R E S
C E E   S N E A D   I R E
O N E A M   E X T R A C T O R
L A N C I A   E E R O
      E X T R A D I T I O N S
D A S   E R I E   S N A I L
E X P O S I T I O N   A T K A
K E A N U   Z O R A   G E E K
E S T O P   Y U R T   E R S E
```

45

```
A C D C   M E S A S   J A V A
W A I L   E X A L T   O X E N
E S A U   T E M P O   W E N T
  A L B E R T   W I L L I E
      L E E C H E D
C L A R E   R H O   O V U M
W O M E N S   A B O   A N I N
T H E M A N F R O M U N C L E
S A B U   L O L   B R Y A N T
  N A S A   R E D   G A P E S
      L A D Y E V E
M I L T I E   F E S T E R
U T A H   S A B I N   A D A M
S E M I   O N E N D   P I C A
T M E N   P I N E S   S T E W
```

46

```
D I T C H   B O G   Q U I E T
I T A L O   A D O   U L T R A
G S U I T   B O A   E N T E R
I M P O S T E R T U N A
N E E   E A R   E M T   T E A
    M A T U R E P I N O T S
  A G I T A T E   N E W A T
E T N A   S H I L L   V E T O
S W A M P   G O O B E R S
  P A T I O M U N S T E R
Y R S   I A N   E S T   K I A
  P E R M U T A T I O N S
S U S A N   A R I   O M A N I
A N T I C   D I M   R I L E D
C O Y L Y   E S E   S N A R E
```

47

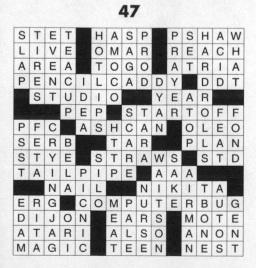

```
S T E T   H A S P   P S H A W
L I V E   O M A R   R E A C H
A R E A   T O G O   A T R I A
P E N C I L C A D D Y   D D T
  S T U D I O   Y E A R
    P E P   S T A R T O F F
P F C   A S H C A N   O L E O
S E R B   T A R   P L A N
S T Y E   S T R A W S   S T D
T A I L P I P E   A A A
    N A I L   N I K I T A
E R G   C O M P U T E R B U G
D I J O N   E A R S   M O T E
A T A R I   A L S O   A N O N
M A G I C   T E E N   N E S T
```

48

```
M O S H   J A I L S   Z E T A
A S T O   A D D U P   I C O N
T H E T O W E L S I N T H A T
T A P I R   S E T T O   O D S
      T A I   E L I
H O T E L W E R E S O B I G I
A T O M   O L A V   S O S A D
R E Y   S N I V E L S   T V S
D R O M E   H E R O   P L E A
C O U L D J U S T B A R E L Y
      B A A   E P A
S E T   T I M E S   A N W A R
C L O S E M Y S U I T C A S E
A B L E   E S T E R   E D E N
M A L E   S T A R E   S E A T
```

49

B	A	T	H	■	B	A	W	L	■	I	N	C	A
A	L	A	I	■	G	E	N	R	E	■	D	E	A	R
S	I	L	L	■	M	E	D	E	A	■	L	A	N	K
H	E	L	L	O	S	T	R	A	N	G	E	R	■
■	N	Y	E	T	■	E	T	T	A	■	B	A	Y
■	L	O	O	K	W	H	O	S	H	E	R	E
S	T	S	■	R	E	S	■	P	O	E	M	S
H	A	N	D	G	U	N	■	N	O	S	I	R	E	E
A	B	O	I	L	■	R	A	W	■	S	D	S
H	O	W	V	E	Y	O	U	B	E	E	N
S	O	P	■	N	O	U	N	■	O	O	P	S
■	L	O	N	G	T	I	M	E	N	O	S	E	E
C	M	O	N	■	U	L	N	A	S	■	D	E	A	L
H	O	W	L	■	R	A	T	S	O	■	L	U	L	L
I	T	S	Y	■	T	W	O	S	■	E	D	Y	S

50

A	E	R	A	T	E	■	M	O	D	E	L	A
R	U	I	N	O	U	S	■	H	E	L	I	X	E	S
C	R	O	S	S	R	E	F	E	R	E	N	C	E	S
T	E	T	■	T	A	D	■	I	V	E
I	K	E	A	■	B	A	N	D	B	■	U	S	E	S
C	A	R	L	Y	L	E	■	A	I	M	L	E	S	S
■	D	O	A	■	G	E	N
P	R	E	A	K	N	E	S	S	S	T	A	K	E	S
S	U	V	■	O	C	T	O	P	U	S	■	E	S	L
S	N	I	P	■	S	A	T	Y	R	■	T	Y	C	O
■	A	L	E	S	■	M	I	R	A
A	R	E	E	L	■	S	A	P	■	A	K	I	R	A
D	A	Y	L	I	G	H	T	S	A	V	I	N	G	S
A	C	E	■	T	E	E	T	I	M	E	■	G	O	P
M	E	D	■	S	T	A	Y	S	I	N	■	S	T	S

51

A	S	T	A	B	■	E	X	E	R	T	■	C	A	M
N	E	H	R	U	■	S	E	N	O	R	■	A	L	E
O	L	E	I	C	■	P	R	A	D	O	■	T	I	N
■	A	S	K	I	N	■	M	I	N	T	S	E	T
K	I	T	T	E	N	■	M	E	N	■	R	E	N	O
G	R	E	A	T	S	E	A	L	■	B	U	Y	E	R
B	A	R	■	S	I	N	S	■	M	E	L	E	E	S
■	R	E	S	T	S	E	A	S	Y
P	T	B	O	A	T	■	E	M	I	T	■	R	E	D
R	H	E	T	T	■	M	U	S	T	S	E	E	T	V
E	R	N	O	■	P	A	R	■	R	E	T	I	E	D
L	E	T	S	E	A	T	■	F	E	L	O	N
I	E	S	■	K	N	U	T	E	■	L	I	S	Z	T
M	R	E	■	E	E	R	I	E	■	E	L	I	E	S
S	S	N	■	S	L	E	P	T	■	R	E	N	E	E

52

M	A	C	S	■	O	R	K	I	N	■	K	U	R	D
I	T	U	P	■	S	O	A	M	I	■	I	R	O	N
N	E	L	L	■	H	I	T	O	N	■	E	S	T	A
C	A	P	I	T	A	L	O	F	J	A	V	A	■
E	R	A	T	O	■	F	A	Q	■	M	A	G
■	M	I	C	E	■	U	S	A	I	R
A	R	S	■	B	R	O	A	D	W	A	Y	J	O	E
S	H	A	G	■	A	T	R	I	A	■	R	O	L	E
C	O	M	P	A	N	Y	P	E	R	K	■	R	I	D
A	D	M	A	N	■	S	U	M	O
P	A	Y	■	T	A	S	■	C	H	A	K	A
■	S	T	I	C	K	I	N	T	H	E	M	U	D
Z	O	O	S	■	C	E	D	A	R	■	M	I	D	I
I	L	S	A	■	T	I	L	D	E	■	A	T	O	M
P	E	A	R	■	S	N	E	A	K	■	N	Y	S	E

53

S	P	A	S	■	L	E	F	T	S	■	O	B	I	T
L	A	I	C	■	U	R	I	A	H	■	F	A	D	E
I	N	S	O	L	V	E	N	C	Y	■	T	W	I	T
D	E	L	T	A	■	C	E	O	■	H	E	D	G	E
■	D	E	S	P	O	T	S	■	R	A	N	I
■	M	S	U	■	S	M	O	G	■	N	A	P
P	A	C	E	■	T	H	E	E	Y	E	■	E	C	O
I	R	O	N	O	R	E	■	G	A	N	G	S	U	P
G	E	M	■	F	A	I	S	A	L	■	A	S	P	S
S	A	M	■	A	G	R	A	■	T	I	M
■	U	R	G	E	■	R	H	Y	M	E	R	S
G	E	N	I	E	■	M	A	E	■	A	S	H	E	S
O	V	I	D	■	M	E	L	A	N	C	H	O	L	Y
R	I	S	E	■	R	E	E	V	E	■	O	N	E	S
E	L	M	S	■	S	K	E	E	T	■	W	E	S	T

54

M	P	S	■	G	R	E	T	A	■	N	A	O	M	I
O	A	T	■	L	O	G	O	N	■	U	R	B	A	N
O	N	E	S	E	C	O	N	D	■	S	E	E	D	S
L	A	N	C	E	■	E	R	E	■	A	D	M
A	M	O	R	■	N	O	D	E	C	I	S	I	O	N
H	A	S	A	C	O	W	■	W	O	N	■	E	N	E
■	P	R	I	E	D	■	P	A	N	E	D
■	M	R	P	E	R	S	O	N	A	L	I	T	Y
S	E	E	Y	A	■	C	I	G	A	R
L	A	S	■	T	A	G	■	L	A	Y	D	O	W	N
O	N	T	H	E	L	E	V	E	L	■	A	R	I	A
■	W	E	E	■	P	I	A	■	I	T	A	L	S
R	E	A	M	S	■	S	P	L	I	T	E	N	D	S
E	L	S	I	E	■	H	O	O	D	S	■	G	E	E
F	L	Y	N	N	■	A	R	T	S	Y	■	E	R	R

55

```
S P A R   W O O D S   P R E K
L E G O   A B B I E   R O T E
A R E A   D E I S M   A O N E
B U D D H I S T H O L Y M A N
      S A N E     L E S
S A W I N G   M A I D   C A W
P R I D E   B A R N   M O P E
A N D E S P A C K A N I M A L
M I E S   O D E S   E N A C T
S E N   A R E S   D A I S E S
      A L T     D O T S
B L A Z E I N B R O O K L Y N
E A S T   C A R O M   I I I I
N I T E   O P I N E   R E N T
E R I C   S A T E D   T U G S
```

56

```
M U F F S   L A W   A D U L T
A T A L E   A S H   C I G A R
D E T A T   S P O R T S H O E
T R A I T S   C R I E R
V O L L E Y B A L L   A B C S
      S E R E   L I E L O W
S T L   I A M B   S L A K E
T H E Y C A N B E S P I K E D
A I R E D   S A L T   E S E
G R O S S E   L A S S
E D Y S   F R U I T P U N C H
      I N G O T   S E N O R A
S H O R T H A I R   A L D E N
T H R E W   S L Y   K I T E D
S H E E T   T E E   S T O P S
```

57

```
O M E G A   T Y P E   N A P S
N A I L S   R E E L   O L E O
O N E S F A N C Y   T O R A
      S A I D S O   T I E U P
T O P S I D E   S C A M
I R A   L E I F   P R E F A B
A I R   S N L   R O T A R Y
R O O S T   S I T   T O R M E
A L L U R E   N H L   R I B
S E E P I N   T E A K   A N Y
      A P O P   A I L A R G E
P L A T E   E S T E E M
H U T U   N O E X P E N S E
I N O N   M A M A   T N O T E
L A N E   E L E M   O D D E R
```

58

```
C R A G   S C U B A   B A A S
R O N A   E A S E L   L U L L
I B I S   W R E S T   O R L Y
B O M B O N B R O A D W A Y
S T E A M   S T R O P
      G A W K   S T I F L E
E A R   N A A C P   P L A Y
S W A Y I N T H E B R E E Z E
S E G O   T I A R A   W E D
O D E S S A   T A B S
      E U R O S   B O A T S
  C O M E D I A N W I L S O N
S A K I   E L S I E   V I N E
A L I T   N E S T S   E D G E
G L E E   T R Y S T   S E A R
```

59

```
R E N E W   S O F A   T A S K
A R O S E   E D E R   B L U E
P E N A L   S E A M A I D E N
      M I L I T A R Y B R A S S
O W E   T O E   B I D
R A M   O U T W O R E   P A R
G I B E D   O D A   M E N U
I V E G O T N O S T R I N G S
E E R O   W I L   E X M E T
S R S   B O X F U L S   A L L
      A R B   N E O   N A E
S A N T A A N A W I N D S
O R C H E S T R A   A D H O C
C I A O   E W E R   N A I L S
K A R L   S T A Y   T Y P E A
```

60

```
G L E N   A C H   C H E Z
R U F U S   B R E A   R O L E
E R I C H   C A N D L E P I N
W I L L A N D G R A C E
  D E E R E   I N D   D A M
      A E S O P   O T S E G O
F A R R   T R O T   V O C A L
A N E W   S E W E R   L O P E
I N L A W   S E R E   A Y E S
T I A R A S   R I D E R
H E X   I C H   I N F R A
  S T A Y I N G A L I V E
H O R S E R A C E   C A P O S
U N I T   S T O W   T R O I S
M O M S   T N T   E N D O
```

61

```
C L A N . S C A R F . E N D S
Y A L E . L O W E R . V I E W
S T O W . I N A N E . I N C A
T H E T I M E Y O U E N J O Y
. . O N L Y . . D E C A Y S .
E V E N L Y . P A I N E . . .
M E N S A . A U R A . S A S S
I N C . W A S T I N G . M A O
L I E U . R E I D . E P O X Y
. . P E C A N . S L A K E S .
M O O L A H . S T I R . . . .
I S N O T W A S T E D T I M E
N A S A . A W A R E . I D O L
E K E D . Y O K E L . N E S S
R A T S . S L E W S . G A T E
```

62

```
E R A S E . A S A H I . J I M
X E R O X . T A L E S . A M O
A L E X C O M F O R T . C P U
M O S . U P S E T . H I K E R
. . E S E . . . N A P K I N .
L I O N E L H A M P T O N . .
E N V Y . S A T Y R S . I S T
F L E A S . I R R . O F F E R
T A R . A S T E R N . A E R O
. B I L L I E H O L I D A Y .
S A U C E R . . W A R . . . .
H E R E S . A M A I N . P T A
A I D . T H E I N N C R O W D
R O E . A I O L I . E E R I E
P U N . X E N O N . T O N G S
```

63

```
A D S . W W W . H E R S E L F
B U M . A H A . A T E A L O T
C H A P L I N . H O T L I P S
. L I L T . P A N D A . . . .
B I L L . E M U S . . A C R O
A M M O . F E R . B E M O A N
S P I T B A L L . L E S L I E
E R N . O C T . F A R . D D S
M O D I N E . R I C O C H E T
E V E N E D . O R K . A E R O
N E D S . B O M B . R A S P .
. O L L A S . E V E R . . . .
B I G F O O T . M A E S T R O
A M I A B L E . A R E . E N D
P A T R O L S . C D S . D A D
```

64

```
A L E C . S P E E D . B A A L
M I D I . P R U D E . A R N O
P E E R . H O R A S . N A T O
U N C L E T O M S C A B I N .
. . L I R E . . . E O N . . .
I R E M E M B E R M A M A . .
S N A R E . L I T E . . O R E
I S I S . S P I N S . P U R E
P U N . S T A N . F E R A L .
. M Y C O U S I N V I N N Y .
. . L O N . . . O I L S . . .
A L L I N T H E F A M I L Y .
P A I N . C A L E B . O Y E Z
S T A G . A R I E L . N O T A
O H M Y . R E E S E . S N I P
```

65

```
L O R D . J E A N . S C H M O
O P U S . A B L E . C H U R N
W H I T E S A L E . R O S I E
M E N . R O Y . S L E P T . .
A L I S O N . C O L E S L A W
S I N U S . C O N A N . E Y E
S A G S . P A N . M E S S E S
. . H E A D S T A R T . . . .
L A R I A T . I R S . O A K S
A B E . T A N G Y . A M P L E
B U C K S K I N . T I P P E R
. A N A I S . K I M . R E P .
A L L O W . S A N D S T O N E
D E L T A . A L O E . O V E N
S I S S Y . N I B S . T E X T
```

66

```
H E L I X . A T O N . L O O T
O R A T E . R E I N . I O T A
S A R A S O T A L E I P Z I G
E T A L . M I S C . T R E S S
. . . I S I S . O N C E . . .
C A L C U T T A L E H A V R E
E L Y S E . R O M . D I E D .
L E I . D O G T R O T . S I G
E R N S . P O I . U P O N E .
B O G O T A L E N I N G R A D
. . T O L D . O M A R . . . .
S I G H T . S A L A . A N T I
T A L E O F T W O C I T I E S
A G A R . T A R S . D E C A L
B O D E . D R Y S . A D E L E
```

67

S	H	I	P			S	K	I	M			P	E	E	P	S
P	A	N	E			H	E	M	I			E	X	T	R	A
A	S	T	R	O	N	A	U	T			O	A	T	E	S	
R	A	H			M	O	N	S	T	E	R	M	A	S	H	
S	T	E	R	E	O				S	L	I	P				
		W	A	L	K	T	O			B	A	L	S	A	M	
J	A	I	M	E			E	S	T	O			E	T	R	E
U	R	N			T	V	S	H	O	W	S			A	C	E
N	I	G	H			I	S	E	E			A	U	G	H	T
E	A	S	I	E	R			A	S	P	I	R	E			
			B	I	G	D			E	D	I	C	T	S	
P	O	T	A	T	O	C	H	I	P	S			O	O	H
I	L	I	C	H			C	O	R	P	O	R	A	T	E
N	I	C	H	E			A	H	M	E			I	C	E	D
T	O	S	I	R			B	O	A	R			O	H	M	S

68

A	B	C	S			B	A	L	S	A			O	P	T	S
D	A	A	E			I	C	E	I	N			B	R	I	T
D	I	V	A			C	H	A	N	D	E	L	I	E	R	
S	T	E	W	S			E	S	E			S	A	M	O	A
			A	N	D	R	E	W			S	T	A	N	D	
S	E	T	T	L	E					R	E	E	D			
A	S	H	E			A	I	S	L	E	S			O	S	S
U	S	E	R			L	L	O	Y	D			O	N	T	O
L	O	P			P	E	L	L	E	T			U	N	I	T
			H	E	A	R				A	L	T	A	R	S	
A	D	A	I	R			W	E	B	B	E	R			
G	O	N	G	S			I	V	E			N	A	G	A	T
O	F	T	H	E	O	P	E	R	A			C	A	T	S	
R	O	O	T			H	E	N	R	I			E	R	I	K
A	R	M	Y			O	S	T	A	R			D	Y	E	S

69

	A	P	P	A	L			S	E	W	N			A	K	A
	P	R	E	G	O			C	R	E	E			L	A	M
	E	I	G	H	T	E	E	N	T	W	E	L	V	E	
K	L	M			A	S	I	N			N	U	N	N	
R	I	M	Y			O	N	E	H	U	N	D	R	E	D
O	K	E	E	F	F	E			E	R	A	S	E	R	
C	E	S	A	R			G	I	G	I					
	T	H	I	R	T	Y	S	E	V	E	N			
		D	A	H	N				E	W	E	R	S	
	B	E	S	A	M	E			S	U	R	E	B	E	T
F	I	F	T	Y	S	E	V	E	N			S	U	L	U
A	G	F	A			E	L	S	E			L	A	B	
T	W	O	T	H	O	U	S	A	N	D	S	I	X		
A	I	R			O	A	S	T			A	G	A	Z	E
H	G	T			E	K	E	S			P	E	T	E	R

70

P	E	S	T			B	U	N	K			A	B	B	O	T
E	L	I	E			A	R	E	A			S	O	R	T	S
N	A	T	T	U	R	N	E	R			T	R	I	C	K	
S	P	U	R	N	S			A	M	O	R	E			
I	S	A	A	C			N	E	T	P	R	O	F	I	T
V	E	T			I	L	E	N	E	S			W	E	R	E
E	S	E			V	E	A	L			B	E	R	E	T
		N	I	T	P	I	C	K	E	R			
S	E	O	U	L			S	H	I	N			V	A	H
A	L	A	I			A	T	T	I	R	E			E	N	E
N	O	T	S	O	F	A	S	T			A	R	R	I	D
	B	A	N	T	U				A	T	E	A	S	E	
E	A	R	N	S			N	U	T	N	H	O	N	E	Y
S	P	A	C	E			T	R	O	T			I	D	E	E
T	E	N	E	T			S	I	N	E			L	A	D	S

71

S	E	M	I	S			B	E	A	U			C	L	E	F
C	A	P	R	A			R	O	W	S			L	I	N	E
I	T	S	A	N	Y	O	N	E	S	G	U	E	S	S	
			T	O	W			R	U	B	O	U	T			
W	H	O	C	A	N	S	A	Y			A	C	N	E	
R	E	P	O			E	L	V	I	R	A			
I	C	E	B	A	G			L	E	A	D	R	O	L	E
S	H	R			B	E	A	T	S	M	E			C	O	N
T	E	A	R	I	N	T	O			A	D	D	E	N	D
		A	G	E	O	L	D			I	A	G	O			
	F	I	C	A			I	D	O	N	T	K	N	O	W
S	A	N	K	I	N			U	N	O					
C	L	U	E	L	E	S	S	R	E	P	L	I	E	S	
A	S	S	T			M	A	I	L			A	I	S	L	E
B	E	E	S			O	P	R	Y			Z	Z	T	O	P

72

O	N	C	E			A	D	D	S			A	C	T	E	D
L	E	A	P			V	A	I	N			C	E	A	S	E
D	E	L	I			E	L	S	E			C	L	I	P	S
	D	I	S	G	R	A	C	E	K	E	L	L	Y		
			O	A	S	I	S			I	D	O			
C	A	N	D	L	E			K	N	E	S	S	E	T	
E	M	A	I	L			O	P	I	E			O	L	E
D	I	S	C	O	U	N	T	D	R	A	C	U	L	A	
A	N	A			L	E	A	D			L	O	S	E	R
R	E	L	E	N	T	S			C	O	M	E	R	S	
		S	I	R			S	C	R	U	M			
	D	I	S	P	A	T	C	H	A	D	A	M	S	
F	A	D	E	S			I	R	O	N			N	O	A	H
A	R	E	N	A			E	A	S	E			D	O	T	E
R	E	S	E	T			S	P	E	D			S	T	E	M

73

```
O L I V E █ C O R A █ R A N K
N A D I A █ A V E R █ A L E E
T W E N T Y S E V E N D O W N
O N A █ D O I N █ █ O N E T O
█ █ S I G N █ S A N E █ █
█ T O P R I G H T C O R N E R
D A V I T █ █ E Y E S █ E A U
E L A N █ S A X E S █ L E V I
A I L █ S H U E █ █ W I D E N
L A S T W O R D A C R O S S █
█ █ R I T A █ G A I N █ █
S L A I N █ E A S T █ A L I
C E N T E R O F T H E G R I D
U N D O █ A R T E █ R E G A L
M O A N █ M E S S █ S T O R Y
```

74

```
M U Z A K █ L O E W █ A W O L
C H I L I █ A N T I █ M E N U
J U N G L O V E R S █ S A L T
O R G A N S █ T E E N █ R Y E
B A Y █ L E I █ A P R S █
█ █ █ F R O M M S C R A T C H
D I J O N █ D E E R █ T H O U
O C A N A D A █ D E S T I N E
F E N D █ E S A U █ H A N E S
F R E U D C H I C K E N █ █
█ F E E L █ R E A █ A H A
A M O █ G A O L █ H Y E N A S
J U N K █ S K I N N E R D I P
A I D E █ S A N E █ S M O T E
X R A Y █ E Y E D █ M A R I N
```

75

```
E R I K █ I S S U E █ J A M B
L O C I █ L L A M A █ O B I E
K T E L █ L E M A T █ W E N D
S C R O O G E █ █ M I L T I E
█ █ B O T C H E D █ █ █
█ O T R A █ S H A █ I V A N A
S C H E M E █ A L A █ A R O N
T H E M A N F R O M U N C L E
U R D U █ D E L █ A N Y H O W
B E A S T █ L E G █ P A Y S
█ █ H O L Y O K E █ █ █
F E S T E R █ █ W I G G I L Y
O M O O █ B A B E L █ O R E O
X M A S █ I D E S T █ B O N Y
Y A K S █ T E N T S █ I N T O
```

76

```
S I R █ L I D O █ M O J O S
O D E █ O V E N █ P A T E N T
N A H █ C A B C A L L O W A Y
A H A █ A N T E D A T E █ █
R O B O T S █ V I A █ A T M
█ C R I █ B R A N █ A R O O
C R E D O █ R U N S █ I A G O
H U N A N █ A B C █ U R B A N
A L T I █ O K I E █ P A C E S
S E E N █ B E N D █ P R O █
E R R █ T E M █ L E M U R S
█ █ C A R E S F O R █ N E T
G R A B C O N T R O L █ T A R
T A K E I N █ D E S I █ R T E
O P A R T █ S E E P █ Y A P
```

77

```
S W I S S █ C A B █ M O L L S
T E N S E █ L E E █ E L I O T
R I D E S █ A G A █ D I N G Y
I G O █ T R Y I N G █ O G E E
P H O B I A █ S P A R S E █
S T R O N G █ O T C █ R R S
█ █ S A S █ G L O A T I N G
B O S S █ E S E █ W E S T
R U T A B A G A █ A T A █
O R E █ B U G █ C R I T I C
█ A C C E S S █ R E N A M E
E L M O █ R H I N O S █ L P S
S A I N T █ E R E █ T H E A S
S I N G E █ L E X █ L E N I N
A R G O T █ L E T █ E X T R A
```

78

```
N E O N █ O C H O █ J O K E R
E L M O █ O L A N █ O D E T O
V I E W █ H I S T █ S E N A T
I O G A L L O N H A T S █ █
S T A D I A █ T E L L S A L L
█ █ A R L O █ D E A R I E
I O O Y E A R S W A R █ D N A
P C T S █ S H H █ B E E P
A A H █ I O O O I S L A N D S
S L E I G H █ G O A D █ █
S A R D O N I C █ F I V E A M
█ I O O O O M A N I A C S
S H Y O F █ T R I B █ B R E D
P E A C E █ A A R E █ E L I O
F L O Y D █ S L E D █ S Y N S
```

79

```
S S S . S T R A P . S C A L P
P I C . P H I L S . E E R I E
A D O . R E L E E . A L T E R
M E T R O S E X U A L S . . .
S A T O U T . A D S . . A P T
. . . S T I R . O P E N B A R
S U I T . N U B . . T I B I A
U N D E R G R O U N D F I L M
S P O R E . . G L O . T E S S
H O L S T E R . T H A I . . .
I T S . . B E E . A G E N D A
. . . S U B W A Y S E R I E S
K A Y A K . A R E S O . E L I
E L A T E . S T A L L . C A D
G A M E S . H O S E D . E Y E
```

80

```
A S C I I . Z I M A . S K I M
S P A M S . E D O M . M E M O
H A P P Y J U I C E . I V A N
E N T R E E S . S C H T I C K
. . . U T E . . . H A H N . .
B O Y D . P I Q U E D . B A T
O T O E . S O U P . T I A R A
S H U N S . W A S . O N C D S
S E R T A . A R E S . T O O T
A R E . L O S T T O . E N R Y
. . T U T U . . . F D R . . .
A C O L Y T E . G A U C H O S
G O A T . F A B E R G E E G G
U S S R . I S O N . I D I O T
E T T A . T E X T . N E R D S
```

81

```
E P E E . C A R O L . P A T S
S A R A . A C E L A . R O A N
Q W E R T Y U I O P . O L I O
U N C L E S . D R O O P . . .
E S T E R . A S D F G H J K L
. . S I L L . . . H E E L S
D I N S . A I D A . A T S E A
R N A . Z X C V B N M . T I T
A N G L E . E D E N . S U N S
N I G E R . . . T E S H . . .
K E Y B O A R D S . P E A R L
. . A S S H E . S U R R E Y
J O A N . T Y P E W R I T E R
A R N O . A M O R E . F I L E
W R E N . R E T I E . F E S S
```

82

```
A S C O T . C U B S . H A S P
C H O R E . I S E E . O T T O
C A P R A . C O N G E R E E L
E L Y . C O E . T A B . A V A
P L E T H O R A . B A S I N
T O D O . H O N D A . N E E D
S W I S S . T E M P T . . .
. . T H I N G A M A J I G . .
. . I S A A C . . S O R E S
B O M B . T Y I N G . C O N E
O C E A N . D O N S H U L A
I T S . O A K . R U M . N A B
L A S T D A N C E . A N D R E
E V E S . R E D S . S I E G E
D E S K . P E S T . H A R E S
```

83

```
S O D A . A P O P . I N C A N
A C E D . B E L A . M O O R E
H A N D Y A N D Y . A T L A W
A N T E S . N I C E N E L L Y
R A I D E D . E O N . E S O
A D S . R A P . D O W A G E R
N A T O . T O T . A P E A K
. . P L A I N J A N E . . .
I S S U E . T A X . S O R T
N O N S T O P . W E B . R E A
A L I . R I D . D A M A S K
D A P P E R D A N . L A N C E
A R I E L . G L O O M Y G U S
Z I N E S . I L S A . B E E T
E A G L E . N Y E T . E S S O
```

84

```
F E S S . H A L T S . T A M E
A R T Y . A T A R I . U L A N
B A R N . S H I E D . T I R E
. . . I C E H O C K E Y T E A M
A S K . N I L . B O U N T Y
N T E S T S . I C A N T . . .
W A T E R H A Z A R D . S T S
A T W T . V A L . S K E E
R E O . S T E A M E N G I N E
. . Q U I C K . N E T P A Y
I M P A L E . T C U . S M A
T U R N U P T H E H E A T . .
A R U T . I T I N A . G O Y A
L A N A . N O T O N . E W E S
O L E S . S P E N T . S N A P
```

85

```
HUT   ATM   AMBIT
OPAL  BRER  TEAMO
MLII  BODE  MADAM
BONDJAMESBOND
RATSO PAILS   RBI
EDS DRE DOT   EAR
   PIE BUT  CAKE
 HOMESWEETHOME
REVS TIE  EON
ERE SAL ARM  ADE
PER ATLAS ESSEX
 TIMEAFTERTIME
SLURP ROOM  ODOR
AURAL DORM  WENT
SCENE  TSA   SSS
```

86

```
CAT  JILL  MURMUR
OVA  OREO  UNEASE
LILIESOF   REAGAN
EDEN    THISLIFE
    ROWS  REC
TOSIRWITHLOVE
EKE GIGO    ESSO
ARAISININTHESUN
MALI    TORE  ARE
   SIDNEYPOITIER
   REM  EYRE
NOWAYOUT   RHEA
OXALIC  THEFIELD
MERINO  OISE  SLO
ENSIGN  PETE  SAG
```

87

```
SLAB  PUTUP  BMOC
HERO  THESE  SARA
ACCT  BARED  IRON
WHOSYOURDADDY
   WEAL  GREGGS
AGHAST AMOI  ORA
TOON  SIEGE  RUN
DOWAHDIDDYDIDDY
AGT AWGEE   NOGO
WOO TANS  PLANES
NOBLER  ASCH
 OLDFUDDYDUDDY
EROO ILIAC  RARE
ICKY NEATH  RYAN
NASD GENES  YOWS
```

88

```
STORM  DEN  TINAS
CARNE  AVE  ANART
APASSAGETOINDIA
MEL SCAR  SLEAZY
   HAMM  ATEE
GARAGEATTENDANT
ADELE  WORD  ROO
MODE LIENS  ESTA
MRI FARE  DROID
ANGELSANDSAINTS
  SOTS  ROME
SARTRE YODA  OER
THEHIDDENAGENDA
ASPEN ATE  ELCID
BOORS BID  DIETS
```

89

```
SHALT  ENDUP  ABS
GOREN  SEATO  FOP
TYRONEPOWER  FRO
STOP RING  SWAIN
  GABLE  ACHING
CHARLESINCHARGE
HANDY  SICEM
EST SQUAT  CHO
  SPITZ  APRIL
GRAPEFRUITJUICE
HUBERT  MEANT
EPICS ABET  SELA
TED ITSELECTRIC
TRE SATED  DEION
OTS TIARA  CRANE
```

90

```
JESS  METUP  STEW
USTO  ERASE  HERO
STUB  TRUER  ENOW
THAIRESTAURANT
SERGIO  SKA  YIN
ORT CROP  ENESCO
  ICICLE  TOAD
 TAICHICHUAN
ADAM  SECANT
FIXINS DLVI  KIM
REB YIP  ETHANE
 TIEUPLOOSEENDS
ETTA HARPO  ISIS
PIES ONEAM  DARE
APSE NELLE  INAS
```

91

```
S P A D E _ T H O M _ R U E D
A R I E L _ E U R O _ O N M E
D I R T F A R M E R _ T I M E
A D E E _ G E E _ T I T T E R
T E R R I E S _ R I C E _ _
_ _ G R E A S E M O N K E Y
H O M E S _ E D E N _ E P A
A M E S _ A S T O R _ S E E P
N A N _ O M I T _ J O N E S
G R U N G E R O C K E R _
_ U R N S _ R E T R A C T
N E S T E A _ E E E _ E L L A
U R A L _ M U D S L I N G E R
M I L E _ E M I T _ S T E E D
B E E T _ N A T S _ P O R K Y
```

92

```
B L O B _ A D E A R _ S S T S
Y U R I _ P A N D A _ C H O P
O L E G _ I N T O W _ R I T A
B U M S T E E R _ O L I V E S
_ _ T E C S _ P N O M _
A C C U S E _ F A I R P L A Y
S H A F T _ T O T O E _ E T A
T U R F _ D A R I N _ G A R R
I T E _ M O T T O _ R O S I N
N E W M O N E Y _ H O O H A S
_ _ E W E R _ S A N D _
A T L A S T _ I T S A D E A L
B R A G _ H A H A S _ E R L E
C A V E _ A T O L L _ E G O S
S P A R _ T E P E E _ D O T S
```

93

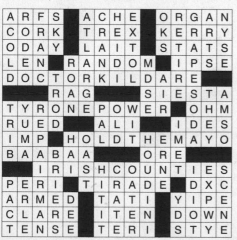

```
M A C H _ S A V E S _ A F R O
O D E A _ I R E N E _ R A I D
P O L L U X B E A N _ I N T O
U R L _ P P S _ M A N A G E R
P E O R I A _ D O T E _
_ U N C L E R O M U L U S
A S K S _ K I R _ R E P O R T
M A N T A _ Z A P _ A S O N E
E G O I S M _ N O R _ I N S I
N E W C H A N G L A N D _
_ E R I E _ M E E K E R
D E B U N K S _ P E R _ L E E
O V E N _ E S A U S F I E L D
J E S T _ T A B L E _ T I E D
O R S O _ S N A P S _ A N D Y
```

94

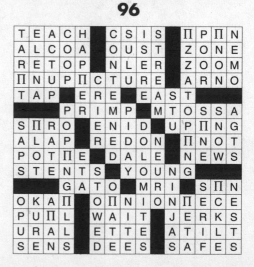

```
O D D E R _ A H A B _ H A H A
C R O N Y _ T O F U _ I M A X
C O N T E N T S F R A G I L E
U N O _ Y E T I _ S H E L L
R E T A K E N _ R O A D _
_ S K I _ D A M P _ A T T Y
I N T A N D E M _ A N Y H O O
V I A _ K E E P D R Y _ I R K
E N C A S E _ L E T M E S E E
B A K E _ N T S _ R A G
_ R H E A _ S C H T I C K
A D L A I _ T I E R _ D O I
P R O T E C T F R O M H E A T
T I N E _ P O S T _ S A U L T
S P E D _ R O O S _ G Y P S Y
```

95

```
A R F S _ A C H E _ O R G A N
C O R K _ T R E X _ K E R R Y
O D A Y _ L A I T _ S T A T S
L E N _ R A N D O M _ I P S E
D O C T O R K I L D A R E _
_ R A G _ S I E S T A
T Y R O N E P O W E R _ O H M
R U E D _ A L I _ I D E S
I M P _ H O L D T H E M A Y O
B A A B A A _ O R E
_ I R I S H C O U N T I E S
P E R I _ T I R A D E _ D X C
A R M E D _ T A T I _ Y I P E
C L A R E _ I T E N _ D O W N
T E N S E _ T E R I _ S T Y E
```

96

```
T E A C H _ C S I S _ Π P Π N
A L C O A _ O U S T _ Z O N E
R E T O P _ N L E R _ Z O O M
Π N U P Π C T U R E _ A R N O
T A P _ E R E _ E A S T _
_ P R I M P _ M T O S S A
S Π R O _ E N I D _ U P Π N G
A L A P _ R E D O N _ Π N O T
P O T Π E _ D A L E _ N E W S
S T E N T S _ Y O U N G _
_ G A T O _ M R I _ S Π N
O K A Π _ O Π N I O N Π E C E
P U Π L _ W A I T _ J E R K S
U R A L _ E T T E _ A T I L T
S E N S _ D E E S _ S A F E S
```

97

```
A D H O C   R A L P H   B L T
B Y A I R   I N U R E   L I E
B E L L Y D A N C E R   O E D
E S T   U R L S   A B A C U S
      A N A T   A C I D
    L U C K O F T H E D R A W
N E E D L E   A M Y   U S A
A R N I E   O K S   B A S I L
S I D   E V E   R E L E N T
H E A D O V E R H E E L S
      C H I N   O A F S
L O W C A L   E R I C   A D O
A L A   R O A S T M A S T E R
M E N   A N D S O   K A R M A
P O T   S E V E N   E M A I L
```

98

```
L E A F   T S P S   S P A R K
A X L E   H A R E   H A D O N
V E E R   E R I E   O Z O N E
A C C R U E A C R E W   R A E
        I N A N E   T R E E
S L A T E R   N E O N A T E
L I M E   T R I O   O G D E N
U M A   P H A N T O M   O R D
G I Z M O   S C A B   P O S E
S T E A L T H   S C A R E D
      A N K A   S P O I L
I B M   A P P A L L A P A U L
F R A U D   A G E E   A W R Y
S A Y S O   N E A T   T O I L
O N S E T   E S T E   E L S E
```

99

```
W A L E S A   A M C S   A S I
A B U S E S   S M U T   I N N
W O R K I S T H E R U I N O F
A O K I   U A E   A C T T W O
      M E A N S   T C U
O B L O N G   P O O R L A W
S R I   V E T O E R   B A L I
C U B B Y   T H E   F I N A L
A N Y A   C O O K E R   A I D
R O A D M A P   D E V I N E
      M E R   E V I T A
E X C E E D   D A B   S A B E
D R I N K I N G C L A S S E S
N A G   E A S E   E L A T E S
A Y S   R C A S   S T R A F E
```

100

```
L U T E S   K A R L   D E E P
O P E R A   O L I O   E C R U
C R E A T U R E C O M F O R T
K I T S   N E C K T I E
U S E   L E A K   S C R A P
P E R S I A   D E S T I N E
      P E R D I E M   M O P
  B E A S T O F B U R D E N
S E A   H O S T L E R
S A R C A S M   S A Y I N G
S U S A N   P A I R   N O R
      I N F E R N O   A S I A
A N I M A L M A G N E T I S M
D I V A   A I D S   T O T E M
O X E N   T R O T   A M U S E
```

101

```
G I A N T   F I R M   J A M B
I G L O O   A R I A   U S M A
R O A D W O R K O N E M I L E
T R I O   P M S   I M P A I R
    F A A   F A I R
  L E F T L A N E C L O S E D
U A R   O S C A R S   P A L E
S T R A P   R A G   M E L B A
E K E D   D O C I L E   V O L
R E D U C E S P E E D N O W
    L E T S   T S U
O R A T O R   D A G   M A D E
F I N E S A R E D O U B L E D
A M O R   C O L A   L E M M E
N Y N Y   T E E M   T R A I N
```

102

```
W A S T E   T A C   H O M E S
I N L E T   A V A   O P E R A
R E A P S S P A R E P E A R S
E R N E   P I N T A S   R O E
R A T E S A R T E S T E A R S
      S O D   T O N
E M U   L E V E R   O P A L
L A R G E R E G A L G L A R E
K O N A   T O P E R   M C I
      Y A P   S I C
T I M E S E M I T S M I T E S
E D O   H E I N I E   C O P A
L E A S T S T A L E T A L E S
C A N T O   E N T   I D E E S
O L S E N   R E S   P A T S Y
```

103

L	A	T	I	N	■	S	L	I	T	■	S	H	O	D
A	T	O	N	E	■	E	A	S	E	■	T	O	N	E
V	O	T	E	R	■	A	I	L	S	■	O	R	A	L
A	M	O	R	V	I	N	C	I	T	O	M	N	I	A
■	■	■	T	E	D	■	■	P	E	P	P	E	R	Y
F	A	B	■	D	I	E	S	■	D	I	S	■	■	■
A	W	E	■	■	O	S	L	O	■	N	O	I	S	E
N	O	N	C	O	M	P	O	S	M	E	N	T	I	S
G	L	E	A	N	■	N	O	S	E	■	A	L	A	■
■	■	M	E	D	■	P	O	L	S	■	L	O	U	■
A	W	A	I	T	E	D	■	■	O	I	D	■	■	■
P	E	R	S	O	N	A	N	O	N	G	R	A	T	A
R	E	D	O	■	I	B	A	R	■	N	A	V	A	L
I	D	O	L	■	R	A	Z	E	■	A	N	I	T	A
L	Y	R	E	■	O	T	I	S	■	L	O	V	E	R

104

J	U	L	E	P	■	V	A	I	N	■	M	A	S	S
A	L	E	V	E	■	E	L	M	O	■	I	L	L	S
M	A	N	E	T	■	R	O	H	E	■	X	O	U	T
■	N	I	N	E	T	Y	S	I	X	H	O	U	R	S
■	■	■	S	R	I	■	S	P	I	E	L	■	■	■
I	T	S	O	P	E	N	■	■	T	H	O	M	A	S
P	A	H	■	A	R	O	A	R	■	■	G	A	S	P
O	C	E	A	N	S	T	W	E	N	T	Y	T	W	O
D	E	B	T	■	■	A	L	L	A	H	■	T	A	R
S	T	A	N	Z	A	■	O	N	E	C	E	N	T	■
■	■	■	O	S	S	I	E	■	C	A	Y	■	■	■
F	A	N	T	A	S	T	I	C	E	I	G	H	T	■
E	L	O	I	■	I	A	G	O	■	S	N	I	P	E
T	E	E	M	■	S	L	E	D	■	L	E	E	K	S
A	X	L	E	■	T	Y	R	A	■	E	T	S	E	Q

105

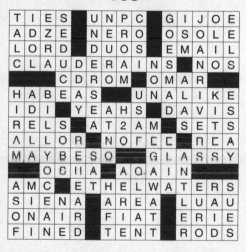

T	I	E	S	■	U	N	P	C	■	G	I	J	O	E
A	D	Z	E	■	N	E	R	O	■	O	S	O	L	E
L	O	R	D	■	D	U	O	S	■	E	M	A	I	L
C	L	A	U	D	E	R	A	I	N	S	■	N	O	S
■	■	■	C	D	R	O	M	■	O	M	A	R	■	■
H	A	B	E	A	S	■	■	U	N	A	L	I	K	E
I	D	I	■	Y	E	A	H	S	■	D	A	V	I	S
R	E	L	S	■	A	T	2	A	M	■	S	E	T	S
A	L	L	O	R	■	N	O	T	E	E	■	N	E	A
M	A	Y	B	E	S	O	■	■	G	L	A	S	S	Y
■	■	O	C	H	A	■	A	G	A	I	N	■	■	■
A	M	C	■	E	T	H	E	L	W	A	T	E	R	S
S	I	E	N	A	■	A	R	E	A	■	L	U	A	U
O	N	A	I	R	■	F	I	A	T	■	E	R	I	E
F	I	N	E	D	■	T	E	N	T	■	R	O	D	S

106

A	P	S	O	■	O	S	C	A	R	■	R	I	N	K
G	A	U	L	■	F	L	A	R	E	■	E	D	E	N
A	U	D	I	■	F	O	R	E	S	T	F	I	R	E
S	L	A	V	■	O	R	A	T	E	■	O	V	A	■
P	I	N	E	S	A	P	■	■	A	C	T	E	D	■
■	■	■	B	U	D	S	■	L	O	S	E	■	■	■
A	N	D	R	E	A	■	D	E	R	E	L	I	C	T
R	O	N	A	■	G	R	E	E	N	■	E	C	O	N
P	R	A	N	C	E	R	S	■	A	B	R	U	P	T
■	■	C	A	S	S	■	S	T	A	Y	■	■	■	■
S	H	A	H	S	■	■	P	E	A	S	O	U	P	■
C	O	B	■	T	O	T	A	L	■	T	U	N	E	■
A	V	O	C	A	D	O	P	I	T	■	A	T	T	N
L	E	V	I	■	D	I	S	C	O	■	L	I	I	I
P	L	E	A	■	S	L	E	E	P	■	K	E	E	N

107

L	I	S	P	■	G	R	A	C	I	E	■	I	L	E
A	S	I	A	■	R	E	R	U	N	S	■	D	O	E
R	I	T	A	■	A	L	A	R	M	C	L	O	C	K
I	N	C	R	E	D	I	B	L	E	H	U	L	K	■
A	T	O	■	L	E	T	■	■	E	X	A	L	T	■
T	O	M	E	I	■	■	U	S	E	R	■	T	E	A
■	■	■	T	S	H	I	R	T	S	■	A	R	T	S
■	■	G	R	E	A	T	G	A	T	S	B	Y	■	■
R	A	R	E	■	T	H	E	B	E	A	R	■	■	■
A	B	O	■	D	E	E	D	■	B	A	B	E	L	■
P	R	O	M	O	■	■	A	C	R	■	I	N	E	■
■	A	M	A	Z	I	N	G	K	R	E	S	K	I	N
T	H	E	R	I	V	I	E	R	A	■	C	I	G	S
O	A	R	■	N	O	T	N	O	W	■	O	N	M	E
P	M	S	■	G	R	E	E	N	S	■	T	I	A	S

108

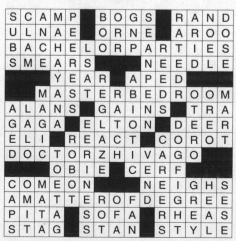

S	C	A	M	P	■	B	O	G	S	■	R	A	N	D
U	L	N	A	E	■	O	R	N	E	■	A	R	O	O
B	A	C	H	E	L	O	R	P	A	R	T	I	E	S
S	M	E	A	R	S	■	■	N	E	E	D	L	E	■
■	■	■	Y	E	A	R	■	A	P	E	D	■	■	■
■	M	A	S	T	E	R	B	E	D	R	O	O	M	■
A	L	A	N	S	■	G	A	I	N	S	■	T	R	A
G	A	G	A	■	E	L	T	O	N	■	D	E	E	R
E	L	I	■	R	E	A	C	T	■	C	O	R	O	T
D	O	C	T	O	R	Z	H	I	V	A	G	O	■	■
■	■	■	O	B	I	E	■	C	E	R	F	■	■	■
C	O	M	E	O	N	■	■	N	E	I	G	H	S	■
A	M	A	T	T	E	R	O	F	D	E	G	R	E	E
P	I	T	A	■	S	O	F	A	■	R	H	E	A	S
S	T	A	G	■	S	T	A	N	■	S	T	Y	L	E

109

R	O	V	E	R		M	O	M	S		F	A	Z	E
E	N	E	R	O		A	L	A	I		A	R	I	D
B	A	R	R	T	E	N	D	E	D		R	I	N	G
A	N	Y			A	M	O	S			E	N	R	A	G	E
			S	T	I	R		W	A	I	F
C	A	S	T	O	R		C	A	R	N	E	G	I	E
A	L	T	A	R		T	R	I	M		T	E	M	P
B	A	E	R		T	H	A	T	S		C	A	S	E
O	M	A	R		R	E	F	S		T	H	R	E	E
T	O	M	S	W	I	F	T		C	H	E	S	T	S
		H	A	F	T		C	O	E	D
A	Y	E	A	Y	E		B	O	M	B		S	H	E
H	A	R	P		C	A	R	R	P	O	O	L	E	D
E	L	I	E		T	R	I	G		S	N	A	R	E
M	E	N	D		A	C	T	I		S	E	V	E	N

110

A	R	A	B	I	C		M	S	G		A	M	A	S
N	I	N	E	T	Y		A	P	E		R	I	L	L
S	C	A	R	E	D	Y	C	A	T		E	D	I	E
E	C	C	E			E	O	N			B	A	D	G	E
L	I	T	T	L	E	A	N	G	E	L		A	N	T
			O	T	S		L	E	E	R	Y
D	E	F	E	N	D		R	E	L	E	A	S	E	R
E	V	I	T	E		F	E	D		D	R	U	I	D
N	E	S	T	L	E	R	S		S	I	E	N	N	A
		H	E	I	N	E		L	I	N
O	C	T		E	V	E	N	I	N	G	S	T	A	R
C	H	A	I	R		T	E	M		M	U	L	E
C	O	I	N		G	R	A	P	E	J	E	L	L	Y
U	R	L	S		P	I	T		S	A	L	L	I	E
R	E	S	T		A	P	O		A	L	L	E	N	S

111

D	I	D	S	O		B	A	T	H		F	T	D
O	M	I	T	S		E	R	R	E	D		R	O	O
P	A	R	I	S	H	H	O	U	S	E		E	R	N
A	C	E	R		O	E	D	S		L	A	S	S	O
			F	A	R	M		S	E	T	S	H	O	T
I	N	P	R	I	S	O	N		L	A	S	H
L	L	O	Y	D		T	E	S	S		T	E	N	D
E	E	L		A	S	H	H	E	A	P		R	O	E
T	R	I	S		A	S	I	T		A	M	B	L	E
		S	H	U	N		S	U	N	V	I	S	O	R
S	C	H	O	L	A	R		P	O	E	T
I	N	H	O	T		A	S	S	N		C	Z	A	R
T	O	A		R	O	S	H	H	A	S	H	A	N	A
A	T	M		A	R	T	O	O		M	U	Z	A	K
R	E	S			Y	A	W	P		A	M	U	S	E

112

D	E	C	O		C	A	P	O		G	L	O	W
E	N	O	L	A		H	O	O	K		R	E	D	O
I	N	D	E	X	C	A	R	D	S		A	M	O	K
S	U	E		E	R	S	T		A	Z	U	R	E
M	I	D	D	L	E	M	A	N	A	G	E	R	S
			E	S	E			O	T	I	S
S	L	A	M		I	O	W	A	N		U	F	O
P	U	T	O	N	E	S	F	I	N	G	E	R	O	N
A	X	E		A	L	L	A	N			K	N	E	E
			E	R	L	E			E	V	E
	P	I	N	K	Y	T	U	S	C	A	D	E	R	O
C	E	D	E	S		L	I	O	N		D	E	G
U	S	E	R		R	I	N	G	L	E	A	D	E	R
S	T	A	G		I	R	A	N		S	P	I	K	E
P	O	L	Y		M	E	S	S		T	E	S	S

113

B	O	O	R	S		H	U	M		U	N	J	A	M
U	B	O	A	T		I	S	O		N	E	A	T	O
D	I	Z	Z	Y	D	E	A	N		E	X	X	O	N
G	E	E	Z	E	R			T	O	A	T
E	S	S			U	T	T	E	R	S		F	W	D
		F	U	Z	Z	Y	Z	O	E	L	L	E	R
H	A	S	A	M	E	A	L			A	O	N	E
O	M	E	N	S		R	E	M		C	U	R	D	S
P	A	I	N			N	O	O	N	D	A	Y	S
O	Z	Z	Y	O	S	B	O	U	R	N	E
N	E	E		C	H	A	L	E	T		S	S	S
		K	E	E	N			I	D	O	T	O	O
M	A	G	N	A		J	A	Z	Z	Y	J	E	F	F
I	N	P	E	N		O	V	A		E	A	T	A	T
G	N	A	W	S		S	E	P		S	I	S	S	Y

114

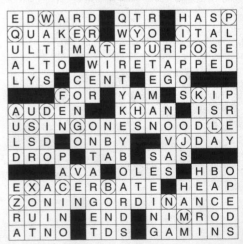

E	D	W	A	R	D		Q	T	R		H	A	S	P
Q	U	A	K	E	R		W	Y	O		I	T	A	L
U	L	T	I	M	A	T	E	P	U	R	P	O	S	E
A	L	T	O		W	I	R	E	T	A	P	P	E	D
L	Y	S		C	E	N	T		E	G	O
			F	O	R		Y	A	M		S	K	I	P
A	U	D	E	N		K	H	A	N		I	S	R
U	S	I	N	G	O	N	E	S	N	O	O	D	L	E
L	S	D		O	N	B	Y		V	J	D	A	Y
D	R	O	P		T	A	B		S	A	S
			A	V	A		O	L	E	S		H	B	O
E	X	A	C	E	R	B	A	T	E		H	E	A	P
Z	O	N	I	N	G	O	R	D	I	N	A	N	C	E
R	U	I	N		E	N	D		N	I	M	R	O	D
A	T	N	O		T	D	S		G	A	M	I	N	S

115

```
A P E S | P A R C H | S K I S
M O M A | A L C O A | K I N K
R U B B E R B A N D | A N T I
A R R I V E | | S I S | N E D
D I A N E | S O U T H B E N D
I N C | R A H A L | E R A S E
O G E E | Y U K | F E A R E D
| S P E L L B I N D | |
P A S T A S | A L F | Y M C A
A L I E N | S W E E P | C O G
J A M E S B O N D | L U C R E
A M P | Y A W | M A R L O N
M E S A | G E R M A N B U N D
A D O S | E T H A N | A R E A
S A N K | L O O P Y | N E T S
```

116

```
Z E S T S | G R A B S | G E E
A F T R A | L A R U E | O L D
G R O U C H O M A R X | L I E
S E W N | O R E | B U R D E N
| M E D D L I N G | A R F
| L E D A | A L L R I S E
A M I E S | S S E | E T S
B E N D I N G T H E R U L E S
A N A | O O P | E N D T O
B U T T S I N | S W A B |
| R A H | G H O U L I S H
T E A B A G | Y R S | A L A R
H A N | R E V E R S E S I D E
O T C | I N A N E | D E C A F
U S E | F E R A L | O D E T S
```

117

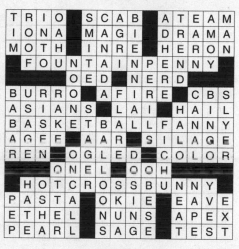

```
T R I O | S C A B | A T E A M
I O N A | M A G I | D R A M A
M O T H | I N R E | H E R O N
| F O U N T A I N P E N N Y
| O E D | N E R D
B U R R O | A F I R E | C B S
A S I A N S | L A I | H A I L
B A S K E T B A L L F A N N Y
A G E E | A A R | S I L A G E
R E N | O G L E D | C O L O R
| O N E L | O O H
| H O T C R O S S B U N N Y
P A S T A | O K I E | E A V E
E T H E L | N U N S | A P E X
P E A R L | S A G E | T E S T
```

118

```
W A L K | P A W N | S A M B A
I L I E | A C H E | U L E E S
R A C E | P R I X | B I Z E T
E M I L I O E S T E V E Z
D O T | L O S T | M E N A C E
| A S S | S I R | N A M
E X T R A E F F O R T | I R A
A H E M | E C O | A N T I
T O L | E L E C T R I C E E L
U S E | D I D | E T E
R A M P A G | G A P E | P A Y
| E A S T E R N E M P I R E
A S T I N | B A J A | A Q U A
L O R N E | R I O T | T U B S
F L Y E R | O N U S | H E A T
```

119

```
A M I E | C H O P S | H O W L
M A L L | H A N O I | A R I A
F U L L T I M E S T U D E N T
M I S S A L | S H U N | O D E
| C D I | E P I C
N E W Y O R K E R | T O T I E
O C H O | E E L | E R R O R
S L E W | N A I L S | N I N O
E A R L E | Z O O | E N I D
S T E E L | H A L F P R I C E
| D I C E | A T E
O T T | T A R A | S T A N Z A
P H A S E S O F T H E M O O N
A R C H | I N T R O | M I N D
L U T E | O S S I E | O R E S
```

120

```
R O I L | F A B L E | T S A R
O R C A | O B O E S | U P T O
O N E W H O C A N T | B E A M
F O R M A T | S E P | E R A
| A I R | R E E L E D I N
C H A N G E H I S M I N D |
A I L | S A P | N O E L S
S E L E C T S | A B Y S M A L
E D D I E | A P E | O N O
| A N D W O N T C H A N G E
B I Y E A R L Y | L E M |
I L L | R I D | O R A T E S
B I O S | T H E S U B J E C T
L A N K | H A T E D | O T O E
E D G Y | E T O N S | R E N T
```

121

I	M	A	C	S		L	A	G		S	C	A	L	A
M	O	R	A	L		O	V	A		C	O	D	E	S
S	P	I	N	A	L	T	A	P		R	U	R	A	L
		D	Y	E	S		B	E	G	O	N	E		
A	B	B	Y		V	A	N	N	A	W	H	I	T	E
F	L	A	B	B	Y		B	I	N		S	T	O	P
A	U	R	A	L		L	A	N	A	I				
R	E	D	R	O	S	E		O	L	D	S	A	L	T
			C	H	E	S	S		E	A	G	E	R	
A	D	E	S		O	Z	S		S	A	Y	I	D	O
B	A	N	K	B	R	A	N	C	H		O	N	A	N
A	T	T	I	R	E		A	E	O	N				
C	I	R	C	A		H	O	L	D	W	A	T	E	R
U	V	E	A	S		A	L	L		E	R	A	S	E
S	E	E	P	S		Y	E	S		D	A	R	T	S

122

P	E	T	E		S	M	I	T		E	F	R	E	M
A	V	I	A		M	A	T	A		M	A	O	R	I
N	O	B	R	A	I	N	E	R		S	T	A	I	N
S	K	I	N	F	L	I	N	T	S		T	R	E	X
Y	E	A		R	E	F		S	I	T	U			
			M	O	S	E	S		N	I	E	C	E	S
P	I	O	U	S		S	T	R	E	S	S	O	U	T
A	M	C	S		S	T	Y	E	S		D	O	R	A
C	A	T	C	H	C	O	L	D		S	A	L	O	N
S	C	A	L	A	R		E	A	R	L	Y			
			E	D	U	C		L	E	E		A	L	E
A	C	D	C		B	O	N	E	H	E	A	D	E	D
S	A	R	A	N		S	C	R	A	P	I	R	O	N
S	P	A	R	E		T	A	T	S		L	E	N	A
N	O	T	S	O		S	A	S	H		S	P	A	S

123

P	I	S	A		A	T	B	A	T		A	T	A	D
I	D	E	S		C	O	R	P	S		R	A	B	E
T	I	C	K	L	E	P	I	N	K		I	C	U	S
T	E	T	E	A	T	E	T	E		L	A	H	T	I
			D	Y	A	D		A	M	I	N	O		
A	R	T	I	S	T		T	I	N	M	A	N		
L	I	O	N		E	X	X	O	N		A	E	R	O
L	A	E			O	X	X			T	E	N		
O	T	T	S		B	O	X	O	F		R	E	N	E
T	A	H	I	T	I		L	E	E	R	A	T		
		E	R	I	C	A		B	A	W	L			
H	I	L	L	S		S	T	A	G	E	A	C	T	S
O	H	I	O		C	H	I	L	D	S	P	L	A	Y
J	O	N	I		S	E	L	M	A		S	A	L	S
O	P	E	N		A	N	T	S	Y		E	M	I	T

124

A	L	A	N		T	A	D	A		E	S	T	E	S
S	A	N	E		O	L	E	S		Q	U	A	K	E
H	U	G	O	B	L	A	C	K		U	M	B	E	R
E	R	R		I	D	S		T	E	A	M	U	S	A
N	A	Y	S	A	Y		M	O	N	T	E			
			P	L	A	Z	A		D	E	R	I	V	E
A	S	S	A	Y		E	R	L	E		S	M	E	W
M	O	W	N		L	A	K	E	R		T	U	N	A
A	L	A	I		A	L	E	G		R	O	S	I	N
J	E	T	S	K	I		T	O	P	I	C			
			H	A	N	K	S		E	D	K	O	C	H
S	E	T	F	R	E	E		S	A	G		C	H	A
E	X	I	L	E		M	I	N	C	E	M	E	A	T
M	E	L	E	E		P	O	O	H		C	A	L	E
I	S	L	A	M		T	C	B	Y		I	N	K	S

125

H	A	R	K		A	W	A	S	H		K	E	L	P
A	S	E	A		R	O	T	T	E	N	I	D	E	A
D	E	E	R	A	F	E	M	A	L	E	D	E	E	R
E	A	S	E	L	S		L	E	N	D	L			
S	T	E	E	L		B	R	I	N	E		W	E	E
			M	I	C	R	O	N		T	E	A	L	
A	P	P		S	A	A	B		I	G	N	I	T	E
D	R	O	P	O	F	G	O	L	D	E	N	S	U	N
M	O	L	I	N	E		C	U	E	R		S	P	A
I	N	I	T		D	O	R	E	M	I				
T	E	C		T	R	I	P	E		A	N	I	O	N
		E	T	H	O	S		O	N	E	T	W	O	
N	A	M	E	I	C	A	L	L	M	Y	S	E	L	F
F	L	A	T	S	C	R	E	E	N		S	M	E	E
L	I	N	E		O	M	A	N	I		E	S	T	E

126

B	A	S	T	E		S	W	A	B		A	B	E	D
A	T	E	U	P		H	A	L	O		S	A	S	E
N	O	D	E	S		A	D	E	N		C	R	A	W
A	M	A		I	T	R	I	E	D	T	O	B	U	Y
N	I	K	O	L	A	I		A	R	T				
A	C	A	M	O	U	F	L	A	G	E	S	U	I	T
			A	N	T		A	M	E	X		T	O	E
F	E	A	R		S	P	Y		C	E	N	T		
O	A	F		S	H	O	E		G	S	A			
B	U	T	I	C	O	U	L	D	N	T	F	I	N	D
		S	A	L		C	A	R	E	F	O	R		
O	N	E	A	N	Y	W	H	E	R	E		T	M	I
S	E	R	A		C	O	I	L		T	E	H	E	E
L	A	I	C		O	R	E	L		C	L	E	A	R
O	R	E	S		W	E	D	S		H	I	N	T	S

127

```
S K I M P █ I L L S █ F E E D
C A R O L █ B E A U █ A X L E
A N I M A L M A G N E T I S M
R E S █ C A S K █ L A T T E S
█ █ █ H A M █ █ R I T E █ █ █
V E G E T A B L E G A R D E N
E C O L E █ E I G H T █ A X E
N O R M █ D A V I T █ F L A W
O L E █ G E T E M █ R E A C T
M I N E R A L D E P O S I T S
█ █ █ M A D E █ █ L S T █ █ █
S A L I N E █ B L U E █ B O Y
T W E N T Y Q U E S T I O N S
A O N E █ E U R O █ T R A C E
G L O M █ S I G N █ A S T E R
```

128

```
L A S S O █ D A D S █ H O T
Y A L T A █ M U S I C █ O L A
C H A R T T O P P E R █ P I N
R E B A █ A D E S █ I T S O K
A D S P A C E █ E P I C █ █ █
█ █ █ █ B E L L B O T T O M S
S A C H E T █ E R N █ H T M L
O B O E S █ B A R █ M E C C A
A L D A █ S E R █ M I S H I T
K E E P A N E Y E O N █ █ █ █
█ █ N E L L █ M U D B A T H
P R A D O █ I M I T █ A L V A
R I M █ N O N E T H E L E S S
I C E █ Z O O M S █ B E R E T
X E S █ O H N O █ W R O T E
```

129

```
W H E W █ E C O L █ O S K A R
R O A R █ N O R A █ P U N N Y
Y E T I █ D R E W █ E M O T E
█ █ T U R N O N A N A X I S █
I T S T R U E █ B E T █ █ █
T U N E I N T O M O R R O W
N S Y N C █ R E M █ A B E D
O K D █ H E Y B A B Y █ L I E
W E E P █ P O I █ A L I G N
█ D R O P O U T O F S I G H T
█ P A C █ T O I L E T S █
T I M O T H Y L E A R Y █
O L I V E █ M I L L █ P E W S
S I R E N █ C O L E █ A V I S
H E A R T █ A N O D █ D A Z E
```

130

```
M A R C H █ T M A N █ A R M S
G L A R E █ A U T O █ C O A L
R O T O R O O T E R █ C L U E
S T E P O N I T █ T I L D E
█ █ █ S I T S █ H A N D S E T
T O R █ N O T █ A F T E R █
A D O B E █ N R A █ N O U N
L I M O █ R A N D R █ T Y P E
K E P T █ I S E █ A S C O T
█ E T A T S █ O W L █ E N S
A C R O B A T █ R A S P █
H A R M S █ P A N O R A M A
E R O S █ R O U N D R O B I N
A L O U █ R U N G █ A T E S T
D A M P █ S I T E █ N O L T E
```

131

```
R O C █ S N A R L █ T E N A M
C L U █ P I X I E █ U V U L A
C D E █ A C E O F S P A D E S
O P T S T O █ T E A █ E X T
L A I C █ J S B A C H █ █ █
A L P H A M A L E █ O U S T
█ █ E R I T U █ W A S T E S
L E A D E R O F T H E P A C K
A R O U S E █ F I O R I █
W A L L █ D E N M O T H E R
█ █ E M B O D Y █ A O N E
A K A █ O R G █ M I L T I E
M A R L B O R O M A N █ K G B
E N L A I █ U T I L E █ E M O
S T O O L █ N O D O Z █ Y A K
```

132

```
A T A D █ S P A T █ A T T A R
L A M E █ T O R O █ N A U R U
I D O L █ A L A N █ G O R E D
T A K I N G A B Y T E █ N A Y
█ █ █ V E E R █ A L A S █
W I P E R S █ R E P O R T S
H O A R D █ D I V E █ M Y T H
I N C █ S L I V E R S █ L E E
P I K E █ A M E N █ O P E R A
█ C O A S T E R █ N U R S E D
█ F R A T █ P I S A █ █
I L L █ N E V E R S A Y D Y E
R A Y E D █ A X I S █ I R O N
A R E N A █ L I M A █ N A U T
N A S A L █ E T O N █ G Y R O
```

133

S	U	B	S		S	L	I	D		S	T	A	M	P
O	G	R	E		T	E	R	I		N	E	P	A	L
F	L	A	T	B	R	O	K	E		E	M	O	T	E
T	I	S	S	U	E		S	T	R	A	P	P	E	D
			S	T	E	M			O	D	E			
N	C	A	A		T	A	P	A	S		R	A	V	E
A	U	D	I	O		R	A	D	I	O		N	I	T
F	E	E	L	I	N	G	T	H	E	P	I	N	C	H
T	I	P		L	O	O	I	E		E	V	I	A	N
A	N	T	S		S	T	O	R	M		E	E	R	O
			P	H	I			E	A	C	H			
I	N	T	H	E	R	E	D		P	E	A	R	L	S
H	O	S	E	R		T	A	P	P	E	D	O	U	T
O	P	A	R	T		C	R	E	E		I	O	T	A
P	E	R	E	Z		H	E	R	D		T	M	E	N

134

P	E	R	E	Z		D	Y	E	R		F	I	S	T
A	L	A	M	O		E	A	V	E		I	N	C	H
S	L	I	P	O	F	T	H	E	T	O	N	G	U	E
T	A	N			E	E	O			V	I	O	L	S
			W	I	N	D	S	O	R	C	A	S	T	L	E
K	E	E	N	E	S	T		O	A	T		S	S	S
G	R	A	T	E			J	O	N	E	S			
B	A	R	R		K	N	O	T	S		I	C	O	N
			O	W	L	E	T			A	T	O	N	E
A	S	P		O	E	R		U	N	W	A	X	E	D
S	Q	U	A	R	E	D	A	N	C	E	R	S		
K	U	R	T	S			T	S	O			W	E	E
F	I	S	H	E	R	M	A	N	S	W	H	A	R	F
O	R	E	O		D	O	R	A		H	O	I	S	T
R	E	D	S		S	N	I	P		A	G	N	E	S

135

G	T	O	S		U	R	S	A		A	B	H	O	R
A	O	U	T		R	O	A	M		T	R	O	V	E
G	O	T	O	P	L	A	N	B		P	A	T	E	S
A	T	O	L	L		D	E	U	C	E		D	R	E
		F	E	A	S	T		S	R	A		O	D	A
D	U	G		T	H	E	C	H	I	C	A	G	O	L
O	N	A	L	E	A	S	H		P	E	W			
S	O	S	A		T	I	C			O	S	A	Y	
		K	E	V		L	O	I	S	L	A	N	E	
S	L	E	E	V	E	L	E	S	S	T		L	O	S
T	I	N		I	R	A		T	R	E	S	S		
E	E	C		L	A	N	C	E		N	E	A	T	O
A	L	O	N	E		D	E	L	I	O	R	D	E	R
M	O	R	E	Y		I	L	L	S		T	I	M	E
S	W	E	D	E		S	T	O	P		A	P	P	S

136

A	D	A	M	S		H	A	M	S		M	R	E	D
R	E	N	E	W		O	M	A	N		Y	O	Y	O
M	A	N	N	A		F	A	T	E		B	O	R	N
	L	A	D	Y	O	F	T	H	E	L	A	K	E	
			B	R	A			Z	E	D				
M	A	C	R	A	E		D	I	E	D		P	G	A
E	T	H	I	C		S	O	F	A		N	O	R	M
C	H	I	C	K	E	N	O	F	T	H	E	S	E	A
C	O	M	E		T	O	N	Y		E	A	S	E	S
A	S	P		H	O	W	E		C	A	T	E	R	S
			E	M	U			B	E	D				
	G	E	M	O	F	T	H	E	O	C	E	A	N	
N	O	R	A		F	O	A	L		A	R	I	E	S
A	N	T	I		E	A	R	L		S	O	L	V	E
P	E	E	L		E	D	D	Y		E	S	S	E	X

137

A	T	O	Z		R	E	H	A	B	S		E	W	E
D	A	V	E		E	D	E	N	I	C		X	E	R
I	C	E	S		G	A	M	E	K	E	E	P	E	R
N	O	R	T	H	A	M	P	T	O	N	M	A		
			S	O	L	E			E	A	R	E	D	
A	R	E		W	E	S	T	P	O	I	N	T	N	Y
L	A	P	S	E		R	A	W		A	N	T	E	
O	T	I	C		J	O	Y	C	E		T	E	R	P
N	I	C	O		I	D	O		A	E	R	E	O	
S	O	U	T	H	B	E	N	D	I	N		S	E	T
O	N	R	I	O			E	N	D	S				
		E	A	S	T	L	A	N	S	I	N	G	M	I
P	L	A	N	E	T	A	R	I	A		A	E	O	N
A	Y	N		R	O	T	T	E	N		F	L	U	X
Y	E	S		S	P	H	E	R	E		U	S	E	S

138

Ⓣ	H	E		J	A	I			I	M	P	A	C	Ⓣ
O	I	L	W	E	L	L		A	R	E	A	M	A	P
Y	E	S	I	S	E	E		M	A	N	L	E	S	S
			N	S	C		Ⓣ	S	Q	U	A	R	E	
P	A	I	G	E		Ⓣ	O	Ⓣ		S	C	I		
A	N	N	E		Ⓣ	E	N	E	Ⓣ		E	N	D	E
L	A	N	D	Ⓣ	A	X		L	O	Ⓣ		D	I	A
A	C	E	Ⓣ	I	C			P	A	Ⓣ	I	O	S
D	I	R		Ⓣ	I	S		N	O	Ⓣ	M	A	N	Y
E	N	C	E		Ⓣ	A	R	O	Ⓣ		O	N	N	O
		I	V	E		Ⓣ	U	Ⓣ		E	B	S	E	N
	C	R	O	S	S	A	Ⓣ		E	L	I			
L	O	C	K	S	I	N		B	U	E	L	L	E	R
A	L	L	E	A	R	S		A	L	G	E	B	R	A
Ⓣ	I	E	D	Y	E			D	A	Y		O	A	T

139

```
S C A T █ A D A M S █ A C H E
H A R E █ R E B U T █ S H O T
I R O N █ E L E N A █ P A T S
P A S S F A I L C L A S S █ █
S T E E R █ █ █ H E S █ E S S
█ █ S E P I A █ █ █ S W A T H
A G A █ Y E S N O A N S W E R
T U T U █ T A T A R █ W A V E
O N O F F S W I T C H █ Y E W
M I N O R █ █ C H O I R █ █
S T E █ A L E █ █ █ R O L E S
█ T R U E F A L S E T E S T █
C L I O █ A L L A H █ A P S O
H A M S █ F A T S O █ T E E N
E Y E S █ S T A T E █ E R N E
```

140

```
E L I A █ A B B E █ █ D R A W
M A R C █ T R A C T █ E A C H
I M A C █ P E T R I █ S P R Y
T E Q U I L A S U N R I S E █
█ █ █ R N A █ █ █ G A G █ █
R E D S K Y A T M O R N I N G
A R I E S █ G E O D E █ T O R
T A M █ █ B O N U S █ █ A T E
E T A █ B A R O N █ F A L S E
D O G D A Y A F T E R N O O N
█ █ A L A █ █ █ A A A █ █
█ A F T E R T H E S U N S E T
A X I S █ E R A S E █ I O W A
M E N U █ A U R A L █ A H E M
A D E N █ E M U S █ S O R E
```

141

```
B O E R █ A S S T D A █ P T A
A R C O █ H O O R A H █ O O P
S A L A M A N D E R S █ I T T
S C A R A B █ O S E █ O N A N
E L I E L █ D I S M A N T L E
T E R R A C E █ E L I T E S
S S S █ Y E A H █ G O O D S
█ █ M I D D L E M A N █ █
S T R A D █ S P A M █ T A S
T H E M E S █ R E S C A L E
P E R M A N E N T █ P O R T A
A S E A █ A L A █ B U N T E D
U P A █ K I L I M A N J A R O
L O D █ O L I V I A █ O R E G
S T S █ A S S E S S █ B E D S
```

142

```
C A R A T S █ C H E █ C R A B
O N E C U P █ H A L █ L A N A
S T U C C O W A L L █ A M E N
A S P █ S T I F F A R M I N G
█ █ F O S S E █ █ O U S T S
J A S O N █ █ C O O P █ █
A L I E █ S P E E D S █ G U Y
W O R S E C O N D I T I O N S
S T E █ G O T T E N █ R I D E
█ C A T S █ █ D O N O R
S W O R D █ A S P E N █
T I M E S T A B L E S █ F A A
E L I A █ B E F O R E H A N D
A C T S █ A R A █ E R M I N E
D O S E █ R O B █ S T O R E S
```

143

```
T A B O O █ G A M E █ B A I T
A L L A H █ I B A R █ O N C E
O P A H S █ J E S T █ S T I R
█ C U T T O T H E Q U I C K
E L K █ O D E █ █ U N C L E
S I T U P S █ G A L A █ S E L
P A I R █ P R O O F S █ █
█ R E L I G I O U S F A S T █
█ S N A P A T █ L I O N
I M P █ E D E N █ T I E D O N
N A A C P █ P O D █ E N E
J O N A T H A N S W I F T █
O R E S █ A R I A █ D A R T S
K I L T █ W E N T █ I R I S H
E S S E █ N A E S █ T E P E E
```

144

```
C H O R █ F O N Z █ █ C E L S
L I N A █ U L E E S █ U F O S
O A S T █ R A T A T A T T A T
S T E R O L █ L O V E █ █
E A T I N █ S M O K E █ L O U
S L S █ E S T A T E S █ E O N
█ █ G U L A G █ █ E N Z O
H A P P Y B I R T H D A Y
S E M S █ C A S E S █
O L E █ O N D A T E S █ F E W
C L X █ K O O L S █ S T A R E
█ S E C S █ █ S O B E R S
D I R T Y H A R R Y █ I R A S
E V E L █ E G G O N █ R O T O
N E M O █ E S O S █ D E A N
```

145

```
M A M M A L _ _ Y E S M A A M
E R I T R E A _ A R R E A R S
S E A S T A R _ C A T N A P S
_ _ _ I O N S _ H O A D _ _ _
A L A N I S _ A T F _ E T C _
C O L A S _ P B S _ D R O O P
C O L I _ A I D _ C O S E L L
E N E _ O C T O P U S _ R O E
N I G G L E _ M O P _ T I N A
T E R R A _ J E D _ S I N E S
_ S O O _ T I N _ S I N G L E
_ W O R N _ T H E Y _ _ _ _ _
R O A D T A X _ B A R T A B S
P R A I R I E _ A R R I E R E
M A R M O T S _ I A M S A M _
```

146

```
T O T A L _ E L L _ I D A H O
A E R I E _ F E E _ G I V E R
B R I D G E F I N A N C I N G
_ _ _ _ P A S T E _ S L I T _
P O L _ C T R _ I T A S C A _
O V E R T H E E D G E _ T O D
D A C H A _ N A H _ E R A S _
_ T R O U B L E D T I M E S _
B I O S _ R A W _ D I E T S _
R O W _ W A T E R F I L T E R
A N N I E S _ D O A _ L D S _
_ _ _ N T S B _ G I N Z A _ _
S O N G B Y P A U L S I M O N
K O A L A _ O W E _ E M P T Y
A F T E R _ E L S _ C A S T E
```

147

```
O R C A S _ R A P _ W E A V E
N E A T O _ I K E _ O L L I E
E L B O W _ V I N E R I P E N
T A B L E T E N N I S _ _ _ _
W I E L D E R _ R E A D E R _
O D D _ T R I K E _ G I V E _
_ _ _ D R A N O _ Q U A I L _
_ A R E N A F O O T B A L L _
P R A D A _ T I L E S _ _ _ _
O C T A _ A S L A N _ _ D I E
T H E M O B _ _ I T S S A F E
_ _ _ F I E L D H O C K E Y _
B U B B L E G U M _ P R O V O
O H A R A _ A L A _ H A T E R
P S H A W _ D U N _ S P A R E
```

148

```
O L D S _ C O M A _ C O O L S
R I O T _ U S E D _ A L C O A
S A G E B R U S H _ N E E D Y
O R G A N _ S O Y A _ A G E _
_ _ _ M A H I _ C O S T N E R
S E S S I O N S _ U T E S _ _
E M T _ W N W _ R A S P E D _
L I R A _ T O U G H _ T R U E
F R I S C O _ N R A _ A R A _
_ P I A F _ G U I L T Y O F _
O C T A V I A _ B R I O _ _ _
P O E _ E X P O _ _ L U C I A
A M A N A _ H O N E Y C O M B
R E S E T _ I Z O D _ A L A I
T R E E S _ D E M S _ N E X T
```

149

```
R I C _ N A D I A _ S I L L _
E N O W _ I S I N G _ A S E A
C A S A B L A N C A _ X R A Y
I N T R A _ A T T _ A D S _ _
T E A M M A T E _ H O P E R _
E R S T _ N A S _ A N A L O G
_ _ _ O C T E T S _ S M I L E
C A R _ H I B A C H I _ S E E
I R E N E _ O T O O L E _ _ _
A T D A W N _ E R R _ M A I L
_ O S H E A _ S E A H O R S E
K F C _ D I X _ _ A T E I N _
A W A Y _ A T B O T H E N D S
R A R E _ D R O N E _ D A R E
T R E S _ S A X O N _ _ S O S
```

150

```
S O L O N G _ G O T T A R U N
T R I B A L _ O K A Y B Y M E
R A M O N A _ P I C K I E S T
A T P E A C E _ E K E D _ _ _
T O E _ E E R _ _ E B B S _ _
A R R A Y _ L O B B Y _ E Y E
_ _ _ L O A _ S A Y O N A R A
F A M O U S L A S T W O R D S
A U R E V O I R _ E L L _ _ _
I R E _ E N D I T _ S O B E R
L A D S _ _ O A K _ _ A V E _
_ _ _ A D D S _ S A T I R E S
H A S B E E N S _ B I S T R O
I S U R E C A N _ O N E A L L
T I M E T O G O _ B Y E B Y E
```

151

```
S A L U D   C R A N E   D E B
A B A S E   O I L E R   U N O
L O B S T E R P O T S   P E P
T O O T   V A S E S   H O S E
    R E B E L       S I N C E
N O D E A L   B A C K S T O P
O R A L S   S A M E A S
W R Y   S U N S P O T   B R O
    D E F I E S   I B E A M
T A N K T O P S   I N L A W S
O V E N S       E G G O N
D E W Y   P E D R O   O P I E
A N A   N E W Y O R K P O S T
T U G   B R E E D   F E L L A
E E E   C U R S E   C R E E L
```

152

```
E S P E R A N T O   W A T C H
C O U T U R I E R   A N G L E
H O T C R O S S B U N N I E S
O N T   M I S   S T U F F S
    P D A     D E A L
H I G H E S T B I D D I E S
A N O D E   A E R O S   N A G
H I S S   A L I E N   A L B A
N N E   O P E N S   A B A L L
  K E E P I N G T A B B I E S
    D U C T     F E E
A W H I L E   A I L   M M E
W H I T E S O X F A N N I E S
L A Y O N   C L A M B A K E S
S M A R T   T E T E A T E T E
```

153

```
T O S C A   S C R I P   M O N
G R I L L   T E A R S   C E E
I D G I V E Y O U M Y   E D T
  I N M A N   L A C O N I C
O N E A   O P S   H A R P O
M A R X   S E U S S   S O U S
E L S E S   S N A G S   E S T
    S E A T B U T I M
A C T   P A L E D   N O A H S
N O R M   S E L I G   B R O S
C H I C O   I S U   I M U S
H A V A R T I   W A L E D
O B I   S I T T I N G I N I T
R I A   O V E N S   E Z I N E
S T L   N O R T H   R E A I M
```

154

```
W I V E S   F A C T   B I K E
E M I L E   I N O R   U K E S
S M A L L   D I M E   R E N T
L U C I L L E S B A L L
E N O S   O L E A T E   T A U
Y O M   S C I   T Y C O O N S
    S P A T E   T I L D E
    S A L L Y S F I E L D
S N A F U   P A R R Y
P O W E R P C   C A N   G A M
A D S   G R A V E N   A R N O
    N E I L S D I A M O N D
L E G O   O L I O   L O U I E
I R I S   R A G U   M U S E S
Z A N Y   I S N T   A R E S T
```

155

```
G A B S   C A V S   R A H A L
A L L A   A L E C   O R O N O
R E A M   V E E R   M I L N E
T R I P L E S P A C E   Y A W
H O R R O R   M I R A C L E
  A G N E W   R O A R
P E P S I   L A I C   H O C K
A L A   C O O L C A T   S H E
W I T H   P I K E   H O S E A
  T A U T   S T A R T
O L Y M P I C   P O T P I E
S O C   S C H O O L B O A R D
C O A T I   A R G O   M B A S
A S K E D   M A R M   A L T E
R E E C E   P L E B   N O E L
```

156

```
A M A S   T O S S   C C V I I
R I T T   E P E E   R A I N S
C L E O P A T R A   E R O D E
A T A R I   B E V E R L Y
N O M I N A L   E P P I E
A N S E   S I L L S   E T C H
    D I T S Y   I S T O O
P A C   S O P R A N O   A P T
C R O A T   I R O N S
S I S I   L U C I A   H I K E
  T R I O S   A M M O N I A
  B U B B L E S   E V A N S
C O M A S   R O S A L I N D E
O B E S E   I M A X   N E L L
E S S E N   D E L E   G R E S
```

157

E	X	C	E	L		S	E	L	M	A		B	B	C
L	E	O	X	1		A	R	O	A	R		A	O	L
F	R	E	E	Z	E	F	R	A	M	E		N	A	E
		C	A	R	E		M	A	N	D	A	T	E	
T	O	F	U		A	S	H		B	A	I	N	E	S
U	N	I	T	A	S		A	S	E		V	A	L	E
B	A	R	E	S		O	T	T	A	W	A	S		
E	N	S		T	O	S	P	A	R	E		P	J	S
		T	R	A	N	S	I	T		N	O	L	I	E
P	O	S	E		N	O	N		S	T	R	I	V	E
O	C	T	A	V	O		S	S	W		I	T	E	M
P	A	R	R	O	T	S		C	A	T	O			
P	S	I		T	I	N	P	A	N	A	L	L	E	Y
E	E	K		E	C	A	R	D		L	E	A	V	E
D	Y	E		R	E	P	O	S		C	S	P	A	N

158

F	L	A	S	K		A	W	E		B	E	E	P	S
L	A	C	T	I		T	H	E		U	L	T	R	A
A	V	E	R	T		O	I	L		Z	O	N	E	S
B	A	D	A	B	I	N	G		E	Z	P	A	S	S
			W	A	D	E		O	N	C	E			
	F	U	H	G	E	D	A	B	O	U	D	I	T	
H	A	R	A	S	S		B	E	S	T		S	A	G
A	N	A	T		B	A	Y			I	L	S	A	
I	N	N		S	P	E	C		K	A	R	A	T	S
	Y	O	U	T	A	L	K	I	N	T	O	M	E	
			P	A	C	T		C	O	I	N			
B	A	D	D	I	E		M	O	B	S	C	E	N	E
O	C	E	A	N		B	A	N		K	A	R	E	N
E	L	A	T	E		U	Z	I		E	G	G	E	D
R	U	L	E	D		S	E	C		T	E	S	T	S

159

S	O	L	A	R	A		F	A	T	S		A	S	S
T	H	E	F	O	G		I	B	E	T		D	R	E
E	D	E	R	L	E		R	O	N	A		O	I	L
P	A	R	O	L	E	R	E	V	E	R	S	A	L	
P	R	E	P	S		I	M	E	T		O	N	A	N
E	N	D	O		A	S	A		S	U	N	N	Y	
			P	A	R	E	N	T	S	T	R	I	K	E
A	L	P		B	T	U		S	H	A		E	A	T
C	I	R	C	U	S	P	A	T	E	N	T			
A	F	O	O	T		T	R	A		A	L	E	R	
P	E	D	I		W	A	W	A		S	P	I	N	E
	B	U	F	F	A	L	O	P	A	W	I	N	G	S
D	O	C		I	G	O	R		D	O	O	G	I	E
R	A	E		E	E	N	S		D	O	C	E	N	T
Y	T	D		F	R	E	T		S	P	A	R	E	S

160

S	A	L	E	M		U	S	E	R		E	M	M	A
O	B	A	M	A		P	A	G	E		R	E	A	L
L	I	T	T	L	E	P	I	G	S		O	N	C	E
E	D	T		A	P	E	D		P	I	T	I	E	S
S	E	E	S	R	E	D		D	I	D	I	N		
			E	K	E		T	I	T	I	C	A	C	A
A	M	B	L	E		T	R	E	E			T	A	R
B	I	L	L	Y	G	O	A	T	S	G	R	U	F	F
E	L	I			R	O	C	S		L	O	B	E	S
D	O	N	T	W	A	L	K		M	I	A			
			D	R	A	T	S		S	A	T	D	O	W	N
H	O	M	A	G	E		N	A	R	C		M	A	O	
A	V	I	D		F	R	E	N	C	H	H	E	N	S
L	A	C	E		U	N	I	T		E	A	G	L	E
F	L	E	D		L	A	N	A		S	T	A	Y	S

161

C	A	C	H	E		T	O	S	S		C	H	I	C
O	C	H	E	R		O	B	O	E		H	O	O	D
S	T	I	N	G	O	P	E	R	A	T	I	O	N	S
T	S	A	R		S	T	Y	E		E	P	P	S	
			I	S	L	E		E	W	E	S			
I	L	K		H	O	N	E	Y	I	M	H	O	M	E
D	E	I	C	E		X	E	D		O	M	E	N	
T	O	R	A		A	M	U	S	E		T	A	T	E
A	N	O	S		M	E	R			U	S	H	E	R
G	I	V	E	M	E	A	B	U	Z	Z		A	D	O
			L	I	N	T		P	A	I	L			
	P	R	O	F		P	A	T	H		A	L	B	A
T	H	E	A	F	R	I	C	A	N	Q	U	E	E	N
W	E	E	D		P	E	R	K		T	R	I	E	D
O	W	L	S		I	S	E	E		S	A	S	S	Y

162

S	P	A	T		M	I	K	A	D	O		A	G	R
U	R	N	S		G	U	N	N	E	R		R	O	E
B	O	O	K	E	M	D	A	N	N	O		M	E	G
P	R	I	E	S	T		V	I	A		S	O	S	A
L	A	N	D	S		N	E	E	D	A	L	I	F	T
O	T	T		O	V	A			A	R	A	R	A	T
T	E	S	T		W	I	N	G		O	P	E	R	A
			I	T	S	F	O	R	Y	O	U			
S	A	U	D	I		S	W	E	E		P	I	C	A
E	L	N	I	N	O		E	N	D			N	O	M
L	I	K	E	A	R	O	C	K		E	L	T	O	N
F	E	N	D		S	R	O		O	L	E	O	L	E
I	N	O		P	I	C	K	U	P	L	I	N	E	S
S	E	W		I	N	H	E	R	E		L	E	S	T
H	E	N		T	O	S	S	I	N		A	R	T	Y

163

H	E	R	D		P	E	D	A	L		A	C	M	E
M	A	U	I		A	N	N	I	E		F	L	A	X
O	R	G	A	N	T	R	A	N	S	P	L	A	N	T
		Z	E	R	O		T	S	E		S	H	E	
C	H	I		W	O	N	T		E	G	G	S	O	N
A	U	S	T	E	N		W	I	N		M	A	L	T
B	E	A	U	S		F	O	R	E		I	C	E	S
	A	N	T	I	O	X	I	D	A	N	T			
L	A	C	E		N	I	T	S		V	O	I	C	E
I	B	A	R		F	E	W		C	A	R	O	L	S
T	A	S	S	E	L		O	R	A	L		N	I	P
E	L	I		O	A	T		E	N	O	S			
R	O	M	A	N	T	I	C	F	A	N	T	A	S	Y
A	N	O	N		E	M	A	I	L		A	N	T	S
L	E	V	Y		D	E	N	T	S		N	O	E	L

164

M	I	R		R	O	L	A	N	D		B	L	A	B
U	N	O		E	R	A	S	E	R		O	I	L	Y
S	A	G	E	A	D	V	I	C	E		Y	E	A	R
K	N	E	L	L		A	S	K	A	R	O	U	N	D
S	E	R	B	I	A				M	A	H			
	B	A	S	I	L	R	A	T	H	B	O	N	E	
A	D	A		T	R	E	A	D		S	O	C	A	L
D	E	C	O		S	A	B	L	E		Y	E	N	S
A	L	O	U	D		R	I	A	N	T		A	A	A
M	I	N	T	C	O	N	D	I	T	I	O	N		
		E	L	L			R	E	D	T	A	G		
H	Y	B	R	I	D	T	E	A		T	O	I	L	E
A	A	R	E		H	E	R	B	G	A	R	D	E	N
F	L	E	A		A	R	A	B	I	C		E	R	E
T	E	A	R		T	I	T	A	N	S		S	O	S

165

T	I	L	T		A	B	O	V	E		F	I	J	I
O	D	O	R		B	O	R	A	X		L	O	O	N
M	A	G	I		A	R	E	N	T		O	W	E	N
	S	O	N	E	S	N	O	S	E		W	A	Y	S
		K	L	E	E			N	Y	E				
S	C	R	E	E	D		U	N	D	E	R	M	Y	
O	R	A	T	E		G	R	E	E	N		I	A	N
R	U	N	S		N	A	I	A	D		A	L	L	A
E	S	C		P	E	N	A	L		M	U	L	T	I
	T	H	R	O	U	G	H		M	E	D	E	A	L
		H	E	R			Z	I	T	I				
Q	U	A	Y		O	P	P	O	S	A	B	L	E	
T	R	I	M		S	A	O	N	E		L	A	T	S
I	D	L	E		I	N	N	E	R		E	C	R	U
P	U	S	S		S	E	E	D	S		S	E	E	P

166

Y	O	G	A		A	T	T	I	C		D	O	C	K
E	A	S	T		B	U	R	R	O		O	T	O	E
S	T	A	L	E	B	R	E	A	D		O	T	B	S
		A	R	E	N	A			A	D	A	R	E	
E	W	I	N	G		S	T	E	A	L	A	W	A	Y
L	A	O	T	S	E		A	D	I	D	A	S		
A	N	T	I		A	G	A	T	E	S				
L	E	A	S	T	R	E	S	I	S	T	A	N	C	E
			U	N	S	E	N	T		I	C	E	T	
P	H	O	N	E	S		E	R	R	A	N	T		
S	L	A	T	E	R	O	O	F		E	L	A	T	E
N	A	M	E	D			I	R	A	N	I			
I	T	L	L		T	A	L	E	S	O	F	W	O	E
P	E	E	L		S	L	E	E	T		T	I	L	L
E	S	T	O		K	I	D	D	O		S	T	E	M

167

H	O	F	F	A		S	K	I		V	I	B	E	S
A	B	D	U	L		P	A	L		U	S	U	R	P
G	I	A	N	T	B	I	L	L		L	A	I	N	E
		N	O	I	R	E		A	C	A	C	I	A	
E	B	A	Y		C	O	L	T	P	A	C	K	E	R
D	A	L	L	A	S			R	I	N				
I	B	E	A	M		S	E	A	S		M	A	Y	O
C	A	R	D	I	N	A	L	C	H	A	R	G	E	R
T	R	O	Y		O	U	S	T		L	O	R	N	E
		X	I	N			E	T	C	E	T	C		
C	H	I	E	F	S	A	I	N	T		T	E	A	K
R	O	N	N	I	E		L	O	T	T	O			
A	W	F	U	L		S	U	P	E	R	B	O	W	L
S	T	O	R	E		O	V	A		A	E	R	I	E
S	O	R	E	S		B	U	R		P	R	E	G	O

168

J	O	G	S		A	G	A	R		O	P	A	R	T
O	R	E	O		R	O	L	E		B	O	X	E	S
T	E	N	D	E	R	L	O	I	N	S	T	E	A	K
S	M	E	A	R		A	T	N	O		A	L	P	S
		P	R	O	M	O		D	O	T				
S	O	L	O		W	E	N	T		L	O	A	T	H
C	H	O	P	I	N		O	R	A	L		H	A	Y
E	G	G	S	S	U	N	N	Y	S	I	D	E	U	P
N	E	O		S	P	E	E		S	E	R	A	P	E
T	E	N	S	E		A	S	I	A		I	D	E	S
		T	I	A		P	A	Y	T	V				
O	A	H	U		C	A	L	M		L	E	M	M	E
P	E	A	C	H	E	S	A	N	D	C	R	E	A	M
T	R	U	C	E		I	T	O	O		E	T	N	A
S	O	L	O	N		F	E	T	E		D	A	N	G

169

```
B A L E   S P E A R   S C R A P
A L A N   A I S L E   T R A S H
S O R T   F E T A L   A O R T A
I F V E G E T A R I A N S E A T
S T A R E       M E L D S
      O S L O   D L I   M O O
E V E L   W A I L   O S W A L D
V E G E T A B L E S W H A T D O
I S A I A H   S A K E   D E E R
L T D   L I P   F I D O
    M E L O N       W A L E S
H U M A N I T A R I A N S E A T
E V E N T   A B O M B   P A G E
L E A S E   T O T A L   I S L E
P A L E D   O B E S E   C H E R
```

170

```
D U S K   P O E M S   U S S R
A S I A   I N D I A   S O H O
D O G B R E E D E R   U F O S
E C H O E R   A N I M A T E S
      B I R D       A L P
L E A   N E U M A N N   A C T
U N C L E   F A T E   S L A W
N O T E S O F T H E S C A L E
A C I D   B E T E   T I T L E
R H O   S I L E N C E   E S T
    N I T       S H A H
D O D D E R E D   E M I N E M
A H O Y   S M I L E Y F A C E
M I L L   V I N E S   I D O L
P O L L   P R O X Y   S A N D
```

171

```
A T O Z   O Y E Z   M I S C
S H O E   M A K E   M A L T A
S A N D W E D G E   A V I A N
T W A   O L D   C R E A T E
    M E A T G R I N D E R
L O O K A T   E L A N
A M A I N   P H O T O C O P Y
R O H E   K R E M E   O R E O
S O U V E N I R S   S H I R K
    M O M A   T O N G U E
A M E R I C A N S U B
D E B U N K   E X E   H E M
L E O N E   S U P E R H E R O
I S L A M   A R I D   E L L A
B E A T   C I A O   X M E N
```

172

```
C R A G   U B O L T   F A Z E
R U L E   S A T I E   E X E C
A M E N   A L I N E   L E N O
B O X O F F I C E H I T
B R I A R   A E R I A L S
E S S   A R M W R E S T L E R
    F I O N A   C O M O
H O L D O N T I G H T
A J A R   D E R R Y
S U I T S T O A T E E   S E C
S T R I K E R   A P P L Y
    F I N I S H S T R O N G
F I J I   N O H I T   A K I N
O K I E   I L I K E   N E N E
B E G S   S E V E R   K N O T
```

173

```
A V O N   I D L E   O R A T E
P A C O   T R A M   B O X E R
A C C T   C A V E   S U E D E
C H U R C H W A R D E N
H E R E I   Y E S D E A R
E L S   V I D A   E S T A T E
    D I C I E R   R U I N
P E R C U S S I O N I S T
H I K E   H O T T I P
B L E A T S   P E O N   E T H
O L D M A I D   E R N I E
    B I C Y C L E R I D E R
A S S O C   I R O N   G O R E
M I C A H   N E R O   E R O S
I S I T I   G E E S   L A D Y
```

174

```
D U M B   I R I S   Z O N E D
I B E T   N A S A   S M I L E
N O N E E D T O T H A N K M E
G A L A X Y   C O Z I E S T
S T O M P   J O H N S
    A L A R M   A S T E R
G L A D T O B E O F   H O P I
N U D I S M   U S E R I D
A L E C   A S S I S T A N C E
T U N E D   A R O S E
    R A Y O N   L A S T S
T E A S E T S   C L I Q U E
I T W A S M Y P L E A S U R E
P A R I S   E V E N   L A N D
S L Y L Y   S C O T   E B A Y
```

175

B	A	H		F	A	L	L		C	A	T	N	I	P
O	R	U		A	S	E	A		A	I	R	A	C	E
A	I	M		C	H	I	C	K	F	L	I	C	K	S
R	A	B	B	I		S	E	N	T		F	R	E	T
		L	E	A	S			E	A	R	L	E	S	S
J	O	E	Y	L	A	W	R	E	N	C	E			
A	M	P		S	A	H	I	B		A	R	N	A	Z
M	A	I	M		B	I	G	O	T		S	E	R	B
S	N	E	R	D		S	O	N	I	C		R	N	A
		C	O	L	T	R	E	V	O	L	V	E	R	
A	L	C	O	H	O	L			O	M	O	O		
L	I	E	F		Q	E	I	I		E	X	U	R	B
C	A	L	F	M	U	S	C	L	E	S		S	O	O
O	R	T	E	G	A		K	I	R	I		L	A	C
A	S	S	E	R	T		Y	A	R	N		Y	M	A

176

D	O	U	S	E		A	L	F		P	I	Q	U	E
I	D	S	A	Y		L	E	A		L	A	U	R	A
S	I	E	V	E		L	A	W		A	M	I	S	S
H	E	R	E	S	J	O	H	N	N	Y		P	A	Y
			H	O	W			A	M	C				
P	A	C	M	A	N		R	E	L	E	A	S	E	D
A	C	R	I	D		G	O	L	D		S	U	M	O
T	H	E	R	E	S	N	O	I	I	N	T	E	A	M
R	E	M	I		M	A	M	A		O	L	D	I	E
I	D	E	N	T	I	T	Y		S	T	E	E	L	S
			G	O	T			V	I	A				
S	A	M		W	H	E	R	E	S	W	A	L	D	O
O	C	E	A	N		Z	E	N		H	O	A	R	D
A	L	I	B	I		R	E	A		I	N	B	A	D
P	U	R	S	E		A	L	L		T	E	S	T	S

177

J	E	D		S	T	A	M	O	S		M	O	J	O
A	M	A		I	M	P	O	S	E		A	W	O	L
B	A	N	A	N	A	B	O	A	T		K	N	E	E
B	I	G	T	E	N		S	K	A	T	E			
E	L	I	A		M	E	A	T	W	A	G	O	N	
D	S	T		P	E	A			O	F	U	S	E	
			R	E	D	R	O	S	E		A	N	U	T
	T	U	R	N	I	P	T	R	U	C	K			
A	R	A	B		A	S	T	A	I	R	E			
H	I	R	E	D			H	E	N		P	G	A	
A	P	P	L	E	C	A	R	T		P	I	E	R	
			B	L	I	G	E		D	I	A	N	N	E
V	E	T	O		G	R	A	V	Y	T	R	A	I	N
A	V	O	W		A	E	R	I	E	S		T	E	A
L	E	N	S		R	E	S	E	D	A		A	S	S

178

O	L	I	V	E	R		O	K	L	A	H	O	M	A
M	I	N	O	S	O		S	P	A	M	A	L	O	T
A	V	A	L	O	N		L	A	V	A	L	I	E	R
R	E	N	T			C	O	X	E	S		N	S	A
R	U	E		T	R	A			D	S	C			
	P	R	O	V	E	R	B	S			H	A	I	R
			C	A	B	A	R	E	T		A	N	N	E
E	C	R	U		E	V	I	T	A		L	Y	N	X
P	H	I	L		C	A	N	D	I	D	E			
A	I	D	A		N	E	O	N	A	T	A	L		
			R	S	A		W	T	S			N	A	T
D	E	N		C	L	O	W	N			F	A	M	E
O	V	E	R	R	I	D	E		J	O	R	D	A	N
C	A	R	O	U	S	E	L		F	R	I	E	Z	E
S	H	O	W	B	O	A	T		K	I	S	M	E	T

179

B	E	T		E	F	F	U	S	E		M	A	Y	S
U	Z	I		F	O	R	A	L	L		A	L	O	E
N	R	C		F	L	O	R	I	D	A	K	E	Y	S
T	A	K	E	A	I	M		M	E	D	I	C	O	S
		E	N	C	A	M	P		S	O	N			
T	A	R	G	E	T		I	N	T	L		J	A	S
A	S	T	A		E	D	G	E		P	L	U	N	K
S	T	A	G	E		O	P	T		H	I	N	D	I
T	O	P	E	R		D	E	S	I		O	K	I	E
E	R	E		O	D	O	N		M	I	N	D	E	D
			A	D	O		S	I	M	M	E	R		
S	I	N	C	E	R	E		S	E	A	L	A	N	T
T	H	I	R	D	S	T	R	I	N	G		W	A	R
L	O	C	I		A	T	E	A	S	E		E	M	I
O	P	E	D		L	A	S	H	E	S		R	E	X

180

S	A	M	I	A	M		A	L	A			T	A	O
A	G	E	N	D	A		W	E	N	T	S	O	L	O
P	E	R	S	O	N	A	L	I	T	Y	Q	U	I	Z
S	E	E			I	F	S			P	U	T	T	Y
			I	S	L	A		S	P	E	E			
P	R	O	Q	U	A	R	T	E	R	B	A	C	K	
L	A	P	S	E		O	R	O			L	A	N	A
E	N	E		D	A	R	K	A	G	E		P	E	T
A	U	R	A		C	O	Y		S	H	R	E	W	
	P	A	T	C	H	W	O	R	K	Q	U	I	L	T
			O	L	E	S		S	A	S	H			
M	T	I	D	A			O	V	I			E	E	E
M	I	N	D	Y	O	U	R	P	S	A	N	D	Q	S
E	M	I	S	S	A	R	Y		E	V	E	N	U	P
S	E	T			K	I	X		R	E	T	A	I	N

181

```
S C A L P ■ A M A S S ■ T D S
O M N I A ■ L A C T O ■ H O T
F O U R T E E N R E D ■ E R Y
A N T I T A X ■ E N A B L E R
■ ■ ■ I C E S ■ ■ ■ A M M O
O L A F ■ H I T M E A G A I N
R O S I E ■ A I D S ■ ■ ■
D O U B L E O R N O T H I N G
■ ■ ■ L E N D ■ A U D I O
I L L T A K E O N E ■ M O T O
M E A N ■ ■ M E T A ■
P A T T E R S ■ S C R A P E R
E S E ■ R O L L T H E D I C E
D E N ■ A D U E L ■ N I E C E
E S T ■ S E E M E ■ A N S E L
```

182

```
W A G S ■ A D D U P ■ E L S E
I D E A ■ L O O S E ■ N O U N
G O L D F I N G E R ■ O W E D
■ ■ D I S S ■ ■ R U S T S
L A M E N T ■ S H R U G ■
E R A S E ■ S T E E L H E A D
T O R T ■ E T E R N E ■ R H O
H U T ■ C L A R E T S ■ R O W
A S H ■ A D L I B S ■ B A R N
L E A D B E L L Y ■ S E N S E
■ ■ V E R S E ■ G O A D E D
A C T O R ■ ■ E L A N
R O A R ■ S I L V E R B A C K
A L G A ■ P R E E N ■ A L O E
B A S K ■ Y E A R N ■ G A N G
```

183

```
S E Z ■ U T T E R ■ R A N D B
I L E ■ N O O S E ■ A D O R E
T I R E S O M E W I N D B A G
A H O L E ■ ■ I N S ■ I T S
T U S K E D W A R T H O G
■ ■ S N O O Z E ■ O L D I E
J A M ■ L E O ■ P R I E S T
P R O M P T S ■ P E T N A M E
E M B E R S ■ R E T ■ L E S
G E S S O ■ H E A R S T ■
■ C A P E A F R I K A N E R
E R E ■ O T T ■ E L E N A
D A N I S H P H Y S I C I S T
G R E T A ■ I M E A N ■ G U T
E A S E L ■ N O N O S ■ H E Y
```

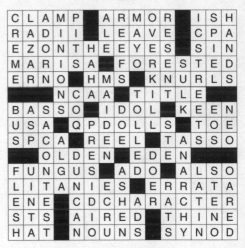

184

```
C L A M P ■ A R M O R ■ I S H
R A D I I ■ L E A V E ■ C P A
E Z O N T H E E Y E S ■ S I N
M A R I S A ■ F O R E S T E D
E R N O ■ H M S ■ K N U R L S
■ ■ N C A A ■ T I T L E
B A S S O ■ I D O L ■ K E E N
U S A ■ Q P D O L L S ■ T O E
S P C A ■ R E E L ■ T A S S O
■ ■ O L D E N ■ E D E N
F U N G U S ■ A D O ■ A L S O
L I T A N I E S ■ E R R A T A
E N E ■ C D C H A R A C T E R
S T S ■ A I R E D ■ T H I N E
H A T ■ N O U N S ■ S Y N O D
```

185

```
S T O I C ■ N E A R ■ C O A T
H O N D A ■ U R G E ■ O A T H
E A T I N G C R O W ■ I S E E
A D O ■ C U L ■ G R A N T E E
■ ■ R E N E E ■ I R E ■
■ T A L K I N G T U R K E Y
J O E Y S ■ C O E N ■ A R E
E R T E ■ C A R T S ■ I S I N
E A R ■ T O N Y ■ A M E N S
P L A Y I N G P O S S U M ■
■ ■ A N D ■ T R E S S ■
D E F R A U D ■ G A I ■ B A A
O V E R ■ C R Y I N G W O L F
C A T O ■ T I M E ■ N O R M A
K N E W ■ S P A S ■ S W E A R
```

186

```
F U M E ■ S E M I ■ B A S I N
U N I V ■ A X E D ■ A C H O O
S I D E ■ L I M E ■ S T E W S
S T A N D A T E A S E ■ D A Y
Y E S S I R ■ ■ S A M B A
■ ■ O B I E S ■ P A R T E D
I C U ■ S E V E N ■ N E E D Y
L A P D ■ D A T E S ■ W A G E
S M A R T ■ C O A L S ■ R E D
A E N E A S ■ F R I T O
■ ■ D I X O N ■ M O P T O P
B A A ■ F L O R I D A T E C H
A S T R O ■ W A C O ■ S R T A
S T E E R ■ A N E W ■ I R E S
H I M O M ■ Y A R N ■ N A T E
```

187

```
T O R M E   D I C E   C L U B
O P I U M   I M A X   R O S E
M I S S I L E U N I V E R S E
S E E K   O D S   T A V E R N
      O O O     A F T A
  T E X T I L E M E S S A G E
R I D   T E E N I E   S O U P
O B E Y S   S A N   E E R I E
T I N A   A L M O N D   T O E
C A S T I L E I R O N P A N
      I N K Y   V A R
C O N T R A   I O U   O S S O
H O S T I L E C O M P U T E R
O N E L   I H O P   A S Y E T
P A C E   S S N S   S T E P S
```

188

```
A D D S   D O W N   B O B S
D I R T   M A C H O   L A R K
U V E A   A C H E S   O K A Y
L A W R E N C E W E L K
I N T   L I A R   J E E R A T
    H U L A   G O D   A C E
R T E S   C L A M B I S Q U E
A R L E S   O S E   N A U R U
F A I R A M O U N T   H E A P
T I N   L E T   H I L L
S L E E T S   F L E D   W P A
    L I T T L E B O P E E P
M A U I   I R A T E   A L A S
R A Z Z   Z E R O S   A C R E
S H I A   O X E N   R H Y S
```

189

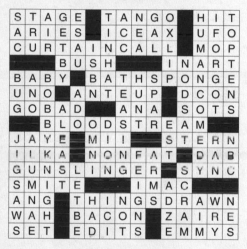

```
S T A G E   T A N G O   H I T
A R I E S   I C E A X   U F O
C U R T A I N C A L L   M O P
  B U S H     I N A R T
B A B Y   B A T H S P O N G E
U N O   A N T E U P   D C O N
G O B A D   A N A   S O T S
  B L O O D S T R E A M
J A Y E   M I I   S T E R N
I L K A   N O N F A T   D A B
G U N S L I N G E R   S Y N C
S M I T E   I M A C
A N G   T H I N G S D R A W N
W A H   B A C O N   Z A I R E
S E T   E D I T S   E M M Y S
```

190

```
L I M E   L A M B   R I O T S
A S E C   A L O E   E R R O R
T A L C   T E R R A F I R M A
H A B E A S C O R P U S
E C A S H   N A B S   C P A
    I A M S   S A S H E S
J O N G   B U L B   L I E N S
A R O N   A B O V O   N E N E
P A D U A   J U D O   E R S T
A T O M I C   C H A Q
N E Z   M U S H   R U S T S
  A L E A I A C T A E S T
S E M P E R I D E M   N E A R
E P E E S   N E R O   O T R A
W A R D S   T R O N   N O S Y
```

191

```
L I T U P   M A S T   F A N S
A R O S E   O K R A   O V A L
G E N E R A T I O N   R O S A
E N G   W O N   L E E W A Y
R E A C T O R   H I T S
    A W L   P A N A T E L A
T E T R A   L I V E S A L I E
A T O B   S E X E S   T I E R
M A J O R E D I N   P I A N O
S T O N E A G E   R E O
    A S H E   S E A N C E S
B L O T T O   A P E   O V O
R A V I   R E V E L A T I O N
O R E O   S P I N   S A N K A
W A R N   E A S T   P O S E R
```

192

```
A C M E   R A N O N   F U R Y
B I A S   I R A T E   O N E A
C O C A   P A N I C   C A P P
  H U M P B A C K W A I L
A V E   A L I   O L D E R
B A T T L E C R E A K   E T E
A L E U T   E R G   I D E A
  F A R M G R O A N
S E C T   A A A   R C P T S
O A R   B E L L A N D H O W L
P R O S Y   T O E   B O Y
  M A K E S A B O O B O O
H A T E   E L A N D   A X L E
E R I E   R U R A L   H E E L
S K A T   A M B L E   U S A F
```

193

```
WASPS  WKRP  MSRP
AGORA  OLIO  OTOE
XAXES  LUGS  OPAL
      *SOFTHETRADE
IMAM PEET  RE*S
QUEENED SUED
TURNED *ISE JIF
EMOTE SODA PINE
SUBS RARE VENTI
TUE HAT* HOAXES
  KIWI TENCENT
 DCIV ROAM EDDY
JEANEKIRKPA*
AIRS ACTE NIECE
NODE OAHU DELLA
EN*Y SLOP ASSET
```

194

```
PATTI  RIFF  ASEA
AVIAN OMAR  PATS
JALFREDPRUFROCK
ALLTIME  GOOP
MOE  TOSS  ONAIR
ANDIE  AWED  URI
 PILSNER ULAN
 JJONAHJAMESON
PIED LEOTARD
AMT BAAS  RAFTS
ZIPPO FEAR  RIP
 LOFT  SERRATE
JDANFORTHQUAYLE
LAND OBOE STEED
ODES NIPS  TEDDY
```

195

```
LOFT  EBOLA  OMSK
IDIO  NORAD  MUNI
FIVESTARGENERAL
TEETER    ALAIN
  COE FIVEBELLS
STETS AFIRST
HANOI TSAR  GAD
EXTENT SICILY
DIS  GULF NOMDE
 TAIPEI PUMAS
TAKESFIVE ONE
ODETS  ARTFUL
QUARTERPASTFIVE
ULNA RABBI OVEN
ETES ATSEA READ
```

196

```
CHALKS  EPEE  CAT
LADIES  URNS  ALE
ASIANS LOVELIFE
STEIN RENO  ERIN
HOUSEPARTY GOES
 ELEV  OSHA
STL NEE  UTICA
TWOKINDSOFBOATS
SIXAM PLO  NRA
 NAPS ACES
BOOS ICEFISHING
LPGA PHIS CUTIE
AIRSPEED MOTIVE
NNE ATME IRISES
DES YSER ATNINE
```

197

```
BOSC  PIGSTY  GRAS
ANKA ENAMOR  LAST
DRIVINGMISSDAISY
MET STOUTS ANSEL
OPT MATTE ENCORE
VOICED  CLIENTS
ERSE PATOIS
 THEBLACKDAHLIA
 RODEOS  ESPN
VASSALS TROUPE
ARETHA MEDIA PET
SCRAM POLITY PAZ
THENAMEOFTHEROSE
LIND ONSITE USER
YEAS STENOS NERO
```

198

```
ATMO  RATED  BOOM
BRIS AGAPE  ERMA
CUSS DENIM  ADEN
 SHOWINGCONCERN
ATM OUT  IHATE
LEASES JOES  LAD
PEST VARLET
 HOLDINGFIRM
 PAULEY  EATS
ALT NEAT IBERIA
SOUSA SNO  IND
PARTINGCOMPANY
ETNA OMANI RATS
CHIN MEGAN TRIO
TEND SNERD YAMS
```

199

N	E	A	L		E	S	T	O	P	S		D	A	M
T	R	I	O		B	O	O	H	O	O		E	T	A
H	O	L	D	S	B	A	R	R	E	D		T	H	E
	S	E	G	O		K	N	O	T		D	E	L	
T	I	R	E	O	F		B	R	A	I	N	E	R	
G	O	O	D	N	I	K		Y	V	E	T	T	E	
I	N	N		R	I	N	G		O	G	E	E	S	
		J	U	S	T	S	A	Y	N	O				
Y	E	T	I	S		S	A	F	E		M	O	P	
A	D	O	N	I	S		F	L	Y	Z	O	N	E	
H	I	T	G	A	M	E		L	E	A	N	E	R	
	T	A	O		A	M	M	O		A	P	I	T	
O	I	L		G	R	E	A	T	S	H	A	K	E	S
V	O	L		A	M	E	L	I	A		T	E	R	I
A	N	Y		L	Y	R	I	C	S		A	R	M	S

200

W	I	S	P		C	R	I	P	E	S		T	I	M
A	L	O	E		D	E	N	A	L	I		O	N	E
F	I	F	T	H	C	O	L	U	M	N		P	A	L
T	E	T	R	A		E	L	I		V	I	L	E	
	T	O	I	L	E	T	A	R	T	I	C	L	E	
T	R	O	L	L	E	D			A	V	A			
I	O	U		S	A	G	E	S		A	L	I	B	I
L	O	C	H		P	A	P	E	R		S	N	U	B
E	T	H	A	N		R	A	D	I	O		T	R	I
		I	F	S			G	O	P	H	E	R	S	
S	C	A	R	L	E	T	L	E	T	T	E	R		
M	A	N	Y		R	O	E		I	S	L	A	M	
I	N	N		B	E	S	T	P	I	C	T	U	R	E
T	O	E		U	N	C	O	O	L		O	D	I	E
H	E	X		B	E	A	N	I	E		N	E	A	T

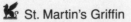 St. Martin's Griffin